POWER IN BRITAIN

Sociological Readings

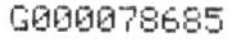

POWER IN BRITAIN

SOCIOLOGICAL READINGS

EDITED BY JOHN URRY
AND JOHN WAKEFORD

Heinemann Educational Books
London

Heinemann Educational Books Ltd
LONDON EDINBURGH MELBOURNE TORONTO
AUCKLAND SINGAPORE JOHANNESBURG KUALA LUMPUR
HONG KONG NAIROBI IBADAN NEW DELHI

Cased edition ISBN 0 435 82900 9
Paperback edition ISBN 0 435 82901 7

First published 1973

Published by Heinemann Educational Books Ltd
48 Charles Street, London W1X 8AH

Text set in 10/12 pt. Monotype Plantin 113, printed by letterpress, and bound in Great Britain at The Pitman Press, Bath

CONTENTS

PREFACE

This book is concerned with certain fundamental features of the economic, social and political structure of modern Britain; and specifically with the distribution of power. In our search for and appraisal of material to include in this volume we have gained the clear impression that this area, key (in our view) to the understanding of the nature of British society, is still relatively neglected. Few studies of ruling classes and power élites have been published and little research in the field appears to be in progress.[1]

Most recent introductory texts published in Britain contain few if any references to conceptual or empirical work on contemporary British élites or the power structure, although the publication of *The State in Capitalist Society* by Ralph Miliband will undoubtedly change this to some extent.[2]

Consequently our intention has been to select material which is representative rather than comprehensive, including extracts from books and reports that do not in themselves provide a systematic analysis but which may provoke and probably direct the reader's attention to some of the major issues in the area. In some cases we have included an article on a specific topic virtually complete. In others the extract is the reproduction of statistical information without detailed commentary. Unfortunately some of the data and discussions are significantly out of date, but they do represent the most recent useful published material on the topic that we could discover. Extracts from classical approaches have not been included partly for reasons of space. Thus we expect that inferences from this volume can be augmented by reference to comparative material and theoretical treatments published elsewhere.

The selection has been made with the interests of the sociology and the politics student in mind, but other social scientists and

[1] See SSRC *Newsletter; Scientific Research in British Universities and Colleges 1970–71* (HMSO London 1972); Carter, M. P. 'Report on a Survey of Sociological Research in Britain,' *Sociological Review*, Vol. 16, No. 1, March 1968, p. 36.

[2] See for instance Worsley, P. et al., *Introducing Sociology* and *Modern Sociology: Introductory Readings* (both Penguin, London 1970) and Giner, S. *Sociology* (Martin Robertson, London 1972).

other readers should find that the book raises major questions for them as well. In our view sociology has become too concerned with relatively trivial and peripheral aspects of our society, encouraged to do so by recurrent 'crises' and perceived social problems. The danger is that the social and political economy of contemporary Britain may be accepted as given, and if our collection encourages greater discussion of the more fundamental issues or helps to stimulate further research, it will have achieved its major purpose. The sooner that much of the material that follows is superseded the better.

A number of friends and colleagues have helped us assemble this book and we are also grateful to Pat Urry for compiling the index, and Jean Simpson and Nan Anderson for their secretarial assistance.

JU
JW
August 1972

ACKNOWLEDGEMENTS

The authors and publishers are grateful for permission to reproduce the copyright material listed below:

Robin Blackburn, 'The Unequal Society' from R. Blackburn and A. Cockburn, *The Incompatibles* (New Left Review, 1967), pp.15–36.

R. J. Nicholson, 'The Distribution of Personal Income' (*Lloyds Bank Review* No. 83, January 1967), pp. 11–21.

National Board for Prices and Incomes, 'The Renumeration of the Top Executives in British Industry', *Report No. 107 Cmnd. 3970*, Chapter 2, Table A and B, and Appendix 3, Table 5.

'The Distribution and Taxation of Wealth', originally appeared as 'The Indefensible Status Quo' (*The Economist*, 15 January 1966).

'The £400m League', from *The Times Business News* of 15 December 1967.

P. Wilsher, 'How the Wealth is Split', from *The Rich and the Super Rich* by Ferdinand Lundberg (Nelson, 1969).

M. Barratt Brown, 'The Controllers of British Industry' from K. Coates, *Can the Workers Run Industry* (Sphere, 1968), pp. 36–9.

S. Aaronovitch, 'The Ruling Class', from *The Ruling Class* (Lawrence and Wishart, 1961), pp. 136, 140–57.

A. Roth, 'The Business Background of MPs' (Parliamentary Profile Services, London 1967), pp. xii–xv.

R. Miliband, 'The Power of Labour and Capitalist Enterprise', *The Capitalist State* (New Left Review, No. 59, 1970), pp. 155–65.

John Hughes, 'Nationalization and the Private Sector' (Universities and Left Review, No. 4, 1958), pp. 44–6.

C. Jenkins, 'Occupational Background of Members of Principal Public Corporation Boards', Table 1 from *Power at the Top* (MacGibbon and Kee, 1959), pp. 42–4.

Michael Hughes, 'American Investment in Britain', © Heinemann Educational Books.

T. Lupton and C. Shirley Wilson, 'The Social Background and Connections of "Top Decision-Makers" ' (The Manchester School, Vol. 27, No. 1, January 1959), pp. 30–51.

W. L. Guttsman, *From* 'The British Political Élite' (MacGibbon and Kee, 1963), pp. 336–7, 359–64 and 367.

H. Glennerster and R. Pryke, 'The Contribution of the Public Schools and Oxbridge: 1 "Born to Rule" ' from *The Public Schools* (Fabian Society, 1964), pp. 17–26.

Public Schools Commission, 'The Contribution of the Public Schools and Oxbridge: 2', *Public Schools Commission: First Report, Volume II* (HMSO), pp. 101, 115, 236–40.

G. K. Fry, 'Recruitment to the Civil Service Administrative Class' from *Statesmen in Disguise* (Macmillan, 1969), pp. 439–40.

C. B. Otley, 'The Public Schools and the Army' (*New Society*, 17 November 1966), © IPC.

Peter Worsley, 'The Distribution of Power in Industrial Society' (*Sociological Review Monographs* 8, 1964), pp. 16–34. Reprinted with the permission of the Sociological Review Monographs, University of Keele, Staffordshire, ST5 5BG, England.

D. Lockwood, 'The Distribution of Power in Industrial Society—a comment' (*Sociological Review Monographs* 8, 1964), pp. 35–41. Reprinted with the permission of the Sociological Review Monographs, University of Keele, Staffordshire, ST5 5BG, England.

T. Bottomore, 'Ruling Élite or Ruling Class?' from *Élites and Society* (Sir Isaac Pitman and Sons Ltd., 1964), pp. 30–41.
Robert A. Dahl, 'A Critique of the Ruling Élite Model' (American Political Science Review, Vol. 52, No. 2, June 1958), pp. 463–9.
Nicol Poulantzas, 'The Problem of the Capitalist State' (*New Left Review*, No. 58, 1969), pp. 67–78.
Ralph Miliband, 'The Capitalist State: reply to Nicol Poulantzas' (*New Left Review*, No. 59, 1970), pp. 53–60.

EDITORIAL NOTE

Obvious misprints in the original articles have been corrected, and spelling and typographical style have been standardized throughout. To avoid confusion, chapter numberings have been added to table captions (i.e. Table 7.10 indicates Table 10 in Chapter 7). However, the original table numbers have been retained, to avoid altering references in the text, and where only part of a paper is reproduced table numbers may thus not always begin with No. 1.

Where bibliographical references were lacking or incomplete in the original essays they have been added, for the benefit of the student. Wherever possible editions in print have been cited, which may post-date the original article. Editorial additions are in square brackets. The style of bibliographical references and footnotes has been standardized.

INTRODUCTION

JOHN URRY

The problem

The concept of power is today enjoying a revival. No longer is it possible to view societies as devoid of power relationships. In the United States the notion of the 'white power structure' has become part of the social consciousness of many black Americans (1). In Britain discussion over the 1971 Industrial Relations Act, 'participation' within the workplace, or the cause of inflation, have all focused upon how the power of contending groups has been affected by and affects these events and processes.

How, then, is power distributed within Britain? What exactly is the effect of a change of government in Britain? Does a change of government make any real difference to the power distribution? These are all questions considered in this book. But they all require that we think very much more carefully about what it is to say that within a particular society the nature of power is such and such. The study of power, if not peculiarly problematic, is so extraordinarily difficult in a number of ways that this collection of readings is as much a case for further study as it is a set of well-defined and closed pieces of information that describe the reality of the nature and distribution of power within the U.K. It is just as much an indication of what needs to be done as a statement of what is already known. But further, it is not simply a question of sending out yet more elaborate teams of research-workers. On the contrary, or perhaps *almost* on the contrary, what is initially more important is that such empirical research must take place within a framework where very much more careful, precise and frankly inspired thought occurs as to what it is that is being studied. That is not to argue for mindless conceptualizing. Rather it is to appreciate that much of the dispute about the empirics of power is in fact a dispute about the concepts of power, of power élites, ruling classes, governing élites, ruling élites and so on. This concern will be partly reflected in the readings in the second section, *The Analysis of Power*, it is also reflected in the present section.

Introduction

The intention here is to outline some of the problems involved in studying power in general and power in the United Kingdom in particular. We hope that this discussion and this book will promote more interest in the subject. Indeed that would not be difficult in Britain. It is a matter of some significance that it would be very much easier to compile such a reader in the U.S.A. (2). There is relatively little empirical work in this field that has been done in this country and, interestingly, much of it is now out of date. But nevertheless we must take what has already been achieved, ask whether it shows what it purports to show, and how far it fills up our profound ignorances. One cautionary word however: much of the empirical information, although in itself interesting and informative, generally indicates less than might be initially presumed.

Power: its meanings and dimensions

Power is defined in very many ways. Thus competing arguments and interpretations generally miss the point that they are often dealing with totally different phenomena. This can be seen in the controversy between Wright Mills and Talcott Parsons over the nature of power (3). On the one hand, power is taken to be something to do with the ability of one man to realize certain objectives against the wishes of another; power is seen as power over others. On the other hand, power is the capacity to realize certain intended states of affairs, it is, for Parsons, a facility which enables the fulfilment of functions in and for society as a whole. Parsons criticizes Mills for not perceiving that power serves the function of increasing the adaptation of the society to its environment. But what in turn Parsons does not seem to realize is that his consideration is essentially the consequence of a relationship of power and is not that relationship itself. Parsons, in taking authority to be the basis of power, ignores that power is in fact power over some-one (4).

There is nevertheless one aspect of Parsons' argument which has considerable significance. This is the fact that he sees power as existing on more than the interpersonal level. There is an appreciation of what Masao Maruyama calls the substantive rather than the functional con-cept of power (5). The strength of this conception is that power rela-tions are not taken to be simply the relationships between individuals but rather as canalized in a definite objective pattern. It is a failing of all definitions following on from Weber (6) that power is only considered microscopically. Now this is highly limited since, although it may be correct to argue that the most useful *definition* of power is one which refers to the power-over-others aspect, it does not follow that this should preclude consideration of how large-scale institutions do, as a matter of fact, possess power. The problems that this causes can be seen from C. Wright Mills' *The Power Élite* (7). What he wants to show is that in the U.S.A. it is the institutions of the economy, politics and the military that are most powerful. But that is difficult to do—just what is the economy, where are its boundaries, how is *it* powerful? Mills, to substantiate his argument empirically, has to study not the economy, but rather the power derived by incumbents (the 'corporate rich') of roles within these institutions (the giant corporations).

A further limitation of the interpersonal focus upon power is that it tends to be associated with the methodological precept that the only way of studying power is to consider the processes of how key decisions come to be made (8). I will return to this consideration later. For the moment I want to make just two points. First of all, the fact that *most* of the discussion of this methodology has related to the study of local community power structures, suggests that it will not be necessarily pertinent to the concern of this work, which is the *national* power structure. Secondly, although the concentration upon the study of how it is that decisions come to be made reveals a pleasantly enthusiastic concern for grasping the realities of power, it is doubtful if any key decisions can ever in themselves indicate who does and who does not possess power within a society. This is so not only for the point above, that it is very difficult to see how the exercise of power by organizations or institutions can be effectively placed within a simple power-over-others model, but also because it ignores the processes by which certain issues come to be defined as decisions and others do not. The study of decisions is the failure to study who has the power to determine what are decisions (9).

Thus, although it has been shown that power should be taken to mean the overriding of the wishes of another to realize certain objectives, this does serve to raise certain somewhat intractable problems. As a consequence the notion of power must be made more complicated. David Lockwood (10) maintains that attention must be paid to the agent's potential to employ sanctions, his capacity to prevent opposition arising in the first place, and his ability to prevent an issue ever coming to the point of decision. He further supports Peter Worsley's argument that if a certain set of institutional arrangements remain intact and if these appear to favour systematically the interests of a particular group then this would appear to provide some evidence about the distribution of power within that society (11).

Worsley's article however raises the further question as to precisely what sorts of groups may be considered as potential beneficiaries of any set of institutional arrangements. He distinguishes between Politics I, the exercise of constraint in any relationship, from Politics II, the specialized machinery of government, administration and party apparati. This differentiation corresponds to the distinction in every day speech. In the first case we say that one is engaging in action which involves manoeuvring, lobbying, and struggling to gain power behind the scenes; in the second we say that 'one shouldn't enter politics', politics here being a cluster of institutions. Worsley makes a plea for the use of politics in the first sense. But if we accept his argument that politics and therefore power is not simply the prerogative of government and parties, of what precisely is it a prerogative? The answer to this question can best be approached through considering what seems confusing in Worsley's treatment. Although it is clear that his identification of these two uses of the term politics is quite justified, he does not satisfactorily indicate the nature of the difference between them. What is important is that Politics I refers to a class of actions, such that we speak of someone acting politically; Politics II refers to a class of institutions. Now clearly Worsley's advocacy of the study of Politics I does serve to counter the simple-minded assertion that a change in the party of government represents *ipso facto* a change in the distribution of power. But to say that the study of power should embrace more than the study of government, administration and party is not to say that one study of politics, that is, of institutions, should be necessarily discontinued or quite submerged in the study of all forms of political action, termed Politics II. It is a similar concern that lies behind the emphasis that Miliband and Poulantzas (12) place upon Politics II, upon what they call the state.

Perhaps one should not carp too much at Worsley's distinction. What he emphasizes is that not all power resides in Politics II; and particularly within Politics I what is important is the continued although modified dominance of the property-owning classes. But this latter argument is to get ahead of ourselves, and to make what is at this stage an unjustified claim. Rather, Worsley is important here in indicating an alternative sort of power to that found within Politics II. As this is based on control over economic resources, we may obviously term it economic power. It is distinguishable from political power, which would appear to result from control over political institutions. But is this classification of types of power satisfactory? Earlier one objection made to studying power simply through the study of how decisions are made was that this ignores the processes by which decisions ever come to be decisions: who does the defining of what is and is not important? And this seems to depend at least in part on who it is that possesses the power to create, transform and interpret the values and norms operative within that society. Now often of course those who actually possess this power are those who also possess political or economic power. But this seems to me at least analytically distinguishable, if the notion of political power is itself redefined. In the writing on politics or the state there is a classical dichotomy between whether its power is thought to rest upon force or upon the pervasion of certain norms and values which serve to legitimate it. Thus three sorts of power are distinguishable: economic power based on control of economic resources, political power based on control of the resources of force, and cultural power based on control of the resources which create, transform and interpret the society's values and norms. I do not want to go into this further except to maintain that this seems a useful classification and one which corresponds with much work within sociology and political science (13). It does suffer, though, from the major limitation that it is very difficult to substantiate empirically since all one can do is to show that any other apparent type of power is in practice reducible to one of these varieties.

The next stage in the argument necessitates a discussion of the sorts of problems that are involved in making assertions of the sort that in particular societies particular dimensions of power predominate. In general it has become fashionable to argue that any single-factor explanation of history is essentially misguided and that the optimum solution is to combine all sorts of different approaches. It is through discriminating eclecticism that the history of any society is to be sought. This view of history has the corollary that in the area of power no one dimension is seen to dominate any other. Consequently, it is quite in order to argue that the political dimension is separate from the other dimensions; however, since it is also believed that there is something special and ultimate about *political power*, this eclecticism in fact allows an implicit single-factor explanation. The political institutions, the state, although customarily a compound of both political and cultural power (because of the need both for ultimate force and legitimation), could be taken as primary. It is this view which is the object of Worsley's attack when he maintains the dominance within the U.K. of the property-owning classes. The difficulty however with his claim is that it may be countered by the eclectic argument above. It is maintained that there cannot possibly be such a single interpretation of power in society, or of the course of history. It must be the outcome of more factors than that. This view had until recently a certain plausibility; it is less plausible now because of the importance of the distinction developed by Althusser between the notion that the economy is always determinant but not necessarily dominant (14). This is more than simple word-play. He argues that the basic moving force of history is the economy, with its internal dynamism and its own laws. He then maintains that depending upon the nature of the economic processes there may be, within any particular stage of history, domination by the economic, or the political, or the cultural, or perhaps by two or three of these. Thus what is special about the capitalist stage of history is that the determinant economy has resulted in a dominance of economic power. Therefore, it can be claimed that politics, the state, is simply the executive arm of the capitalist ruling class. It is the economic dimension which dominates the nature of political and cultural power.

Clearly not everyone would accept this particular account. However, that does not mean that Althusser's basic distinction between determination and domination need be discarded. One might say in opposition that changes in the determinant economy have created a situation in recent years where no single power dimension dominates, or that the political or the cultural now dominates the economic. One might go further, although I would not, and maintain with traditional political philosophy that what is the moving force of history is the state and that its nature determines which sector is dominant. The importance of this distinction lies in the fact that should one conclude that power relationships within one dimension are dominant, one is not thereby committed to an 'over-naïve' interpretation of society.

Now we may justifiably turn to the empirical evidence to see both whether there are significant inequalities and whether differences of power within one dimension are the result of differences elsewhere.

Power dispersion, power élite, or ruling class?

What can we conclude from the evidence? Does the considerable inequality of power enable us to conclude that Britain is ruled by a power élite or ruling class? Robert Dahl's argument (15) contains two important points. One is to show the danger of some interpretations of an élite which are based upon an infinite regress of explanation. But though this is an opportune warning, if it is, as a matter of fact, true that the 'real' rulers in a situation are at many stages removed from view, the only valid explanation will be one based upon what *appears* to be infinite regress. Secondly, Dahl maintains that the hypothesis of the existence of a ruling élite can be strictly tested only where this élite is a well-defined group, where the preferences of this hypothetical élite run counter to those of another group in a number of key political decisions, and where the preferences of the élite regularly prevail. If value could be attached to these criteria, it would certainly be impossible to conclude that there was a ruling élite in Britain. But there are in fact tremendously serious problems involved in the use of these criteria. I think that a brief discussion of these points will help to clarify the problems involved in this sort of argument.

First of all, Dahl argues that an élite cannot be said to exist unless it is well-defined, that it meets presumably what Meisel calls the three C's—group consciousness, coherence and conspiracy (16). I do not want to object to this criterion except to say that it excludes consideration of all those situations where the powerful are merely the category of those with an extraordinary amount of power, and where the degree of power inequality is more pronounced than where there is a conscious, coherent, conspiratorial élite. Indeed there is a certain probability that anyone armed with Dahl's criterion would tend to miss this category of the powerful in the search for a well-defined self-conscious group of rulers. The second criterion is even more troublesome. Who is to decide the number of decisions to be considered, who decides what is a decision, what consideration is paid to the process by which some issues never become *political* decisions at all, and what importance is to be paid to the argument that the hegemony realized by the ruling élite may have served to ensure that there are no basic differences of preference? (17) The final criterion, as Dahl admits, is difficult because without a definition of a *key* decision the 'élite's' rate of success cannot be interpreted. These are, I would argue, totally damaging criticisms. But they are not just criticisms that we can make of Dahl and then ignore. What he tried to do was to make explicit the sorts of criteria that we have to use in approaching this sort of study. We should appreciate his attempt to be explicit, and be grateful to him for thus clarifying certain problems.

In Britain there are two sets of difficulties involved in the attempt to analyse whether there is a power élite (with or without group consciousness, coherence and conspiracy) or a ruling class. The first is lack of information: this book is an attempt to gather together the best that is available. The second is that the interpretation of this evidence very much depends upon the general picture that one has of the workings of society as a whole. And this in turn depends both on a vast variety of information about other social phenomena as well as the general structure of concepts with which one approaches such a study. The empirical information simply prevents one from saying certain things: that there is income equality, that the economically powerful are *ipso facto* directly politically powerful, or that there is no consciousness, coherence and conspiracy among the powerful. The empirical information cannot in itself confirm or refute the hypothesis that there is a ruling class unless two other conditions exist. One is that specific criteria of this concept must be provided. The other is that a concept only makes sense and its value judged when it is placed within a whole set of other concepts which are theoretically related.

The first point is difficult; thus certain variants of the power-élite thesis may specify the same criteria that have been posited as indicating the existence of a ruling class. At this stage, though, I think it is useful to consider Poulantzas' article (18), since his argument specifically refers to both this and the second point above. He argues that there is no difficulty about the relationship between economic and political power. The specification of a definition of the ruling class and the indication of empirical information is here irrelevant. By definition there is an objective relation between the bourgeois class and the state; the latter is dependent upon the former and there is thus a ruling class. Miliband (19) criticizes Poulantzas' analytic statement because of its lack of amenability to empirical confirmation or refutation. Although I have some sympathy for Miliband's criticism, Poulantzas' argument is particularly interesting: firstly, for providing a singularly clear example of a claim presumed true by definition, and which cannot be refuted. Other examples exist within this area but they are rarely made so explicit. Secondly, Poulantzas makes it quite clear that he rejects the notion of an élite because of the unpredictable consequences that its importation would have upon his *own* framework of concepts. Again Miliband disagrees, as does Bottomore (20), who provides the best descriptive account of the differences and compatibilities between these concepts. But Poulantzas does have a point, a very important one at that. This can be seen if one considers what it is to talk of a power élite. In Wright Mills' book of the same name what is significant is that the notion of a power élite on the one hand implies the mass society on the other. This arises because an unblessed, and thus undifferentiated, majority is a necessary implication of a blessed minority. Neither the division of society into classes nor the possibility that the values held by members of that society are in fact implicit justifications of the position of one or more of those classes, are part of the perspective of the power élite theorist. To be fair to Miliband's criticism of Poulantzas, the latter does not provide any substantiation of the uncontrollable consequences brought about by the importation of the concept of the élite. I think that Poulantzas' case is overstated, but nevertheless it is true to say that to talk of the notion of a power élite is to place one's analysis within a particular framework. And thus, as asserted earlier, whether one interprets the evidence on power in Britain as indicating the existence of a power élite will depend upon all sorts of other information available, and the assumptions that one makes. The acceptance of a statement that 'Britain has a power élite', is the acceptance of a particular view of the totality of that society and of the way in which it should be studied.

This is very important. It means that certain relevant questions cannot be answered within the contents of this book. This is because any account of the nature of power *per se* is necessarily partial. It is only a set of observations upon one aspect of social life. The problem of the power concept is that, however well it may be used to categorize interpersonal relationships, it is difficult to use it as a means of analysing more significant institutional structures. This was well seen above when we considered Dahl's criteria of a ruling élite. One objection that I made then was to his notion that there had to be a difference of preference between the potential ruling élite and an alternative. He objected to the argument that it is the most effective ruling élites who manage to generalize a consensus and thus do not meet the criterion of a difference of preference. His argument in support of this is that since he is studying American communities and not totalitarian dictatorships it is not difficult to find differences of viewpoint between citizens.

But that, sadly, is too naïve. If there is a power élite or a ruling class, is it sensible to expect that it would have no effect upon the ideas that we hold? It is clearly untrue to say that we all think the same in Britain. But surely we all tend to think within the same sort of range. There is a Marcusian 'repressive tolerance' (21), the liberty to think and act within constraints. How does this range come to be established, who defines it, what maintains its existence? These are all questions that relate to what we called cultural power. They are central to the study of power within Britain. They emphasize the inappropriateness of customary ways of analysing power. It is as a result a matter of regret that this book cannot answer these questions, although some answers are offered to other questions and problems. The inappropriateness of customary ways of thinking about power suggests the need for alternatives.

One crucial consideration in any such approach would have to allow for a point so far only implied. Robert Wolff (22) maintains that the U.S.A. is not ruled by a power élite because major issues of social importance are not the object of anyone's decision at all. Thus American cities are allowed to decay into slums simply because there is no group of individuals willing and able to exercise power to prevent such deterioration. The same argument might be roughly applied to the United Kingdom. In other words, Britain is not ruled by a small self-conscious conspiratorial group of men. On the contrary, both decisions and non-decisions emerge from the interdependent actions of a number of men within large institutions, who may at times be in much competition with each other, the important thing being that in a sense no one exercises centralized power. The final outcome may be unintended by anyone—although that is not to say that there is no such thing as power inequality.

Again this complicates our analysis. For the present, if we take Worsley's definition of people in power, i.e. those who benefit from the existing arrangements, then we may note with interest that the institutions of the property-owning classes are still in existence.

NOTES

(1) See, for example, S. Carmichael and C. V. Hamilton: *Black Power* (Penguin, London 1969).
(2) See, for example, M. Zeitlin (ed.): *American Society Incs.* (Markham Publishing Co., Chicago 1970); and M. E. Olsen (ed.): *Power in Societies* (Macmillan, London 1970).

(3) See C. Wright Mills: *The Power Élite* (Oxford University Press, New York 1959), and T. Parsons: 'Power in American Society', *World Politics*, 10, 1957, pp. 123–43.
(4) See A. Giddens: 'Power in the Recent Writings of Talcott Parsons', *Sociology* 2, 1968, pp. 257–72.
(5) M. Maruyama: 'Some Problems of Political Power', in *Thought and Behaviour in Modern Japanese Politics* (Oxford University Press, London 1963), pp. 268–99.
(6) 'Power is the probability that one actor within a social relationship will be in a position to carry out his own will despite resistance, regardless of the basis on which this probability rests', M. Weber: *The Theory of Social and Economic Organization* (Free Press, New York 1964), p. 152.
(7) See Wright Mills, *op. cit.* For a collection of most of the useful commentaries and criticisms of *The Power Élite*, see G. W. Domhoff and H. B. Ballard (eds.): *C. Wright Mills and the Power Élite* (Beacon, Boston 1968). Also see A. Hacker: 'Power to do what?', in I. Horowitz (ed.): *The New Sociology* (Oxford University Press, New York 1964), pp. 134–46 on how Mills is essentially referring to the power of organizations rather than personalities.
(8) This has given rise to a voluminous literature, particularly among pluralist writers. See, among many others, N. Polsby: *Community Power and Political Theory* (Yale University Press 1963).
(9) See the by-now classic articles: P. Bachrach and M. S. Baratz: 'Two Faces of Power', *American Political Science Review*, 56, 1962, pp. 947–52; and 'Decisions and Nondecisions: An Analytical Framework', *A.P.S.R.*, 57, 1963, pp. 632–42. They are both reprinted, together with many other useful articles on the concept of power, in R. Bell, D. V. Edwards, R. H. Wagner (eds.): *Political Power: A Reader in Theory and Research* (Free Press, New York 1969).
(10) See below, pp. 266–272.
(11) See below, pp. 247–265.
(12) See below, pp. 291–314.
(13) See among many others, H. H. Gerth and C. W. Mills: *From Max Weber. Essays in Sociology* (Routledge, London 1948), pp. 180–95; A. Etzioni: *A Comparative Analysis of Complex Organisations* (Free Press, New York 1965); W. G. Runciman: 'Class, Status and Power' in J. A. Jackson (ed.): *Social Stratification* (Cambridge University Press, London 1968), pp. 25–61; and G. K. Ingham, 'Social Stratification: Individual Attributes and Social Relationships', *Sociology* 4, 1970, pp. 105–13.
(14) See L. Althusser: *For Marx* (Allen Lane, London 1969); and M. Godelier: 'System, Structure and Contradiction in "Capital",' *Socialist Register*, 1967, pp. 91–119.
(15) See below, pp. 282–290.
(16) See J. H. Meisel: *The Myth of the Ruling Class: Gaetona Mosca and the Élite* (University of Michigan Press 1962); and in general see G. Parry: *Political Élites* (Allen and Unwin, London 1969), who adopts this position.
(17) On the notion of hegemony see G. A. Williams: 'The Concept of "Egemonia"' in 'The Thought of Antonio Gramsci: Some Notes on Interpretation', *Journal of the History of Ideas*, 21, 1960, pp. 586–99, 1960. Dahl himself argues that this may be important in *A Preface to Democratic Theory* (University of Chicago Press 1956), pp. 132–3, 137 and 139.
(18) See below, pp. 291–305.
(19) See below, pp. 306–314.

(20) See below, pp. 273–281.
(21) See H. Marcuse: 'Repressive Tolerance', in R. P. Wolff, B. Moore Jr., H. Marcuse: *A Critique of Pure Tolerance* (Jonathan Cape, London 1969), pp. 95–137.
(22) R. P. Wolff: *The Poverty of Liberalism* (Beacon Press, Boston 1968), p. 118.

PART ONE

THE DISTRIBUTION OF POWER

A

INCOME AND WEALTH

INTRODUCTION

A relatively small minority of the population own, often by inheritance, the majority of the private wealth in Britain. A similar overlapping minority command incomes from all sources which are ten to fifteen times as large as those received by the average working man. This small number can be seen as at least part of a dominant power-group in British society—partly because they have been able to maintain the institution of private economic power and large inequalities of wealth and income during a period in which successive governments have proclaimed their intention to lessen these inequalities. As a group it is not well defined; it has numerous associations and it has to some extent eluded the systematic attention of social and political scientists. Yet despite nationalization, education acts and legislation to moderate its power, this minority must be the starting point in any analysis of power in Britain.

In this first section we aim to establish, with a selection of the most recent systematic material, the broad outlines of the distributions of income and personal wealth in the U.K. It should be emphasized that there are considerable methodological limitations because the only data available are incomplete and collected for other purposes. For instance, many of the figures depend upon the practices employed by the Inland Revenue, and this means that inequalities of income and wealth are under—rather than over—represented.[1]

The selection from Blackburn's contribution to *The Incompatibles*, a reader on the relationship between unions and management in modern Britain, provides a comprehensive and systematic survey of the current situation. He details the distribution of domestic and productive property and the distribution of income, and analyses the interrelation between the two. He discusses the payments to different factors of production, movements of relative wages, and the redistributive character of the Welfare State. Nicholson's important article develops in more detail some of the problems involved in changes in the distribution of income before and after tax. He shows that, in

[1] See R. Titmuss, *Income, Distribution and Social Change* (Allen and Unwin, London 1962).

contrast to popular opinion, in the fourteen years up to 1963 there was a progressive lightening of the tax burden on the higher income groups. He concludes with a discussion of how this came about.[1]

This section concludes with three shorter and more specific contributions. The three tables from the P.I.B. report on top salaries in 1969 provides some indication of the earnings and fringe benefits of members of boards of directors and senior executives in various sectors, both public and private, of British industry.[2] The second is a reprint in full of a well-known article first published in *The Economist* and already quoted by Blackburn. Not only does this indicate how inadequate has been the statistical basis for previous indications of the distribution of wealth in Britain but also the ineffectiveness of death duties as a tax on capital. The final piece, published in *The Times* when it became possible to investigate directors' capital assets as well as their salaries, lists about forty company directors holding over £1m of equity capital in a single company. It is not implied however that those owning considerably lower proportions of equity in other companies are necessarily less powerful in their company than those owning a higher percentage, as Sargent Florence demonstrated some years ago.[3]

[1] See for further discussion and amplification: A. L. Webb and U. E. Sieve, *Income Distribution and the Welfare State* (G. Bell, London 1971).

[2] A similar recent study shows that between one-quarter and one-third of executives, chairmen and managing directors get additional income from profit-sharing. Over 40 per cent benefit from a top-hat pension scheme and free life assurance; less than 5 per cent receive no fringe benefits at all. The median working week is under fifty hours. See Social Organisation Ltd, *Work, Remuneration and Motivation of Directors* (London 1970).

[3] P. Sargent Florence, *The Logic of British and American Industry* (Routledge, London 1953).

1

THE UNEQUAL SOCIETY

ROBIN BLACKBURN

Introduction

Hostility to the unions, and even demoralization within them, partly stems from the feeling that they are no longer necessary. It is thought that the rise of wage levels has greatly reduced inequalities of wealth and income and that such inequalities as remain are mitigated by high taxation and generous welfare services. By continuing to press a sectional interest the unions are failing to recognize the new economic facts of life. In post-war Britain the type of class conflict with which the unions and the Labour movement have been associated in the past has become obsolete. Affluence and greater social justice have abolished the old conditions which gave birth to militant trade unionism. A modified version of this theory is to be found within the trade union movement itself. It stresses the historical contribution which the unions have made to a prosperous and welfare-oriented society. Having established a position of considerable power, the unions should use it responsibly and for the common good. By co-operating with employers and with the State, the unions can help to ensure a better standard of living for all.

In this article I wish to question these assumptions. I think it can be shown conclusively that disparities in income and wealth are as great now as they have ever been. Indeed the well-being that is enjoyed by some, makes the survival of poverty in our society even more shameful. Inescapably, my account will be couched primarily in economic terms. It is a feature of market-dominated societies that man is defined, above all, by his economic situation. Riches are intimately correlated with personal security, educational opportunity, the scope for travel and recreation, diet, health and the general pleasantness of everyday living. Traditionally the unions have striven for a more egalitarian society in which the fruits of society's collective labours are more equitably distributed. They have never confined themselves purely to wage bargaining. The fate of the old and infirm, and the life chances of

First published as 'Inequality and Exploitation' in New Left Review, 1967.

the young, have always been of concern to the trade unions, not least because they touch the interests of every one of their members. Even on the most narrow definition of the trade unions' proper sphere of activity, the continuing necessity for trade union militancy can easily be demonstrated. As *The Times* recently remarked: 'The British worker's status has suffered a relative decline. In fringe benefits generally, security against arbitrary dismissal, redundancy procedures, security of income, training and retraining, the right to a say in the conduct of his workplace, he lags behind most workers in Western Europe' (*The Times*, 9 July 1964).

That Britain can be shown to remain a country where the concentration of wealth is still one of the highest in the world is a fact that has significance for all societies of the capitalist type. After all, Britain has had one of the strongest Labour movements of any advanced capitalist country. The fifth Labour government now enjoys office, while the British trade unions, unlike their counterparts on the continent, are not divided on political or religious lines. The experience of two world wars provided particularly favourable contexts for reformist action, as did the general advance to prosperity of the economy. Yet the relative positions of the major social classes have not changed in this century. Britain today is not a significantly more equal society than when the Labour Party was brought into existence by the unions over sixty years ago. In the intervening period the Labour movement has succeeded in maintaining but not improving the relative economic position of those it represents. In certain favourable conjunctures it has been able to win particular, notable advances, such as the Health Service, only to see them eroded in the subsequent period.

The British Labour movement has always drawn back from a serious confrontation with the power of private capital. Whether during the General Strike of 1926 or the Labour Government of 1945–51—at the decisive moment caution prevailed. Thus the forces making for social inequality remained, and remain, unscathed. Private property, installed at the heart of the productive system, survived to generate the inequalities displayed below.

The distribution of wealth

Two recent investigations give us a picture of the distribution of private wealth in contemporary Britain. According to estimates published in *The Economist* the richest 7 per cent of the population owned

84 per cent of all private wealth, while the richest 2 per cent accounted for 55 per cent of the total (1). Very similar conclusions were reached by J. R. S. Revell of Cambridge University who estimated that the top 5 per cent of the population owned 75 per cent of all personal property while the top 1 per cent owned 42 per cent of all such property. The results of both studies are summarized in Table 1.1 and 1.2.

Table 1.1. The Distribution of Personal Wealth in the U.K.(2)

% of the population	As a % of total personal wealth			% of personal pre-tax income from property, 1959
	1936–8	(1954)	1960	
1	56	(43)	42	60
5	79	(68)	75	92
10	88	(79)	83	99

Table 1.2. The Distribution of Personal Wealth in U.K. 1959/60 (3)

Size of fortune (in £s)	% of taxpayers	% of total wealth	Average size of fortune (in £s)
Below £3,000	87·9	3·7	107
£3–10,000	5·1	12·0	6,000
£10–25,000	4·9	29·0	15,200
£25–50,000	1·2	16·6	36,250
£50–100,000	0·6	15·1	68,250
£100–200,000	0·2	10·6	136,400
£200,000 and over	0·1	13·0	334,100

The following points are worth noting:

1. The vast majority of the population owns very little wealth at all. As shown above, according to *The Economist* the 87·9 per cent of the population who own less than £3,000 have an average holding of only £107.

2. Both estimates are ultimately based on estates assessed for the collection of death duties by the Inland Revenue. They are liable to understate the degree of concentration of property ownership as the wealthy are known to evade this tax systematically. Much property is either given to younger members of the family, exported abroad, or

placed in family trusts which escape the Inland Revenue assessors and is not liable to duty.

However, even the information from this source shows that the inherited element in most large fortunes is as significant now as it was forty years ago. C. D. Harbury, in a study of the Inland Revenue material, has concluded that there was 'no very marked change in the relative importance of inheritance in the creation of the personal fortunes of the top wealth leavers in the generations of the mid 'twenties and mid 'fifties of this century. For either, the chance of leaving an estate valued at over £100,000 or even over £50,000, was outstandingly enhanced if one's father had been at least moderately well-off'(4).

3. The fact of tax avoidance, which as *The Economist* notes, is 'inevitably more widespread in the top wealth brackets' makes comparison of the figures over time very difficult. It is all the more remarkable that the top 5 per cent owned roughly the same proportion of the total in 1960 as they did in 1936–8.

4. Revell's figures (Table 1.1) show that property income is even more highly concentrated than property ownership, so that the richest 10 per cent of the population actually receive 99 per cent of all property income. *The Economist* survey similarly notes that 'the rich do not only have more money; they also make it multiply faster'. The main explanation for this is that the rich can devote a larger proportion of their wealth to investment in equity shares, with the high yields and capital gains which these produce. *The Economist* estimates that only 5 per cent of fortunes under £10,000 consist of shares, compared with 56 per cent of fortunes over £250,000. 'As a result, the average capital appreciation of the assets held by the wealthiest group on this average composition has been 114 per cent between 1950 and 1964; while the assets of the £3,000–£10,000 group have appreciated by only 48 per cent' (5).

Share-ownership is in fact much more concentrated than the ownership of other types of property. Only 4 per cent of the adult population hold any shares in commercial or industrial companies, according to a recent Stock Exchange survey (6). An earlier investigation found that the top 1 per cent of the adult population owned 81 per cent of privately owned company shares (7). *The Economist* comments on the composition of the large fortunes as follows:

> . . . there is undoubtedly a permanent built-in tendency to inequality here. It is not just that the wealthy are financially more sophisticated; they are also genuinely better placed to take risks and need to keep a smaller proportion of

their money as a liquid reserve. The awkward fact is that any tendency towards a more even distribution of wealth in Britain is being counteracted all the time by these differences in its composition (8).

We are here dealing with the ownership not just of wealth, but of the country's productive system. Even when the economy only expands at a moderate pace, as it has done over recent years, the private ownership of the means of production powerfully generates inequality. This is the heart of a system which has systematically defeated egalitarian attempts, which fail to encroach on property rights in this vital sphere. Taxation on capital has been either low or easy to avoid; had it not been it might have risked reducing the rate of investment. So long as productive resources are in private hands, they must be allowed to produce a sufficient reward to maintain growth. Indeed the present Labour government, which in the past derided the 'capitalist begging-bowl', has now introduced an investment grant scheme to pump public money into a flagging private sector. The combined effect of all taxes on capital (capital gains tax, death duties, etc.) remains very mild: according to *The Economist* they 'amount to a property levy well under 1 per cent a year'.

The existence of a large public sector, following the nationalization of certain industries, might be thought to modify the picture presented above. The value of public property, no less than 42 per cent of the total, does not offset the great concentration of private wealth. The national debt actually exceeds the value of all public property by some 14 per cent, £28 million as against £21 million in 1960. All public property is hopelessly mortgaged to the private sector—the estimates cited above have already taken account of this, as they included the ownership of government securities and other items of the national debt. Professor J. E. Meade has commented on this situation that, 'as far as the net ownership of real wealth is concerned we live, not in a semi-socialist state, but in an anti-socialist state' (9). Where nationalization involves compensation to the former owners—and compensation has always been generous in Britain—the distribution of property ownership is not much affected. Moreover, the publicly-owned industries have predominantly been those which were unlikely to be profitable—either declining industries (railways and coal-mining) or infant industries unlikely to be profitable for some time (atomic power). Marx's dictum still holds: 'The only part of the so-called national wealth that actually enters into the collective possession of modern peoples is their national debt.'

The distribution of income

We have seen (Table 1.1) that income derived from property is more concentrated than property ownership itself. Table 1.3 sets out information on the distribution of all personal incomes from all sources

Table 1.3. Distribution of Personal Income, 1964 (10)

Income before tax (in £s)	% of a total number of incomes	% of total income before tax	% of total income after tax
50–500	36·6	12·95	14·4
500–1,000	34·5	31·3	33·04
1,000–1,500	19·9	28·8	29·5
1,500–3,000	7·45	17·0	16·04
3,000+	1·47	10·0	7·02

derived from the Board of Inland Revenue statistics. It is important to note that these figures are collected for taxation purposes rather than with the aim of discovering the true distribution of income. Scrutiny of the Board's information has revealed how inadequate it is for the latter purpose. This is the conclusion of such critiques as *Income Distribution and Social Change* (1962) by Professor R. M. Titmuss and *Efficiency, Equality and the Ownership of Property* (1964) by Professor J. E. Meade. The publication of the former work brought about something of a revolution in the climate of informed opinion on the subject. Uncritical acceptance of information derived from the Inland Revenue has led to the belief that during the war and immediate postwar period a permanent egalitarian shift had occurred in the distribution of the national income. Titmuss's study revealed the faulty statistical basis of this view and led to a renewed awareness of the powerful forces making for inequality in contemporary Britain. To give some idea of the main gaps in the Board's information, the following should help:

1. The tax-free character of many fringe benefits has given them increasing importance in recent years. The contribution to incomes made by company cars, subsidized housing, subsidized school fees, meals, etc., has recently been estimated by *The Economist*. The

following table shows that the importance of fringe benefits rises with income, not only absolutely, but also proportionately:

Table 1.4. Fringe Benefits as a Percentage of Salary (11)

£s per year	%
1,000	11
1,600	15
3,500	19
4,200	21
7,000+	31

These tax-free fringe benefits help to explain the statistical invisibility of really high income-earners.

2. Dividends and interest taxed at source are often not reported by taxpayers to the Inland Revenue. In 1958–9 the Board estimated that these omissions amounted to £260 million (12). As we know that property income is highly concentrated this substantial tranche would undoubtedly increase the inequalities of distribution in Table 1.3.

3. We have already noted the effect of capital gains on the distribution of wealth: from the income perspective they are also important. In Meade's words:

> In the United Kingdom there is a special reason why the figures of personal incomes derived from income tax returns (as in Table 1.3) will seriously underestimate personal incomes from property. They exclude capital gains. But the increase in the value of company shares which is due to the accumulation of undistributed profits represents in effect a personal income for the shareholders which has been saved for them by the companies themselves (13).

In a memorandum of Dissent to the *Report of the Royal Commission on Income Tax*, Nicolas Kaldor, George Woodcock and others stated that 'the long term rate of capital appreciation in this country in all forms should be put at a minimum of £600 million to £1,000 million a year' (14). This estimate was made in 1954, prior to the boom in share prices and property values in the 'fifties and early 'sixties. By mid 1966 (July 1), *The Economist* Extel Share Index stood at 445·8 with 1953 as the base line (1953 = 100). The fact that capital gains have been untaxed or only lightly taxed naturally led shareholders to prefer to receive additions to their resources in this manner rather than as dividends. Taking into account both dividends and capital gains the rate of return on capital between 1919 and 1966 on a lump sum investment in a standard share index has been calculated to amount to 8 per cent per year *after* tax and *after* allowing for inflation. This notable long-term rate of real return after tax is a tribute to the resilience of the profit system, when it is remembered that, in the words of the authors of the above estimate, 'this period included some twenty years of relative depression, a costly war and its aftermath of austerity, shortages and controls, and a postwar rate of growth in real national income which has scarcely been remarkable' (15).

4. Professor Titmuss has written: 'The British fiscal system is almost unique in the Western World in its generous treatment of wealth holders in allowing them to use family settlements, discretionary trusts, gifts, family covenants and other legal devices for redistributing and rearranging income and wealth' (16). Thus, the income from accumulation trusts set up in favour of children under 21 simply adds to the capital value of the trust eventually received by them when they reach the necessary age.

5. Income which accrues to life insurance and superannuation funds is also not included as part of individual income, though it clearly confers at a later date an important financial advantage to certain sections of the population. Meade estimates certain additions to such funds to have been £236 million in 1959. Though a relatively large number of salary earners benefit in some way from such arrangements, the upper income brackets benefit even more. For example, the top 1 per cent of incomes accounted for one seventh of the Inland Revenue relief offered as a 'special indulgence' to life assurance holders in 1959–60 (17).

6. An estimate of the rentable value of owner-occupied houses must naturally be made if we wish to know the income, or income equivalent, derived from property ownership. Meade puts this figure at £301 million for 1959–60. Again, the rich are not only more likely to own their own houses but they are more likely to own more expensive houses.

This list by no means exhausts the *lacunae* to be found in the statistics of income distribution.[1] The net effect on distribution of the

[1] Changes of composition in the tax population provide another area of problems making intertemporal comparisons very difficult: e.g. a husband and wife are usually counted as one unit for tax purposes, thus 'the phenomenal rise in the amount of marriages and in the number of early marriages is one of the major factors in producing statistical illusion of greater income equality' (R. M. Titmuss, *Income Distribution and Social Change*, Allen and Unwin, London 1962).

factors in question is impossible to quantify with any precision, though the overall inegalitarian impact they have on income distribution is manifest. Meade concludes as follows:

> It would seem that personal incomes from property . . . may be under-estimated by as much as £1,500 million (£200 million for certain deductions allowed by the Inland Revenue, £800 million for under-estimated profits net of depreciation, £200 million for the income of life assurance funds, £300 million for owner-occupied houses) (18).

Only the most visible items have been included here. If the calculations are even roughly accurate then they raise the share of property income in total national income to the range 15 per cent to 25 per cent. According to Meade the consequence of this value for property income is to raise the share of the top 1 per cent of income to a total amount equivalent to that received by the bottom 36 per cent of incomes. As we can see from Table 1.3 the bottom 36 per cent of incomes put together received 12·95 per cent of total income before tax and 14·4 per cent of total income after tax, in 1964. Meade shows that if the share of property income in total income is between 15 per cent and 25 per cent then the absolute share of the top 1 per cent of incomes in total income is in the range 12–16 per cent. Meade's estimates are, of course, based on figures for 1959–60, and it seems probable that between 1959 and 1964 there was 'a slight increase in inequality' (19). But these figures are only offered as orders of magnitude to establish the striking fact that the top 1 per cent of incomes and the bottom third of incomes receive roughly the same share of total income.

On one point Meade himself uses an Inland Revenue figure that should be subjected to closer scrutiny—the figure for profits net of 'depreciation'. The concept of depreciation used by the Inland Revenue refers to that portion of gross profits which are covered by Depreciation Allowances and hence are not taxed. These allowances have been greatly increased over the last decade as an encouragement to investment, and government statisticians make it clear that they bear no necessary relation to real depreciation costs (this is explained in an appendix to the *National Income and Expenditure* blue book for 1965, p. 38). Thus, while 'depreciation' was only £521 million in 1954 it had risen to £1,967 million by 1964. *As a consequence of this rise British companies were actually paying £135 million less in taxes in 1964 than they had been paying in 1954.* The latest figures show that whereas company taxation raised £881 million revenue in 1955 this had dropped to £580 by 1965 (20). Given the erosion of money values over this period and the considerable rise in overall tax revenue, this declining contribution in money terms has meant that the share of companies in total tax has fallen to less than half its value in the course of ten years. Deliberately generous depreciation allowances have offered innumerable ways of avoiding tax on profits. No doubt it is because the category 'depreciation' so often merely refers to untaxed profits that capital gains have been so important over the last ten years. The effect of reinterpreting Meade's estimates in this way would be to increase the share of property income by a large, but indeterminate, amount.

Factor incomes

The approach adopted above was to attempt to discover income distribution by reworking Inland Revenue information. The results of such a scrutiny must remain to some extent inconclusive, though with the strong probability that income inequality has been maintained at a high level, or that, in Titmuss's words: 'Ancient inequalities have assumed new and more subtle forms (21).' However it will be useful, as a check, to look at incomes from another perspective: that of the ratio of profits to wages and other employment incomes.

In 1938 the ratio of gross profits to all employment incomes was 1–4·5, in 1962 it was 1–4·8 and in 1965 1–4·2 (22). The considerable stability of this ratio is maintained over quite long-term periods, with short-run fluctuations cancelling out. (Profits tend to fluctuate more than employment incomes in the short run.) Between 1870 and 1950 the share of wages in the national income varied between 36·6 per cent and 42·6 per cent (23): during the years 1960–2 wages comprised 42 per cent of national income. Changes in the definition of what constitutes 'wages' and 'employment incomes' complicate this picture, as do changes in the composition of the working population. It seems that both employment incomes and property incomes have grown at the expense of incomes from self-employment in this century, with the former, as one would expect, gaining more. The complicating factors to some extent offset one another, leaving the broad relation between the different categories as they were. This, at least, seems to have been the case over the last few decades. The author of an analysis of income distribution in 1959 compares his findings with those made by Professor T. Barna for the year 1937 in the following terms: 'the degree of inequality of producers' or pre-redistribution income seems to have been very similar in the two years' (24). Although year to year variations can be partially correlated with union strength, the constancy of the share of labour in the national income in the long run shows within what narrow limits the unions operate in a capitalist society. Even in the short term it is favourable overall conditions in the economy and labour market which give unions the chance to raise slightly the share of wages.

In his book *Contemporary Capitalism* John Strachey was prompted by facts such as these to reflect that: 'Capitalism, it has turned out, is a Red Queen's sort of country from the wage-earner's point of view. They have to run very fast for a long time to keep in the same place *relative* to the other classes' (25).

Any capitalist economy is a complex ensemble of economic variables: a change in one variable (for example, money wages) triggers off changes in other factors, for example the value of money, which restore the *status quo ante*. This *Alice in Wonderland* logic of a capitalist system from the worker's point of view has again became apparent from a new study of the movement of wages and salaries between 1906 and 1960 published by the National Institute of Economic and Social Research (26). The author, G. Routh, writes that: 'As with Alice, it is sometimes necessary to run faster and faster to stay in the same place . . . the Unions then act as agents for hurrying things along' (27). However, Routh goes on to note that, 'in the race, transient advantages may be of considerable importance to the parties concerned, and may give groups of workers advantages that are obscured in long term comparisons'. Investigations into the economic role of unions tend to indicate that the more militant or the union which finds itself in a more favourable economic conjuncture can raise its members' wage rates considerably in the short term (28). However the self-equilibrating nature of even an imperfect market economy seems to ensure that such 'transient advantages' simply maintain the share of labour in national income rather than significantly increase it.

Routh's study gives valuable information concerning the movement of different types of pay. He concludes that between 1906 and 1960 'the outstanding characteristic of the national pay structure is the rigidity of its relationships'. Table 1.5 compares the position in 1960 with that in 1913.

Table 1.5. Movement of Pay, 1913–60 (Men) (29)

	Movement of pay 1960 as % of 1913
Managers	108
Clerks	81
Foremen	106
Skilled manual workers	94
Semi-skilled workers	99
Unskilled workers	100

The total effect of movements over the period has been somewhat to reduce differentials between male employees, though this reduction disappears if women's pay is also included. The managerial group registers the largest gain over the period, though still a modest one. As this group is composed of very different levels of management some larger changes may be hidden here. Routh's conclusions bring us back again to the role of unions:

> It is a mistake to imagine that there is a sharp division between unionized and ununionized workers, for trade unions cannot do much more than institutionalize and direct drives and aspirations that are already present in individual workers. Unions protect workers against arbitrary acts; they give collections of workers more control over their own destiny than they would have as individuals and present the possibility of attaining social ends that might not otherwise have been obtainable (30).

The welfare state

The discussion so far has not explicitly confronted the redistributive effects of the taxation system and of social welfare when looked at as a whole. An *Economist* survey again provides a useful summary of the significance of the total tax burden in Britain:

> Contrary to undying popular belief Britain is not one of the most heavily taxed countries in the world. True taxes of all kinds devour about one third of the national output. But this is well below the figures of between 40 per cent and 45 per cent which hold good in France, Sweden and Germany. Even Americans suffer 30 per cent of their total incomes to be claimed back in taxes. . . . Partly these differences reflect accounting practice. But a more important factor is the view a country takes about the level of social services it provides. France and Germany give a lot; Britain, like Switzerland, is only middling (there goes another popular myth); and America takes a 'low' view. Both Britain and America, in fact, would appear even lower in the tax burden table if it were not for armaments expenditure (31).

More important than the absolute size of the tax bill is the question of which groups pay it.

Two recent attempts have been made to assess the distribution of the tax burden between different income levels. The assessments take into account not only taxes on wealth and income but also those on consumption (these latter taxes can be imputed on the basis of Family Expenditure Surveys). These studies agree closely on one very important point: the failure of the British tax system to tax the rich significantly more heavily than the poor. Professor A. J. Merrett, summarizing the investigations he conducted with D. A. G. Monk, writes as follows: 'The basic conclusion is therefore that the great bulk of all taxes are in fact paid by tax-payers with relatively modest levels of income.' He adds that 'the percentage of income paid in total taxes tends if anything to be somewhat *higher* at the lower ranges of income' (32). These conclusions are substantially borne out by J. L. Nicholson's investigation of the same problem, which has been summarized as follows: '. . . families within a wide range of income, from nearly the lowest to nearly the highest, constituting in fact the great bulk of the population, pay taxes at an almost uniform rate (33).

Although the income tax is 'progressive' (i.e. taxes the rich more heavily than the poor) this is not the case with the other taxes which are so important in Britain, a number of which are actually regressive. Thus the total revenue raised from all the taxes of wealth and profits (surtax, death duties, profits and excess profits tax) amounted to £933·5 million in the fiscal year 1965–6; this was *less* than the revenue raised by the tax on tobacco alone (£1,014·9m).

Whether the tax system is ultimately redistributive finally depends on the pattern of government expenditure. Fortunately the government publication *Economic Trends* publishes information which relates directly to this problem. The direct and indirect taxes paid by the different income groups are computed against the direct and indirect benefits which, on average, they receive. The evidence suggests that redistribution *within* social classes is more significant than redistribution *between* them. Single adults, and couples before they have children, tend to subsidize larger families and to finance state pensions for the old. Thus in the income range £676–816 per year a single adult would suffer a loss of income of 31 per cent after allowing for both taxes and benefits. A man in this income range with a wife and two children would experience a net loss of income of 5 per cent, while if he had four children his income would actually increase by 23 per cent (34). The income range £816–988 per year exhibited a very similar pattern. Comparing across income ranges one finds that a single adult in the income range £382–460 suffers a loss of income very much the same as the couple without children in the £2,122–2,566 income range: the former suffers a net loss of 24 per cent, the latter of 29 per cent. Or again the couple with an income between £816–988 and one child experience a net reduction of 17 per cent compared with a net reduction of 18 per cent for the couple with two children in the income range £2,122–2,566 (35).

There remains, of course, some element of 'vertical' redistribution between income groups: but this is to be found in most societies and is not a special consequence of the 'welfare state'. J. L. Nicholson's conclusion, after examining both the incidence of direct and indirect taxation and the provision of social services, is that 'there appears to have been little increase in the amount of vertical redistribution between 1937 and 1959' (36).

Comparison over this period of time conceals the more egalitarian effects of total tax and benefits produced by the war and maintained by the Labour Government for a certain period of time after it. There seems to be some parallel between the effect of union activity and the effect of political representation of labour through the Labour Party. When circumstances are favourable both can obtain real advances for those they represent. But in the longer term the logic of a private enterprise system erodes these gains and re-establishes the former relative position. It seems that the power of the labour movement in capitalist society is never a static quantity. This power must expand until it encroaches on the property system, or it will be subject to erosion by the unchallenged momentum of capitalist accumulation. Further aspects of this question will be examined later. At this point it is enough to note that the present Labour government has abandoned any policy which threatened to produce a significant redistributive effect. In the ill-fated National Plan the share of Gross National Product devoted to expenditure on Social Security, Education and Public Housing was to be increased by a modest amount, while that for Health and Welfare Services was to be slightly reduced. The government was envisaging an increase in the relative size of the social security sector in the period 1964–70 which was to be something about half as large as the increase actually achieved between 1957 and 1963 (11 per cent as against 23 per cent). During this same period (1964–70) the overall population is expected to increase by 14·8 per cent and the number of people aged 65 or over to increase by 11·1 per cent. These demographic changes indicate how inadequate were the government's plans, even if all had gone well. And as these plans were to be financed by economic growth, we may assume that they will certainly not be achieved now the growth targets announced in the Plan have been abandoned.

The methods used by J. L. Nicholson and by *Economic Trends* to investigate redistribution are necessarily somewhat crude when it comes to imputing the value of benefits received by the different income groups. They probably underestimate the extent to which the middle and property-owning classes gain from the formally equal system of welfare provision. In a class society, it is difficult, if not impossible, to ensure that publicly-provided welfare services will not be more intensively used by the richer sections of the population. Just as the recent rate rebate scheme was taken advantage of more readily in middle-class areas than it was in working-class ones, so in the case of the social services. It is this factor that partly explains the different rates of infant mortality to be found in different social classes. A recent study revealed that death near or at birth is twice as common in the lower working class as it is in the upper middle class (37). Perhaps the best researched example of the unequal use of a public service is provided by the workings of the educational system. As with other forms of social provision there is, in the educational field, also a private sector receiving indirect public subsidies through tax rebates. As if in imitation of the economy the education system is pervaded by a competitive and utilitarian ethos and the chances are always stacked in favour of the offspring of the richer sections of the population. A recent study sub-titled 'The Trend of Class Differentials in Educational Opportunity in England and Wales' (38) came to the following conclusions. Class differentials in educational opportunity 'result in the elimination of some 96 out of every 100 manual working-class children from formal full-time education before the age of 17'. The authors note that:

> . . . as this process of elimination goes on, so the relative prospects of survival as between children of different social origin become steadily less equal. At 11–13 a professional or managerial family's child had nine times as high a chance of entering a grammar or independent school as an unskilled worker's child. Some years later, at 17, he had nearly thirty times as high a chance of still being at school.

J. W. B. Douglas has shown that even among children whose performance in the eleven plus was similar, the child of the upper-middle class was three times as likely to go to a grammar school or public school as the lower manual-class child (39). The expansion of the comprehensive type of school is unlikely to modify these class differentials as it has already shown that streaming produces much the same results (40). Moreover the privileged private enclave of education continues to exist with teaching conditions much superior to those found in the public sector: for example a staff/pupil ratio of 1/11·5 instead of 1/18 as in the grammar schools (41). Little and Westergaard point out that 'there are certainly no indications of any narrowing of class differential in access to the universities over the generations'. If, as the Robbins Report shows, the proportion of male students from the working class has not changed since before the war, with all the social upheaval of these two decades, then future change is likely to be lethargic. As it is, 'an unskilled manual worker's daughter has a chance of only one in five or six hundred of entering a university: a chance a hundred times lower than if she had been born into a professional family' (42).

In education, as in the economic field, a general rise in standards has not produced a big change in the relative position of the social classes. This has considerable implications for rates of social mobility. The evidence available on social mobility in the first five decades of this century indicates that rates between the major social categories did not vary (43).

In the past it seems likely that internal promotion within companies, the civil service, etc., contributed to this social mobility. There is reason to believe that educational qualifications are becoming increasingly important for jobs in these fields. In consequence, overall rates of social mobility are unlikely to rise as the educational system will return class differentials to the occupational hierarchy in the next generation. As all this suggests, given the commanding position which it occupies in any capitalist society, it is difficult to confine any discussion of economic equality to the purely economic sphere.

A further check remains to be carried out before exploring why it is that inequality has persisted undiminished in British society. If wealth has accumulated at one pole of society, then we would expect relative poverty to remain at the opposite pole, if indeed the overall relation between social classes has not changed. And in fact that is exactly what we do find.

Evidence concerning poverty in Britain today is drawn together and analysed by Brian Abel-Smith and Peter Townsend in a recent book,

The Poor and the Poorest (Bell, London, 1965). After careful calculation their conclusion is:

> In 1960 approximately 18 per cent of the households and 14·2 per cent of the persons in the United Kingdom, representing nearly 7,500,000 persons, were living below a defined 'national assistance' level of living. About 35 per cent were living in households primarily dependent on pensions, 23 per cent in households primarily dependent on other state benefits, and 41 per cent in households primarily dependent on earnings (44).

The plight of old people has been an open scandal for some time, yet a significant proportion, amounting to something like a million pensioners, still falls below the National Assistance level, while one half of all pensioners are solely or primarily dependent on the state, which means that they exist at or slightly above National Assistance levels (45).

There are two curious types of government-sponsored poverty which are less well known than that of the pensioners—those who are denied the full National Assistance either because of 'the wage stop' or because their rents are too high. Sickness and unemployment benefit must, according to the regulations, never exceed the wages a man would earn if he was employed. It is thought that without this 'incentive' to return to work the unemployed worker would be happy to live on the dole. Even during the autumn of 1965, when unemployment was very low, there were nearly 15,000 families who were denied the full National Assistance for this reason. And as large families are the ones most affected by the 'wage stop' provision, the number of children involved at this time was nearly 60,000. Usually National Assistance covers rent, but if rents of private accommodation are considered to be too high they will not be fully met. At the end of 1964, 20,000 households (with approximately 60,000 children) were in this position. All these groups are of direct concern to the trade union movement: the old, unemployed or sick worker needs union defence of his interests just as much as the worker on the job. But the most striking feature of the Townsend and Abel-Smith survey is the high proportion of *currently* employed workers who fall below the officially defined poverty threshold. On 20 July 1965 it was announced in the House of Commons that between 150,000 and 250,000 families had incomes below the National Assistance minimum level. Anne Lapping commented in *New Society* on this figure that: 'The average number of children in these families is probably something over three. This means that at least 450,000–600,000 children in Britain today live in homes that cannot afford what the NAB considers the minimum essential even when the breadwinner has work' (46).

The government's Family Expenditure Survey for 1964 showed that 15·7 per cent of all male manual workers earned less than £12 per week and that no less than 42·7 per cent earned less than £15 per week. These figures give a more accurate picture of the low wage sector than the frequently-quoted statistics of the industrial wages released by the Ministry of Labour. Thus, according to the Family Expenditure Survey, 68 per cent of the manual workers earned less than £18 per week in a year when the Ministry of Labour estimated average earnings at £17 12s in April and £18 2s in October. The Survey's own average for the year is £16 9s. *Labour Research* commented on this as follows: 'The reason for this discrepancy is undoubtedly the relatively narrower categories for which the Ministry of Labour collects figures—they exclude for instance, agriculture, railways and distribution' (47).

Another circumstance which leads to a certain underestimation of the incidence of poverty is the way in which the cost of living index is composed. The commonly quoted index naturally includes all those items which a middle-income family purchases. The pattern of expenditure of the poorer sections of the population is known to be very different and hence the real price index of the goods they buy. Thus the purchase of consumer durable goods figures significantly in the budget of the middle-income family but not in that of the poorer family. The ownership of televisions is relatively widely diffused—only 20 per cent of households are without them. But, according to the Family Expenditure Survey of 1964, 47 per cent of households do not possess a washing-machine, 66 per cent are without a refrigerator and 63 per cent are without a car. The price of these goods has actually tended to fall over the last decade or so, compared with steep rises in the price of items which comprise the greater part of the poorer families' budget (rent, food, fuel and light, etc.). According to the Ministry of Labour, the cost of living index in August 1966 had risen

	January 1952–62	January 1962–4	January 1952–64
Pensioner's index	+44%	+11%	+60%
Index of retail prices	+36%	+9%	+48%
High income index	+31%	+7%	+40%

to 117·3 from a base line in January 1962. The cost of durable consumer goods had risen by 10 per cent less than the general price rise while the cost of living had risen 12·2 per cent more, fuel and light by 3 per cent more. A Fabian group has devised the above comparison of the general index with an index based on the known expenditure pattern of pensioners, and another on the expenditure pattern of 'high-income' families (48).

The general effect of price changes over the past decade or more has clearly been to reinforce powerfully the inegalitarian tendencies which were noticed in the section above on the overall distribution of wealth and income.

Before the 1964 election the Labour leaders promised that a Labour government would make a serious onslaught on the shameful survivals of poverty in Britain today. Indeed such measures as a minimum income guarantee and pensions at half pay were offered to the trade union movement in exchange for their co-operation in the Incomes Policy. On 23 September 1964 Wilson gave the following pledge on television:

> What we are going to do now—we are going to do it early because it is urgent in the first few weeks of a Labour government—is to provide a guaranteed income below which no one will be allowed to fall.

We now learn that such a guarantee is unlikely to be introduced before 1970. According to the National Plan: 'An income guarantee would not contribute towards faster economic growth'(49). The scheme to make pensions equal to half pay has gone the same way. According to the National Plan:

> From studies so far undertaken, it is clear that radical changes in pension arrangements are bound to take some time to carry out, if they are to be soundly based to meet the needs of coming generations and if care is to be taken that the cost can be met without damage to the economy. Although, therefore, work is proceeding on a pensions scheme, it will not have any significant effect on expenditure up to 1970 (50).

The Labour government has made a few changes, 'National Assistance' has been renamed 'Social Security', but on the whole the promised new deal in welfare has been sacrificed to maintain sterling and the East of Suez policy. The government's present policy on welfare questions was briefly summarized in the House of Commons by one of the ministers concerned: 'We are now engaged in an urgent study of the whole problem and have been for a long time' (51).

My whole discussion of inequality in Britain has been primarily statistical. But how revealing of capitalist society that the deprivation and class division that it produces can be crudely indicated in this way. The true differences between men and women are incommensurable—it is in this sense that they should be equal. Any purely quantitive equality would violate the socialist principle, 'From each according to his ability, to each according to his need'. Capitalist society effects a reduction of quality to quantity; a price is put on everybody and human labour is bought just like any other commodity. The corrosion of human relations produced by a class society is more profound than anything than statistics can reveal:

> Considered only in terms of opportunity and power, class appears as a unilateral possession of privileges, a greater accumulation of benefits and powers in one sector of society than in another. But class is clearly more than this: it is a universal loss. There is one human need it violates in all members of society, oppressors and oppressed alike: the need of men for each other. It is its aspect as a pure human *division*, rather than an economic or political disparity, which is most often ignored and yet which most wholly describes class (52).

NOTES

(1) 'Still no Property-owning Democracy' in *The Economist*, 15 January 1966.
(2) J. E. Meade, *Efficiency, Equality and the Ownership of Property* (Allen and Unwin, London 1964), p. 27. The figures for 1954 (in brackets) are from H. F. Lydall and D. G. Tipping, 'The Distribution of Personal Wealth in Britain' in *Oxford Bulletin of Statistics*, February 1961.
(3) *The Economist*, 15 January 1966.
(4) C. D. Harbury, 'Inheritance and the Distribution of Personal Wealth' in *Economic Journal*, vol. 72, 1962.
(5) *The Economist*, loc. cit.
(6) 'Shareholders: Why So Few?' in *The Economist*, 2 July 1966.
(7) H. F. Liddell and D. G. Tipping, 'The Distribution of Personal Wealth in Britain' in *Oxford Bulletin of Statistics*, February 1961.
(8) *The Economist*, 15 January 1966.
(9) J. E. Meade, *Efficiency, Equality and the Ownership of Property* (Allen and Unwin, London 1964), p. 69.
(10) *National Income and Expenditure*, H.M.S.O., London 1966.
(11) *The Economist*, 27 August 1966.
(12) R. M. Titmuss, *Income Distribution and Social Change* (Allen and Unwin, London 1962), p. 115.
(13) J. E. Meade, op. cit., p. 79.
(14) *Final Report*, Royal Commission on Income Tax, Cmd 9474, 1955, pp. 380–1.
(15) A. J. Merrett and A. Sykes, *District Bank Review*, September 1963. The return between 1919 and 1966 comes from the same authors in 'Return on Equities and Fixed Interest Securities, 1919–1966', in *District Bank Review*, September 1966.

(16) R. M. Titmuss, 'Goals of Today's Welfare State' in *Towards Socialism* ['New Left Review', ed. Peny Anderson and Robin Blackburn] (Collins, London 1965), p. 361.
(17) R. M. Titmuss, *Income Distribution and Social Change* (Allen and Unwin, London 1962), p. 167.
(18) Meade, op. cit., p. 80.
(19) 'Rising Inequality' in *New Society*, 22 September 1966.
(20) *National Income and Expenditure*, H.M.S.O. 1966.
(21) R. M. Titmuss, op. cit., p. 199.
(22) *Annual Abstract of Statistics*, 1956 and 1963; *National Income and Expenditure*, 1966. It should be noted that employment incomes includes managerial salaries and directors' fees.
(23) E. H. Phelps-Brown and E. P. Hart, 'The Share of Wages in the National Income' in *Economic Journal*, Vol. LXII, 1952.
(24) J. L. Nicholson, *Redistribution of Income in the United Kingdom* (Bowes and Bowes, London 1965), p. 61. The redistributive effects of taxation in these years will be considered later.
(25) John Strachey, *Contemporary Capitalism* (Gollancz, London 1956), p. 150. Strachey quotes the following passage from *Alice in Wonderland:* 'Well in our country', said Alice, still panting a little, 'you'd generally get to somewhere else—if you ran very fast for a long time, as we've been doing.' 'A slow sort of country,' said the Queen. 'Now *here*, you see, it takes all the running you can do to keep in the same place.'
(26) Guy Routh, *Occupation and Pay in Great Britain, 1906–60* (National Institute of Economic and Social Research, London 1965).
(27) Routh, op. cit., p. 152.
(28) cf. Albert Rees, *Wage Inflation*, National Industries Conference Board (U.S.A. 1957).
(29) Routh, op. cit., p. 152.
(30) Routh, op. cit., p. 153.
(31) *The Economist*, 26 June 1966.
(32) A. J. Merrett, *Sunday Times*, Business Section, 25 September 1966. His conclusions are based on 'The Structure of U.S. Taxation 1962/3' by A. J. Merrett and D. A. G. Monk, in *Oxford Bulletin of Statistics*, August 1966.
(33) *Income and Wealth*, Series X, edited by Colin Clark and Greer Stuvel (Bowes, London 1964).
(34) 'The Incidence of Tax and Social Service Benefits in 1963 and 1964' in *Economic Trends*, August 1966.
(35) All examples from *Economic Trends*, August 1966.
(36) J. L. Nicholson, *Redistribution of Income in the United Kingdom* (Bowes and Bowes, London 1965), p. 61.
(37) Neville R. Butler and Denis G. Bonham, *Perinatal Mortality* (E. and S. Livingstone, London 1963).
(38) Alan Little and John Westergaard, *British Journal of Sociology*, December 1964, pp. 301–16.
(39) J. W. B. Douglas, *The Home and the School* (MacGibbon and Kee, London 1964), p. 122. The tests used in the educational system and the nature of what is taught, all contribute to class differentials. Douglas's study shows that the measured 'intelligence' of working-class children actually deteriorates while they are at school, a fact which should lead us both to question the evidence of intelligence tests and the values which permeate education and society (cf. Basil Bernstein: 'Language and Social Class' in *British Journal of Sociology*, Vol. XI, 1960, p. 271).

(40) H. Glennerster and R. Pryke, *The Public Schools*, Fabian Pamphlet, 1964. This pamphlet points out that 'at the growing points of power, in the large industrial firms, the influence of the Public schools has been growing'.
(41) cf. D. N. Holly's article in *British Journal of Sociology*, June 1965.
(42) Little and Westergaard, op. cit.
(43) cf. David Glass (ed.), *Social Mobility in Britain* (Routledge, London 1954).
(44) Abel-Smith and Townsend, op. cit., p. 65.
(45) Peter Townsend and Dorothy Wedderburn, *The Aged in the Welfare State*, Occasional Papers in Social Administration, no. 14, 1965.
(46) Anne Lapping, 'The Unknown Depths of Poverty' in *New Society*, 9 December 1965.
(47) 'Family Incomes' in *Labour Research*, Vol. LV, no. 8, June 1966.
(48) *Ministry of Labour Gazette* data in 'A Plan for Incomes', Fabian Society, 1965, p. 7. *Labour Research* for June 1964 also discussed the problem of using the cost of living index.
(49) 'The National Plan', H.M.S.O., London 1965, p. 204.
(50) ibid.
(51) Douglas Houghton, *Hansard* 23 February 1965, quoted in J. Kincaid, 'The Glossy Soup Kitchen: Social Security under Labour' in *International Socialism*, Summer 1966.
(52) Perry Anderson, 'Sweden: a study in Social Democracy' in *New Left Review*, May 1961.

2

THE DISTRIBUTION OF PERSONAL INCOME IN THE U.K.

R J NICHOLSON

In 1957, Professor F. W. Paish contributed to *The Lloyds Bank Review*[1] in which he examined the changes in the distribution of personal income over the years 1938–55, and two years later Dr H. F. Lydall, in a contribution[2] to the *Journal* of the Royal Statistical Society, made a more detailed study of the changes over the longer period 1938–57. These writers showed that the concentration of personal income, both before and after tax, in the hands of the top 5 per cent of income recipients was substantially reduced after the war, compared with 1938, and that this tendency towards greater equality continued during the post-war years which their analyses covered. Indeed, Lydall found that, 'If anything the tendency towards reduced inequality of pre-tax income seems to have been accelerating.' The present article, linking up with this earlier work, examines the distribution of personal income in the period 1949–63 to see what light more recent data shed on the trends found for the earlier post-war years.

Defining personal income

Both Paish and Lydall used the estimates of personal income as set out and tabulated in the national income and expenditure accounts for the U.K. These figures have been criticized, however, particularly by Professor Titmuss,[3] as being inadequate for studying changes in the distribution of incomes. A further analysis based on these data thus requires some preliminary justification.

[1] 'The Real Incidence of Personal Taxation', January 1967.
[2] 'The Long-term Trend in the Size Distribution of Income', *Journal of the Royal Statistical Society*, Series A, 122, Part 1, 1959.
[3] R. M. Titmuss, *Income Distribution and Social Change* (Allen and Unwin, London 1962).

First published in Lloyds Bank Review *No. 83, January 1967.*

First, it is argued that the number of incomes in the national income tabulations is a compromise between the number of family incomes and the number of individual incomes, since it is derived from Inland Revenue records in which the incomes of husband and wife are counted as one, and all other incomes are counted separately. Hence, the distribution of personal income could be affected by changes in the age of marriage and by changes in the proportion of the total population married and of married women going out to work. These changes may be important when pre-war and post-war distributions of income are compared, because considerable sociological movements took place as a result of the war, and it was in connection with such comparisons that Titmuss made his sharpest criticisms. However, these demographical and sociological changes have been less rapid since 1949 and would not distort comparisons of income distributions over the last decade.

Secondly, this definition of personal income is criticized on the ground that certain claims on wealth are excluded: for instance, undistributed profits and 'tax avoidance' incomes which fall outside income-tax regulations. The effect of extending the definition of personal income to include these other claims on wealth is by no means certain and there are, anyway, differences of opinion as to what the appropriate definition should be, e.g. whether companies' undistributed profits should be included. It is probable that the shape of the income distribution, i.e. the proportionate shares of different income groups, might be modified, but it does not follow that the *trend of changes* in income distribution derived from the national income tables would be discredited. Indeed, even in pre-war/post-war comparisons, Lydall's estimates suggest that the trends would not be fundamentally altered. In the national income figures of personal income we do, at least, have a consistently-defined aggregate which must account for a major proportion of total income on any definition and one which is adequate for picking out changing trends in the distribution of incomes in post-war years.

In the following tables, comparisons are made between various levels of income and shares of particular groups in terms of incomes ranged in order of size. For example, the top 1 per cent of incomes all receive more than a certain amount, those in the top 5 per cent are all above a lower figure, those in the top 30 per cent are above a still smaller figure, and so on. Thus, Table 2.1 shows that the top

1 per cent of incomes were all above £1,861 in 1949 and exceeded £3,364 in 1963, while the top 40 per cent of incomes had a minimum of £304 and £773 in these two years. These money incomes which divide off the top 1 per cent, top 5 per cent, top 10 per cent and so on of incomes may conveniently be referred to as 'percentile incomes'.[1] Secondly, the distribution of incomes can be considered in terms of percentage shares. From Table 2.3 on page 42, for example, it will be seen that in 1963 the top 1 per cent of incomes received 7·9 per cent of the total, the next 4 per cent received 11·2 per cent, and those in the range from the 11th to the 40th percentage bands from the top shared 39 per cent of the total.

Incomes before tax

Percentile incomes before tax are shown in Table 2.1 and index numbers derived from them in Table 2.2.

Table 2.1. Incomes Before Tax

	1949	1957	1959	1960	1961	1962	1963
	£	£	£	£	£	£	£
Top 1% at least	1,861	2,545	2,839	3,039	3,162	3,255	3,364
„ 5% „ „	763	1,198	1,350	1,442	1,526	1,592	1,697
„ 10% „ „	565	940	1,068	1,151	1,215	1,273	1,357
„ 20% „ „	427	773	844	909	966	1,028	1,067
„ 30% „ „	353	667	718	776	828	865	899
„ 40% „ „	304	577	613	653	719	742	773
„ 50% „ „	259	491	514	543	612	621	645
„ 70% „ „	122	304	315	331	374	378	400

Between 1949 and 1957, the lower the income the greater the rate of increase of income (first column, Table 2.2). Without exception, the growth-rate increases as one moves from the upper to the lower income ranges. These trends, which have been studied in detail by

[1] This method of using 'percentiles' was that employed by Lydall. Alternatively, using Paish's method, the comparisons could be made in terms of the shares of specified *numbers* of incomes. In view of the gradual increase in the number of incomes over the years the percentile-income method is preferable. All the numerical results given in the present article have been obtained by logarithmic interpolation into the published distributions.

Table 2.2. Index Numbers of Incomes Before Tax

	1957 (1949 = 100)	1959 (1957 = 100)	1960	1961 (1959 = 100)	1962 (1959 = 100)	1963
Top 1%	137	112	107	111	115	119
„ 5%	157	113	107	113	118	126
„ 10%	166	114	108	114	119	127
„ 20%	181	109	108	115	122	126
„ 30%	189	108	108	115	121	125
„ 40%	190	106	107	117	121	126
„ 50%	190	105	106	119	121	126
„ 70%	249	104	105	119	120	127

Lydall and Paish, indicate some reduction in the inequality of incomes in the post-war years up to 1957.

The next column, however, shows a different picture. Between 1957 and 1959 the top three percentile incomes increased most rapidly, the rates of increase of the lower ranges being progressively less, so that the lowest pre-tax incomes show the least rate of growth. This represents a movement away from equality, the higher incomes pulling away from the lower ones. Over the period 1959–63 all incomes, except the top one, increased in about the same proportion. It is clear, therefore, that since 1957 the trend towards equality in incomes before tax has ceased.

An alternative way of showing these trends, and one which brings out clearly the changes in the distribution of incomes over time, is to set out the percentages of total income held by selected groups of income-recipients, counting from the richest to the poorest.

Table 2.3. Percentage Distribution of Incomes Before Tax

Group of income-recipients	1949	1957	1959	1960	1961	1962	1963
	%	%	%	%	%	%	%
Top 1%	11·2	8·2	8·4	8·5	8·1	8·1	7·9
2–5%	12·6	10·9	11·5	11·4	11·1	11·1	11·2
6–10%	9·4	9·0	9·5	9·8	9·7	9·7	9·6
11–40%	34·9	37·6	38·4	38·5	37·6	38·6	39·0
41–70%	19·2	23·1	22·5	22·1	23·5	22·6	22·6
Bottom 30%	12·7	11·3	9·7	9·8	10·0	9·8	9·7

The most considerable change is that which took place between 1949 and 1957. Between these two years the proportion of pre-tax income accounted for by the top 10 per cent of incomes fell from over 33 per cent to 28 per cent, while that of the middle 11–70 per cent increased from 54 per cent to nearly 61 per cent. The share of the bottom 30 per cent fell slightly, so that, as Paish has noted, the redistribution was from the extremes to the middle ranges. The percentage shares from 1957 onwards, however, show no continuation of these trends. Apart from a reduction in the proportion going to the bottom 30 per cent, the distribution since 1957 has not significantly changed.

Incomes after tax

Because of the stability that we have just noted in the distribution of pre-tax incomes since 1957, changes in rates of income tax and surtax may be important in affecting the distribution of incomes at the actual disposal of persons. The table below will serve to summarize the way tax rates have changed. It shows, in the form of index numbers for two specimen families of different composition, the amounts of earned income taken in tax at different levels of income for the tax years 1956/57 to 1962/63.

Table 2.4. Index Numbers of Amounts Taken in Income Tax and Surtax

	Married couple without children					Married couple with 3 children			
	(Pre-tax earned income £)								
	600	1,000	2,000	5,000	10,000	1,000	2,000	5,000	10,000
1956/57	100	100	100	100	100	100	100	100	100
1957/58	100	100	100	89	92	84	97	85	89
1958/59	100	100	100	89	92	84	97	84	89
1959/60	88	91	91	83	87	73	88	79	84
1960/61	88	91	91	83	87	73	88	79	84
1961/62	88	91	91	61	66	73	88	59	64
1962/63	77	87	90	61	66	66	87	59	64

Clearly, there has been a general reduction in rates of direct taxation, but the most considerable fall has been in the rates on higher incomes since 1960/61. On an income of £1,000, a married couple with three children paid in tax in 1960/61 rather less than three-quarters of what they paid in 1956/57, and two-thirds of this sum in 1962/63. If their income had been £5,000, however, while in 1960/61 they would still have paid 79 per cent of their 1956/57 tax total, in 1962/63 their tax liability would have dropped sharply to 59 per cent. This greater proportionate reduction was, in fact, experienced by all those with annual incomes of about £3,000 and upwards, i.e. incomes in the top ranges.

Under a progressive tax system, the effect of reductions in tax rates can be offset by the effect of inflation on money incomes. As Paish pointed out:

> During a period of rising prices, a man who succeeds in increasing his income before tax by an amount just enough to offset the rise in the cost of living, so that his *real* income before tax remains constant, is continually tending to move into higher tax brackets. With a system of progressive taxation, he will therefore pay in tax a constantly increasing proportion of a constant real income, even if rates of tax are not raised.

To show how tax changes have affected the distribution of incomes Tables 2.5 and 2.6 below repeat the foregoing analysis for percentile incomes (as defined on page 41) and the shares of groups of income-recipients for incomes after tax.

Table 2.5. Incomes After Tax

	1949	1957	1959	1960	1961	1962	1963
	£	£	£	£	£	£	£
Top 1% at least	1,270	1,822	2,073	2,161	2,327	2,406	2,545
„ 5% „ „	660	1,038	1,212	1,292	1,357	1,427	1,480
„ 10% „ „	520	860	965	1,036	1,087	1,164	1,205
„ 20% „ „	382	701	787	831	868	933	973
„ 30% „ „	317	593	655	711	761	794	819
„ 40% „ „	277	526	557	588	633	667	699
„ 50% „ „	250	439	478	508	540	557	576
„ 70% „ „	115	281	287	305	333	336	356

Incomes after tax over the period 1949–57 (except that at the 50 per cent mark) show the same trend towards equality as incomes before tax. The changes between 1957 and 1959, similarly, bring this trend to an end with higher post-tax incomes increasing more than those in the lower ranges. Between 1959 and 1963 all incomes

Table 2.6. Index Numbers of Incomes After Tax

	1957 (1949 = 100)	1959 (1957 = 100)	1960	1961 (1959 = 100)	1962	1963
Top 1%	144	114	104	112	116	123
,, 5%	157	117	107	112	117	122
,, 10%	165	112	107	113	121	125
,, 20%	183	112	106	110	119	124
,, 30%	187	110	109	116	121	125
,, 40%	190	106	107	114	120	126
,, 50%	176	109	106	113	117	121
,, 70%	245	102	106	116	117	124

increase by about the same amount. This pattern of change is confirmed by the distribution of incomes after tax, as given in Table 2.7.

Whether taken before tax or after tax, therefore, the distribution of incomes shows the same general trends, with the tendency towards greater equality ceasing after 1957. However, some slight difference between the two bases is shown by the results for the very high incomes. Before tax, the highest percentile income (i.e. that relating to the top 1 per cent of incomes) increased less rapidly than the others over the period 1959–63: by 19 per cent, against 25–27 per cent for the rest (Table 2.2). After tax, however, the increase is the same as for the other groups (Table 2.6). Similarly, the proportion of incomes before tax taken by the top 1 per cent class fell over

Table 2.7. Percentage Distribution of Incomes After Tax

Group of income-recipients	1949	1957	1959	1960	1961	1962	1963
	%	%	%	%	%	%	%
Top 1%	6·4	5·0	5·2	5·1	5·5	5·5	5·2
2–5%	11·3	9·9	10·6	10·5	10·5	10·7	10·5
6–10%	9·4	9·1	9·4	9·4	9·1	9·4	9·5
11–40%	37·0	38·5	39·8	39·8	38·9	39·2	39·5
41–70%	21·3	24·0	23·7	23·5	24·3	23·6	23·5
Bottom 30%	14·6	13·4	11·2	11·7	11·9	11·7	11·8

this period, from 8·4–7·9 per cent (Table 2.3), whereas on a post-tax basis the share was unchanged, at 5·2 per cent (Table 2.7). Thus, tax changes underline the ending of the movement towards equality, since their effect is to improve the relative position of the top income groups—a somewhat striking result, conflicting with what might have been expected from a tax system in which rates are steeply progressive.

The burden of taxation

Table 2.8 shows that between 1949 and 1957 the proportion of total tax collected from the top 5 per cent of incomes fell from 69½

Table 2.8. Percentages of Total Income Tax and Surtax Raised from Specified Groups of Income-recipients

Group of income-recipients	1949	1957	1959	1960	1961	1962	1963
Top 1%	46·0	35·3	34·5	34·4	30·0	28·4	28·0
2–5%	23·6	18·9	20·1	19·7	19·9	18·5	19·3
6–10%	8·6	9·0	10·2	10·0	10·0	10·8	11·0
11–40%	16·2	24·9	24·8	25·4	27·6	29·7	29·8
41–70%	4·4	11·2	9·7	9·7	11·4	11·8	11·3
Bottom 30%	1·3	0·7	0·6	0·8	1·0	1·0	0·6

to just over 54 per cent, while that raised from the middle 11 per cent–70 per cent band increased correspondingly, from 20½–36 per cent. This shift in the burden of taxation reflects the combined effects of three factors: changes in the tax rates, which were reduced during these years; the inflation of money incomes—so that equivalent real incomes are taxed at higher proportionate rates; and the redistribution of pre-tax income away from the highest income groups taxed at the highest rates, a development which Paish has called the 'loss of taxable capacity'. This loss of taxable capacity (shown by the figures in Table 2.3) was the main cause of the shift. Although tax rates on the highest incomes fell proportionately less than those on lower incomes, the percentages of pre-tax income taken in direct taxes (shown in Table 2.9) fell for the top 5 per

Table 2.9. Percentages of Pre-tax Income of Specified Groups of Income-recipients Taken in Direct Taxes

Group of income-recipients	1949	1957	1959	1960	1961	1962	1963
Top 1%	48·8	45·5	43·1	46·1	41·5	39·7	39·1
2–5%	22·4	18·4	18·3	19·7	20·0	19·9	19·0
6–10%	10·9	10·7	11·3	11·6	11·5	12·6	12·5
11–40%	5·5	7·1	6·8	7·5	8·2	8·8	8·4
41–70%	2·7	5·2	4·5	5·1	5·4	5·9	5·5
Bottom 30%	1·2	0·7	0·7	0·9	1·1	1·1	0·6
All incomes	11·9	10·6	10·5	11·4	11·2	11·4	11·0

cent of incomes but rose or remained constant for the 6 per cent –70 per cent band.

Between 1957 and 1963 the tax burden continued to be lightened on the highest incomes. The proportion of total tax collected from the top 5 per cent of incomes fell from 54–47 per cent, but that from the 6–10 per cent band rose from 9–11 per cent and that from the 11–70 per cent band increased from 36–41 per cent (Table 2.8), the major part of these shifts occurring after 1960. How did this happen?

During these years, as we have seen, the distribution of income before tax was virtually unchanged. There was, therefore, no further significant loss of taxable capacity. The shift in the tax burden must, then, have been the result of the greater proportionate reduction after 1960 in tax rates on the highest incomes (Table 2.4). Indeed, as Table 2.9 shows, it was only for the top 1 per cent that there was a fall in the percentage of income taken in direct taxes over the period 1957 and 1963, a fall proportionately greater than that between 1949 and 1957. For all other ranges of income the reduction in tax rates has been offset by the inflation of money incomes, with a corresponding rise in the relative amounts taken by the tax collector.

Thus, although the burden of direct taxation has shifted over the whole period 1949–63 the explanation of the shift has changed. Before 1957 it was due to loss of taxable capacity in the highest income groups; since then it has been due to changes in tax rates.

Reasons for check to greater equality

The trend towards the reduction of inequality in the distribution of personal income seems to have come to an end by 1957. Indeed if, as is sometimes suggested, certain 'tax avoidance' incomes and other claims on wealth outside personal income have increased over the last decade and are concentrated more among higher income-recipients, it is possible that the distribution of incomes on some wider definition may have moved towards greater inequality. This, however, is conjectural. In the context of personal income as defined in the national income accounts, a comparison of Tables 2.3 and 2.7 shows that the significant change has been the end of the trend towards equality in incomes before tax. Why has this occurred?

The reasons for the continued movement towards equality after the war were rising prices, continuously high demand and the virtual elimination of unemployment, all of which led to earned income rising faster than other forms of personal income. Lydall's view was that, so long as these trends were unchecked, the tendency towards equality would continue. There was certainly no failure of demand after 1957—gross domestic product grew at a marginally faster rate 1957–63 than over the years 1949–57—and employment was no less full. What, then, has happened? It is true that consumers' prices increased at a faster average rate in the years 1949–57 than in the later period 1957–63: at 3·9 per cent, against 2·0 per cent, a year. This may have been a contributing factor to the end of the movement towards equality but is unlikely to be the whole explanation. More important has been the change in the rates of growth of different forms of personal income. (Table 2.10.)

The first two columns of this table, covering the periods during which reductions in inequality of personal income have been demonstrated by Paish and Lydall, show that the most rapidly growing sector of personal income was income from employment, growing faster than total self-employment income and incomes from rent, dividends and interest.

Since 1957 the pattern has changed. Growth of employment income has slowed down relatively to that of self-employment income and, within employment income, the rate of growth of wages has slowed down relatively to that of salaries. In self-employment income, that of professional persons has expanded most rapidly,

Table 2.10. Growth of Forms of Personal Income

	1938–49 (1938 = 100)	1949–57 (1949 = 100)	1957–63 (1957 = 100)
Wages	231	173	129
Salaries	237	190	157
Total employment income	240	179	140
Professional persons	189	129	136
Farmers	509	129	118
Sole traders	179	129	125
Total self-employment income	216	129	125
Rent, dividends, interest	104	142	172
Transfers	271	170	179

faster, in fact, than wages. The most striking change, however, has been the accelerating rate of growth of rent, dividends and interest after the war, emerging as the most rapidly-growing sector of personal income since 1957.

Some light on the relative growth-rates of total wages and salaries is shed by the figures below, derived from the national income accounts, showing numbers of wage- and salary-earners, and average wages and salaries in manufacturing industry.

Between 1949 and 1957 the average wage in manufacturing increased by 73 per cent and average salary by only 54 per cent. Up to 1955, moreover, the number of wage-earners increased more than the number of salary-earners. Since 1957 average salaries have caught up, and increased at much the same rate as average wages: between 1957 and 1963 the increases in manufacturing industry were 35 per cent for salaries and 31 per cent for wages, rates of growth confirmed by the Ministry of Labour's indexes of salaries and average earnings (which include industries and services outside manufacturing). The number of wage-earners, however, has fallen since 1955, whereas the number of salary-earners has continued to rise, indeed by nearly one-fifth since 1957. Thus, with the average salary increasing as fast as the average wage, the relatively greater rate of growth of *total* salaries than of wages since 1957 is due to the continued increase in the number of salary-earners. Table 2.11 shows also that the average salary is about 50 per cent greater than the average wage but, of course, salaries reach up into much higher income ranges than wages.

Table 2.11. Wages and Salaries in Manufacturing Industry

	1949	1955	1957	1963
Wage-earners ('000)	5,870	6,340	6,290	6,150
Salary-earners ('000)	1,170	1,500	1,600	1,890
Average wage (£)	290	444	503	659
Average salary (£)	489	661	754	1,020

It is not possible to obtain estimates of numbers or average incomes of those classified in the national income accounts as professional persons, but since these include doctors, dentists, lawyers and architects, average professional incomes are certainly very much higher than wages. Rent, dividends and interest, like salaries and professional incomes, are usually associated with higher incomes and it is, therefore, the more rapid growth of these three forms of personal income, particularly rent, dividends and interest, compared with that of wages, that has ended the trend towards equality in income.

Dr Lydall, writing of the years up to 1957, saw the trend to greater equality, though unlikely to continue as rapidly in the future as in the immediate past, as a long-term development which might be stopped or reversed only by the onset of a major slump. Professor Paish was more doubtful:

> It seems likely, however, that the process of redistribution would tend to slow down even if prices continued to rise. . . . Most of all it could be because investors and others . . . will increasingly seek out means for ensuring that their money incomes rise at least part of the way with them.

The more rapid growth of the incomes of professional people and of rent, dividends and interest since 1957 supports Paish's view. A particular instance of the latter is seen in the increased buying of equities by private individuals, either directly or through unit trusts specializing in high-income yields adding to income or in capital growth adding to wealth (which is more unequally distributed than income) and making for future capital gains. How far these tendencies will be offset by the capital gains tax or by changes in rates of income tax which, under a Labour government, may reverse recent trends and become more steeply progressive, it is impossible to say. The corporation tax introduced in April 1965 is intended to give a strong inducement to companies to plough back more of their profits for expansion. It is possible, therefore, that the proportion of company income distributed as dividends—which has increased over the past decade—may decline. Nevertheless, the aggregate amount distributed as dividends can be expected to increase as total profits increase, so that personal income from dividends will continue to grow even if, possibly, less rapidly than in the past.

At the other end of the scale, the increases in pensions introduced in 1965 will raise some incomes in the lower ranges, but it is unlikely that this will bring about any fundamental change in the distribution of incomes, because relatively small amounts are involved and increases in pensions tend to lag behind increases in other incomes. Certainly, the present deflationary policies, the incomes freeze and the slowing down of the growth of the national product, following the stability of the income distribution since 1957, must make it doubtful whether the trend in the distribution of incomes for the immediate future is set in the direction of greater equality.

3

THE REMUNERATION OF THE TOP EXECUTIVES IN BRITISH INDUSTRY

NATIONAL BOARD FOR PRICES AND INCOMES

First published in Report No. 107 cmnd 3970 *Chapter 2, Table A and B, and Appendix 3, Table 5, National Board for Prices and Incomes.*

Table 3.1. [Chapter 2: Table A] Pay[a] of Top Executives—Averages, Medians and Quartiles

Category of executive	Sector of industry						
	Nationalized	Nationalized excluding British Steel	Private[c]				Financial
			Group A	Group B	Group C	Total	
	£	£	£	£	£	£	£
Main Board Members							
Average	10,540	8,860	18,760	15,650	12,380	13,310	13,170
Median	9,290	8,910	16,480	14,720	11,590	12,210	12,170
Upper quartile	12,220	9,940	24,130	18,380	15,090	16,150	15,870
Lower quartile	8,080	7,890	12,810	12,340	9,050	9,700	9,650
Senior Executives[b]							
Average	6,880	6,270	9,790	8,040	6,470	6,940	7,800
Median	6,520	6,330	9,090	7,910	6,240	6,650	7,320
Upper quartile	7,480	7,190	11,800	9,490	7,740	8,520	9,780
Lower quartile	5,560	5,470	7,410	6,450	5,080	5,320	5,550

[a] Pay includes salary, directors' fees and bonus.
[b] Selected sample of executives in senior positions in the firms covered.
[c] Group A are companies with net assets of £250m or more, group B—assets between £100m and £250m, and group C—assets between £11m and £100m.

Table 3.2. [Chapter 2: Table B] Type and Cost of Fringe Benefits

Category of executive	Proportion of executives receiving benefit				Average annual cost of providing benefits[b]
	Company car	Free or assisted housing	Assistance towards school fees	Other fringe benefits[a]	
	%	%	%	%	£
Main Board Members					
Nationalized	63·2	2·6	—	39·5	64
Total private	84·4	2·5	0·2	22·3	187
Senior executives					
Nationalized	43·3	3·0	—	48·8	26
Total private	83·2	3·4	2·2	23·7	126

[a] Includes e.g. medical benefits, subsidized lunches, theatre tickets and company products or services at concessionary rates.
[b] Cost to the employer during the last tax year before September 1968 averaged over all executives.

Table 3.3. [Appendix 3: Table 5] Average Pay of Top Executives by Position in Organization

Position in organization	Average pay[a]						
	Nationalized		Private				Financial
	Including British Steel	Excluding British Steel	Group A	Group B	Group C	Total	
	£	£	£	£	£	£	£
Highest-paid executive[b]	12,720	11,410	32,000	25,190	16,780	18,420	21,060
Main Board members[c]	10,540	8,860	18,760	15,650	12,380	13,310	13,990
Senior executives[c]	6,880	6,270	9,790	8,040	6,470	6,940	7,150

[a] Salary, director's fees and bonus, September 1968.
[b] Highest-paid full-time executive in each company covered by the survey definition.
[c] Including highest-paid executive.

4

THE DISTRIBUTION AND TAXATION OF WEALTH

THE ECONOMIST

The Indefensible Status Quo

When the new capital gains tax is in full operation total taxation of wealth in Britain will be over £500 million a year. This is three times the revenue from surtax and about 15 per cent of the revenue from income tax. By past standards, Britain is therefore now imposing substantial taxes on wealth. But they still amount to a property levy of well under 1 per cent a year, and fall in many of the wrong places.

Total personal wealth in Britain in 1963 is officially—but probably wrongly—estimated at about £64,000 million. This represents about £4,000 per household or about £1,200 per head of the population. But three-fifths of the population still has no significant wealth at all; of the wealth owned by the rest the latest figures suggest that 7·1 per cent belongs to those with fortunes of over £200,000, 15·7 per cent to those with between £50,000 and £200,000, and 77·2 per cent to those with less than £50,000.

These data are based on the death duty statistics of the Inland Revenue. The essential assumption underlying these estimates is that the recorded wealth of individuals dying in different age-groups is representative of the wealth of the living in each particular age-group. Then, from statistics of the proportion of individuals likely to die in the various age-groups in any year, it is possible to multiply the death duty figures to obtain estimates of the total wealth of at least that portion of the population with sufficient wealth to be assessed for death duties.

Faults in the official figures

But these extrapolated estimates have a number of weaknesses. The numbers dying in the younger age-groups but in the higher

First published as 'The Indefensible Status Quo' in The Economist, *15 January 1966.*

wealth-groups are too small to give an accurate projection. More seriously, a lot of wealth is transferred by gifts *inter vivos*, and escapes death-duty taxation if made five years before death. Since death duties take 80 per cent of estates over £1,250,000, avoidance is inevitably more widespread in the top wealth brackets. (Hence the apparent poverty at death of bankers and property magnates who were known to possess very substantial fortunes in their lifetimes.) A considerable amount of property is also held in discretionary trusts—that is, trusts that have legal discretion as to who they make beneficiaries of the monies in trust. The beneficiaries of the trusts, while they may enjoy very considerable benefits in their lifetime from the trusts, appear to have no wealth from this source at the time of their death. These and other well-worn devices to avoid death duties mean that the revenue figures of total wealth may appreciably underestimate the amount of wealth held or enjoyed by the upper wealth groups.

Moreover, the official statistics relate to the wealth of individuals; but a more relevant consideration for assessing the distribution of wealth is wealth enjoyed by families. It is clearly misleading to classify with the genuinely poor the wives and children of millionaires, merely because they may have little property in their own right. But that is what estimates based on death-duty statistics do.

An alternative estimate

It is possible to cut through some of these difficulties by basing the estimates not on the recorded wealth of the small sample of the dying, but on the recorded investment income of the living. This not only avoids the distortions caused by gifts, trusts and the rest; it also relates to the total number of taxpayers, and thus treats husband and wife as one person. The breakdown of wealth into various types of asset can itself be taken from the Revenue estimates of total wealth. From the estimated yield of the different assets it is then possible to project the amount of wealth which must lie behind the Revenue figures of investment incomes.

The latest available figures of investment income are for 1959/60. In that year the total personal wealth implied by the investment income figures (including owner-occupied houses) was about £54,100 million. This is probably about 10 per cent higher than estimates based on the death-duty method of estimation at that time. The distribution of this wealth is shown in the table.

Table 4.1. Distribution of Wealth, 1959–60[a]

Range of wealth £	% of taxpayers	% of total wealth	Average wealth held £
Below 3,000	87·9	3·7	107
3,000–10,000	5·1	12·0	6,000
10,000–25,000	4·9	29·0	15,200
25,000–50,000	1·2	16·6	36,250
50,000–100,000	0·6	15·1	68,250
100,000–200,000	0·2	10·6	136,400
Over 200,000	0·1	13·0	334,100
All ranges	100·0	100·0	2,576

[a] These are unofficial estimates of personal wealth based on official figures of investment income. The total number of taxpayers to which the percentages in the second column are related is 21 million. The total personal wealth to which the figures in the third column refer is £54,100 million.

On this estimate, about 84 per cent of wealth seems to be owned by the top 7 per cent of taxpayers; indeed, as much as 55 per cent is owned by the top 2 per cent of taxpayers. This shows an even more uneven distribution than the Inland Revenue estimates. And the reason for this extreme concentration is not that a few have such vast wealth. It is that so many have virtually no wealth. The average size of fortune in the top range (of over £200,000) is £334,000; and this range accounts for 13 per cent of total personal wealth. Of the 55 per cent of wealth owned by the top 2 per cent of taxpayers, some three-quarters is owned by taxpayers with fortunes between £25,000 and £200,000. Meanwhile, 88 per cent of taxpayers probably had an average wealth of less than £300; our table suggests that their average holding is only £107, but this may be an underestimate because of the substantial under-reporting of investment income by the lower income groups.

These estimates (like those of the Revenue) are subject to appreciable margins of error. For this reason it is almost impossible to measure small changes in the distribution of wealth. The strongest conclusion to which most experts in this field are prepared to commit themselves, on the basis of the Revenue figures, is that there may have been a slight decrease in the wealth concentration in terms of the percentage of wealth owned by the top 10 per cent—this percentage having possibly declined from 88·5 per cent in 1936 to 79·5 per cent in 1954.[1]

Why death duties have failed

Why have Britain's not inconsiderable taxes on capital failed to achieve any significant redistribution of wealth? Four reasons stand out:

1. Death duties are readily avoidable simply by transferring wealth by gifts *inter vivos*, as described above.

2. Even when death duties are effective, they may have little direct effect in increasing wealth at the bottom end of the scale. In general they simply enable the government to reduce, or rather to check the increase in, the national debt. And while this reduces the amount of wealth held by the upper wealth group, it does not directly increase the wealth held by the rest.

3. Government help to the lower income groups has not generally taken the form of adding to their wealth. Thus these groups have been given pension rights and national assistance rather than investments; and the right to live in council houses at subsidized rents rather than property. These and other benefits can logically be regarded as the equivalent of capital held in trust by the government for these groups, in the same way as trusts hold property on behalf of the upper wealth groups. To some extent, therefore, the true wealth possessed by the lower wealth group is appreciably underestimated owing to the special legal form it takes.

4. A fourth reason why the distribution of wealth has changed only marginally is to be found in the type of asset in which the wealth is held. Briefly, the rich do not only have more money; they also make it multiply faster. Thus cash and fixed-interest securities represent 45 per cent of the wealth of individuals with less than £10,000, and equity shares only 5 per cent. By contrast, equities represent 56 per cent of the wealth of those with over £250,000, and cash and bonds only 22 per cent. As a result, the average capital

[1] H. F. Lydall and D. G. Tipping, 'The Distribution of Personal Wealth in Britain', *Oxford Bulletin of Statistics*, 1961.

appreciation of the assets held by the wealthiest group, on this average composition, has been 114 per cent between 1950 and 1964; while the assets of the £3,000–£10,000 group have appreciated by only 48 per cent.

To some degree the figures given in that last sentence may have been exceptional, because the equity boom between 1950 and 1964 was probably exceptional, too. But there is undoubtedly a permanent built-in tendency to inequality here. It is not just that the wealthy are financially more sophisticated; they are also genuinely better placed to take risks, and need to keep a smaller proportion of their money unprofitably as a liquid reserve. The awkward fact is that any tendency towards a more even distribution of wealth in Britain is being counteracted all the time by these differences in its composition.

5

THE £400M LEAGUE

THE TIMES

About forty company directors headed by Sir John Ellerman and Sir Harry Pilkington hold shares worth approaching £400m; as many as ten of Britain's largest and best known companies are under the effective control of a single family group; Britain's leading families who created companies like Pilkington, The Thomson Organization and Marks and Spencer each control wealth running into tens of millions of pounds. These are some of the conclusions of a pioneering study carried out by *Business News*. Under the 1967 Companies Act, it is possible for the first time to investigate not merely directors' salaries (discussed in *Business News* on November 4 and 11) but also their capital assets.

The results of the *Business News* inquiry, which covered in all 45 leading companies, are summarized in the table. This sets out the name of the director or directors concerned; the name of the company; particular features of the holding; the value at current stock-market prices, and finally the percentage of total equity or total votes which these interests represent.

Before analysing the figures, it might be useful to set out precisely what information is available. Sections 27 to 29 of the new Companies Act—which came in force on 27 October—require companies to provide a special list of a director's shareholding in his own concern and its associates. That forms the basis of the details given in the table.

The first qualification to the table is that the directors' shareholdings in non-associated companies are not available. Secondly, even in the case of parent and associated companies, shares held in discretionary trusts are excluded. Thirdly, directors do not have to break down the shares in which they are interested—notably between beneficial and trustee interests. Directors do not have to say whether shares are held jointly, so holdings may be double counted—as is almost certainly true of Marks and Spencer.

First published in the Times Business News, *15 December 1967.*

Finally, the table aggregates holdings of the director, his wife, children and the trusts of which he is a trustee. In almost all cases the whole of a joint holding has been attributed to the director concerned. For the two unquoted companies, Pilkington Bros. and Ellerman Lines, the former has been valued on a p/e ratio of 20, while the latter has been reckoned at asset value, making allowances for the discount current on shipping shares.

One poignant fact illustrated by the table is that the largest single holding, the £80m-plus Leverhulme Trust, was built up before the war. The others break down into three broad categories.

The first are family businesses, headed by Pilkington Bros., which remain wholly privately owned. One which does not feature in the table is Lord Cowdray's interests: the S. Pearson register gives him only a 13 per cent stake in that company's capital.

Secondly come the major industrial fortunes that have been built up over the past forty years, or in many cases since the last war. This group includes Lord Thomson, Sir Isaac Wolfson, the Sobell-Weinstock holdings in G.E.C., Sir Jules Thorn and Mr Clore. It seems probable that the table considerably understates Mr Clore's personal wealth, which has been reckoned to approach £50m.

The third group of companies includes the old-established trading and banking families—notably the Sieffs of Marks & Spencer, the Salmons and Gluckste ins of Lyons, and the Kleinworts of what is now Kleinwort Benson.

There is a striking contrast between the large companies controlled by single groups, and the big public companies which are run by highly professional managers with a relatively small stake in the equity. In Imperial Chemical Industries, for example, Sir Paul Chambers' holding (his salary is not known) is worth about £80,000, while Lord Beeching's holding of just over 2,500 shares compares with his £40,000 a year salary; the average director's holding in I.C.I. is worth some £22,000.

In Shell the average is only half that, £11,000, omitting Peter Samuel's £1m holding. (Mr Samuel is, of course, descended from Marcus Samuel, the Shell founder.) In Unilever leaving aside the Leverhulme Trust and the Staff Pension Fund, the average director's holding is only £9,000.

The information processed to produce the table throws up a miscellany of interesting facts. For example, Sir Keith Joseph, former Conservative Minister, holds just under £500,000 worth of shares in Bovis, of which he is deputy chairman. Option details are also available and those show, for example, that Joe Hyman has an option over 300,000 shares in Viyella, of which he is chairman.

At least one myth is exploded, namely, the alleged wealth of directors of the City's biggest discount houses. In Alexanders and Union Discount the directors between them hold only £150,000 and £30,000 respectively. One remaining mystery is P & O, which pleaded exemption from the provisions of the Act because of their Royal Charter.

Table 5.1

Director	Company		Value of equity holding (£m)	% of equity
1. Lord Cole and Dr Woodroofe	Unilever	Held with Lord Leverhulme and others as trustees for Leverhulme Trust	83	18
2. Sir Isaac Wolfson	Great Universal Stores	£140,000 beneficially held; remainder held with others as Wolfson Foundation trustee; percentage = percentage of ordinaries	34	48½
3. D. Phelps	Pilkington Bros.	Mainly trustee; estimated value	30	29
4. Sir Harry Pilkington	Pilkington Bros.	Mainly trustee; estimated value	24	24
5. Sir John Ellerman	Ellerman	Unquoted; estimated value	24	100
6. Lord Thomson	Thomson Organisation	Registered in name of Thomson Scottish Associates and its nominees. Thomson Television controls 80% of the voting shares in T.S.A. and Lord Thomson owns all the voting shares in T.T.	23	78
7. David Lewis	G.E.C.	Mainly trustee; before A.E.I. merger	22	9
8. Sir Jules Thorn	Thorn	Includes £9m held jointly by Sir Jules and others	20	13
9. Kenneth Bond	G.E.C.	Mainly trustee; before A.E.I. merger	19	8
10. A. Pilkington	Pilkington Bros.	Mainly trustee; estimated value	15	14
11. Lord Cozens-Hardy	Pilkington Bros.	Mainly trustee; estimated value	13	13
12. Sir Harold Samuel	Land Securities	£3,900,000 held beneficially	11	16
13. Ivo Forde	Kleinwort	Nearly all trustee	9·2	25
14. Bruce Goodman	Marks & Spencer	Trustee	8·1	2
15. Lord Rank	Ranks Hovis	£7m as trustee	7·5	8

16. Lord Sieff, Joseph Sieff, Marcus Sieff and Michael Sieff	Marks & Spencer	£1,600,000 beneficial; double-counting likely	6·9	1
17. L. H. Pilkington	Pilkington Bros.	Mainly trustee; estimated value	6·7	7
18. Leonard Sainer	Sears	Percentage = percentage of ordinaries	6·5	64
19. Michael Sacher	Marks & Spencer	£2m beneficial	5·9	1
20. Robert Maxwell	Pergamon	Includes large family holding	5·5	34
21. Charles Clore	City Centre		5	12
22. Ernest Kleinwort	Kleinwort	Nearly all trustee	5	15
23. Arnold Weinstock	G.E.C.	Before A.E.I. merger	4·7	2
24. Sir Isaac Wolfson	Drage's	Nearly all trustee; G.U.S. register not ready	4·3	24
25. Alec Lerner	Marks & Spencer	£1,700,000 beneficial	3·6	Under 1
26. Cyril Kleinwort	Kleinwort	Nearly all trustee	3·4	9
27. Charles Forte	Forte's	Taking the 'B' at same value as ordinaries. Percentage = percentage of the votes	2·9	38
28. Gabriel Sacher	Marks & Spencer	£1,300,000 beneficial	2·9	Under 1
29. Sir William Butlin	Butlin's	£1,500,000 trustee	2·7	9
30. W. Shapland	Bernard Sunley	Nearly all trustee	2·1	28
31. Joe Hyman	Viyella		1·8	9
32. Sir S. Warburg	Mercury Sec.	Mostly in joint names	1·7	6
33. Louis Freedman	Land Securities	£1,600,000 held beneficially	1·7	2
34. Leonard Sainer	Hill, Samuel		1·6	8
35. Nine Salmons, three Glucksteins and Sir N. Joseph	J. Lyons	Beneficial as a family group: including both classes of proportional profit share	1·6	Only 9,000 voting ords
36. Trevor Watts	Butlin's	Trustee	1·5	5
37. Julian Hodge	Hodge Group	Excluding 25m deferred ordinaries	1·4	32
38. Anthony Samuel and Peter Samuel	Hill, Samuel		1·3	6
39. Lord Bearsted	Hill, Samuel		1·1	4
40. Leonard Sainer	British Shoe	Also holds £1·5m of 7% unsecured loan	1	1
41. Peter Samuel	Shell		1	Under 1

B

BRITISH CAPITALISM AND POLITICAL POWER

INTRODUCTION

This section is intended to establish the relationship between the distribution of income and wealth and the nature of political power. The first extract links the sections by setting out the personal, family and trustee holdings of certain individual shareholders in a number of important British companies. Michael Barratt-Brown's readable and well-documented article surveys the workings of 'the controllers' in British industry and government. Particularly important are his tables detailing directorships interlocking banking, insurance, industry and commerce. His final table lists the merchant bankers with their membership of toy company boards. The sections from Aaronovitch outline the importance of such finance capitalists in more general terms, in particular in the nationalized industries, the Cabinet, quasi-governmental bodies from the Bank of England to the B.B.C., and in the Departments of State. The close link between business and the Conservative Party is illustrated by the extract from Roth's study of the business background of M.P.s. The extract from Miliband serves to counter both the general argument that there is a plurality of power in Britain and the specific argument that labour and business are more or less equally placed in the power struggle. Two further pieces are included for their illustrative discussion of the nature of the nationalized industries, despite the fact that they are somewhat out of date. In the first, a review of *The Insiders*,[1] John Hughes specifies the character of the relationship between the nationalized industries, the private sector and the government. Clive Jenkins in the second excerpt details the degree to which the members of the boards of the nationalized industries in 1956 were members of other bodies, private or public. The section concludes with a review by Hughes of the role of the multinational corporation and of American investment in Britain.

[1] Clive Jenkins, 'The Insiders', *Universities and Left Review* Supplement 1957.

6

HOW THE WEALTH IS SPLIT

P WILSHER

First published in The Rich and the Super Rich *by Ferdinand Lundberg, Nelson, 1969.*

Table 6.1. How the Wealth is Split

Company	Holder	Personal beneficial holding	Value 11 February 1969	Non-beneficial family and trustee holdings	Value 11 February 1969
Distillers	Lord Forteviot	1,333,849 10s. Ord.	£1·84m	1,220,633	£1·68m
Cadbury Group	Brandon Cadbury	137,939	£0·48m	977,278	£3·4m
	C. L. Cadbury	171,035	£0·60m	1,840,953	£6·7m
	J. C. Cadbury	85,000	£0·30m	1,022,341	£3·6m
Scottish & Newcastle Breweries	Sir William McEwen Younger	80,000	£0·32m	323,880	£1·3m
	E. H. M. Clutterbuck	108,634	£0·43m	384,091	£1·5m
Arthur Guiness	Earl of Iveagh	956,878	£1·4m	6,283,867	£9·4m
	Lord Moyne	375,959	£0·56m	6,531,466	£9·8m
English China Clay	Lord Aberconway	740,114	£1·9m	804,216	£2·1m
United Biscuits	Hector Laing	1,613,393	£3·8m	2,813,857	£6·7m
Chubb	Lord Hayter	456,227	£1·28m	192,779	£0·55m
Weir Group	Viscount Weir	1,505,521	£2·1m	750,960	£1·1m
Firth Cleveland	John Haywood	4,094,760	£4·7m	Interested as trustee in 9,973,784	£11·5m
C. T. Bowring	I. E. B. Bowring	Ord. 77,428	£0·29m	515,137	£1·97m
		'A' —	—	151,100	£0·57m
		Ord. 250,460	£0·95m	320,520	£1·20m
	E. H. Bowring	'A' 112,076	£0·44m	79,325	£0·30m
Bunzl Pulp and Paper	G. G. Bunzl	1,000	£1,660	1,543,680	£2·5m
	J. S. Bunzl	1,600	£2,660	1,538,404	£2·5m
	R. H. Bunzl	537,568	£0·89m	419,132	£0·70m

Table 6.1.—(contd.)

Company	Holder	Personal beneficial holding	Value 11 February 1969	Non-beneficial family and trustee holdings	Value 11 February 1969
Scottish & Universal Investments	Sir Hugh Fraser	7,387,184	£7·1m	250,000	£0·24m
Freemans	Anthony Rampton	903,309	£1·1m	715,163	£0·87m
	D. G. Jones	1,242,789	£1·5m	864,632	£1·05m
Hoveringham Gravels	H. Needler	300,000	£0·25m	3,610,950	£3·0m
	Plus restricted voting Ordinary, 36,000, and Deferred Ordinary, 2,187,560, in family trusts				
Joseph Dawson	Alan Smyth	956,377	£1·6m	4,051,172	£6·6m
Hardy & Co. (Furnishings)	M. L. Slotover	Ord. 767,698	£0·96m	1,313,655	£1·64m
		'A' 686,116	£0·76m	745,954	£0·83m
H. Samuel	S. R. Gentilli	Ord. 2,283	£5,300	1,487,022	£3·5m
		'A' 1,771	£4,100	1,199,188	£2·8m
Large holdings not split between director and family:					
Tesco	J. E. Cohen	12,384,628	£11·7m		
	H. Kreitman	12,783,618	£12·0m		
	L. Porter	12,036,384	£11·4m		
Slater, Walker Securities	J. D. Slater	800,000	£3·0m		
Allied Breweries	K. S. Showering	251,334	£0·26m plus 2·23m Deferred Ord.		
	F. E. Showering	1,473,606	£1·5m plus 0·8m Deferred Ord.		
	H. M. V. Showering	1,774,500	£1·8m plus 0·95m Deferred Ord.		

7
THE CONTROLLERS OF BRITISH INDUSTRY

MICHAEL BARRATT BROWN

We may start by summing up the kind of economic system in which British industry today is operating, and then go on to examine in detail how far different groups in industry and finance may in reality be found to have different interests—and some of these interests, as Peter Shore avers, that might be said to be in line with those of the Labour Movement.

1. Why modern capitalism needs controllers

A modern capitalist economy may be distinguished from its forerunners by at least two major factors:

(i) The rapidly increasing size of plant, and associated with this, the growth in the size of companies from national to international scale (see Table 7.3).
(ii) The growing role of the State both in providing a certain intervening force in the economy, as a source of funds for industry . . . and as a market for goods and services (see Table 7.4).

It may be distinguished from a socialist economy by two other major factors:

(iii) Economic forces in the market (and not any plan, though the market is subject to some state intervention) determine the allocation of the nation's resources, capital investment, imports and exports, movement of labour, etc.
(iv) The market mechanism is operated by the search of individuals and companies for private profit, subject only to state taxation, subsidies and monetary controls.

First published in Can the Workers Run Industry *by K. Coates, Sphere, 1968.*

Table 7.3. Concentration of Assets and Income in British Industry 1953–4 to 1961–3

A. All Industry

Company range (cumulative)	1953–4 Net assets %	1953–4 Gross income %	1957 Net assets %	1957 Gross income %	1961–3 Net assets %	1961–3 Gross income %
Top 50	24 (29)[a]	13 (19)[a]	26·5	17	33 (41)[a]	18 (29)[a]
Top 100	31·5	18·5	34	20	40	23
Top 150	36·5	22	40	24	49	30
Top 300	46	27·5	48	29	58	33
Top 500	51	30·5	53	33	64	37
Top 2,000	60	34	64	40	75	44
All other companies	40	66	36	60	25	56
	100	100	100	100	100	100
Total in £m	12,000	3,800	16,000	4,600	22,000	5,700

[a] Figures for 1953–4 include companies engaged in shipping and property, but those operating wholly or mainly overseas are excluded throughout. If Shell and B.P. were included the figures would be as in the parentheses.

Table 7.3.—(contd.)

B. Manufacturing Only

Company range	1953–4		1957		1961–3	
	Net assets %	Gross income %	Net assets %	Gross income %	Net assets %	Gross income %
Top 50	37	27	44	(33)[b]	52·5	(40)[b]
Top 100	50	35	55	45	60	(50)[b]
Top 150	56	40	58·5	(50)[b]	70	57
Top 300	66	49	70	62	78	66
Top 1,500	(87)[b]	(65)[b]	90	77	95	80
All other companies	13	35	10	23	5	20
	100	100	100	100	100	100
Total in £m	7,000[c]	1,850	10,000[c]	2,000	14,000[c]	2,500

[b] Estimates.

[c] Net assets in manufacturing are estimated on the assumption of the same relation between gross assets and net assets for manufacturing companies as for all vehicles, plant and machinery.

Sources:

National Income Blue Books, 1966. For Totals see Tables 30, 35, 66 and 67.
N.I.E.S.R. *Classified List of Large Companies Company Income and Finance*, 1949–53.
Board of Trade: Company Assets and Income in 1957.
Company Assets, Income and Finance in 1960.
Company Assets in 1963.

Table 7.4. Share of the State in the British Economy 1938–65 with National Plan Estimate for 1970
(All figures are percentages of GNP except the last two lines)

	1938	1948	1957	1965	1966	Estimate 1970 (1964 prices)
A. *Types of Public Authority Expenditure*						
Expenditure as % of National Product:						
All Government Expenditure (current and capital)	31	40·8	36·5	41·5	42·5	43
Payment to persons:						
Debt interest	5·4	5·5	4·1	4·3	4·5	5·0
Pensions/Subsidies	5·9	6·9	8·5	9·5	11·5	10·25
Current purchases of goods and services:						
Arms	4·9	7·1	7·8	6·65	6·75	5·75
Health, Welfare/Education	5·8	5·4	6·9	7·9	7·35	9·0
Other	4·3	11·1	4·5	4·5	5·4	4·75
Fixed capital investment	4·4	4·6	4·2	4·9	5·1	5·15
Loans at home and overseas	0·5	1·3	1·0	2·0	1·8	2·0
B. *Public Corporation Expenditure*	—	13·9	18·2	17·5	17·7	—
Purchase of goods and services	—	5·1	7·2	6·4	6·4	—
Wages and salaries	—	6·4	7·0	6·7	6·8	—
Fixed capital investment	—	2·4	4·0	4·4	4·5	4·35
C. *Public Share of Investment and Consumption*						
Government and Public Corporations Investment as % of all capital investment	30	46	44	45[a]	47	39
Government Current Civil Purchases[b] and Public Sector Housebuilding as % of all consumption and house-building	12·5	13	13·5	15·75	15·1	16

[a] Add another 1·5% for nationalized steel.
[b] i.e. excluding defence and overseas expenditure.

Sources: National Income Blue Book for 1966.
Annual Abstract of Statistics 1938–48.

One must add a fifth factor which distinguishes a modern capitalist economy both from its forerunners and from a socialist economy, viz. that:

(v) A great measure of economic power is concentrated in the hands of a small number of men, who control the main sources of capital, who sit on the boards of banks and insurance companies, the giant industrial and service companies, who sit on nationalized industry boards and other official and semi-official advisory committees, who direct the trade associations and industrial federations.

The reason for this concentration of power arises precisely from the combination of the first four factors. Large-scale plant is not only expensive to build, requiring a great accumulation of capital, but also it is only profitable if run near to full capacity; it requires a whole complex of planned and co-ordinated inputs, and a controlled market for its output. In an unplanned market, subject only to erratic government interventions, capital investment can easily be unprofitably duplicated, unprofitably sited and unprofitably timed. Men with simultaneous contacts in industry, finance and government are thus required to provide some element of planning and control in an otherwise unplanned economy. In Germany and Japan this role has been played by the commercial banks; in Britain in the past, by the merchant banks. In the United States great groups of combined finance and industry and even individual giants like General Motors and Du Pont, have exercised control; similar groupings are developing in Britain and on the continent with the increasing size of the giant industrial companies and their ability to find finance from their own resources (see Table 7.3).

We have already written at length about the so-called 'managerial revolution', but we left out the question of the numbers and motives of managers on the boards of large companies. It is part of the thesis of the 'managerial revolution' to suggest:

(*a*) That boards of directors now consist no longer of owners of capital or even of the private owners' nominees, but are largely made up of managers of technical processes.
(*b*) That these managers are no longer therefore motivated by considerations of the most profitable return to capital, but may

have longer term interests in economic progress and a livelier sense of overall social responsibility.

Whether our controllers are themselves private owners of great wealth or controllers of other people's wealth is in fact not important. They are likely to be both, since the concentration of wealth in Britain is still very great (1 per cent of adults own over half the company capital) and company directors are the most highly remunerated persons in our society in terms of salary, superannuation, expense accounts, etc., and many enjoy stock options and other opportunities for private investment. Company boards are, as we shall see, very far from being made up only of managers of technical processes or managers of labour; but even if they were, we have seen that they must still operate in a system where competition, national and international, can destroy individual companies which fail to pass the test of profitability.

Monopolistic and semi-monopolistic positions provide high profits for expanded investment, but such positions are intrinsically unstable, as British Railways and the National Coal Board discovered. What B.R. and the N.C.B. failed to do (because they were not allowed to) was to accumulate high profits when they had a monopoly and move them into another product or service when competition appeared. This is the pattern of enterprise of the giant companies that have survived. We may instance Cunard's entry into air transport, Rank's bowling alleys and Xerox Process, Gussies' Mail Order business, or Hoover's gas appliances. What they have a monopoly of, compared with the rest of us, is capital. To keep it, they must keep it growing.

Of course, there are other motivations besides maximizing profit:

(*a*) Monopoly profit may not always be pushed as far as it might be for fear of encouraging new competition, e.g. from men like John Bloom.

(*b*) Top management may prefer bigness and merging with competitors rather than profitability and beating them, since salaries at the top tend to depend on the number of steps up to the top rather than on the rate of return on capital.

(*c*) Controllers may have an interest in preserving not merely the position of the companies or group of companies with which they are associated, but also the position of the national economy in which they are based *vis-à-vis* other economies.

(*d*) Finally controllers may have a certain interest in the preservation of the capitalist system as a whole, nationally and internationally, since this is the basis of their own power (and probably of their own wealth).

The importance of the work of co-ordinating investment has been much enhanced as a result of the recent increase in mergers and take-overs, as British industry has rather belatedly begun to rationalize in line with foreign competitors. From 1959 onwards the sums spent by quoted British companies on buying subsidiaries and on other trade investments, which had been running at about £150 million a year, was suddenly stepped up to £400 million a year. This step involved the mobilization of huge sums of capital, since there was no reduction in the sums spent on new fixed assets (see Table 7.5). There have been six main sources for these funds:

(*a*) The largest source, amounting to some 70–80 per cent of the addition to gross assets, has been the internal reserves and depreciation funds of companies, but we noted earlier the dependence of the faster growing companies on the capital market.
(*b*) Internal funds are now being augmented by government tax concessions and grants for investment.
(*c*) Institutional investment has been increasing at a much faster rate than the issue of new shares, so that the proportion of total shares held by institutions has been increased to nearly a quarter of the ordinary shares, nearly a half of the preference and over three-quarters of debenture and loan capital (Table 7.6).
(*d*) Bank advances have been greatly increased from about 30 per cent of bank deposits before 1959–60 to over 50 per cent in 1965–6. Many of these advances are to individuals and small businesses, but large companies also use them widely for short-term finance. This is reflected in an annual increase in amounts owing by the quoted companies to banks from an average extra £60 million a year before 1960 to an average extra £160 million thereafter.
(*e*) Companies can be taken over precisely because they hold liquid or other realizable assets or assets that were not being fully utilized.
(*f*) The capital market remains an important source of capital for nearly all companies when they embark upon a rapid rate of growth.

Table 7.5. Sources of Quoted Company Finance and their Uses 1954–63

Year	Total funds £m	Increase in gross assets £m	Sources of funds internal sources as % of increase in gross assets %	External sources as % of increase in gross assets			Uses of funds as % of gross assets	
				Total %	Ordinary shares %	Long-term loan %	Expenditure on fixed assets %	Investment in subsidiaries and others %
1954	1,236	820	85	15	6	9	70	15
1955	1,483	1,017	77	23	13	8	70	11
1956	1,468	1,059	75	25	12·5	10	85	13
1957	1,553	1,189	70	30	16	13	99	13
1958	1,271	945	80	20	11	8	100	16
1959	1,881	1,361	89	21	9·5	5	68	25
1960	2,327	1,528	78	22	20	2	70	26
1961	2,135	1,480	69	31	23	7	90	31
1962	1,901	1,490	72	28	9·5	14	85	30
1963	2,310	1,510	81	19	9	9·5	82	26

Note: The figures in the Uses of funds column that add up to more than 100 are due to changes in depreciation funds and increases in debts to banks and other trade creditors.
Source: Economic Trends, February 1966.

Table 7.6. Institutional Holdings of Industrial Companies' Assets 1953–5 and 1963–5

	Annual investment (average) £m		Share of all holdings %	
	1953–5	1963–5	1953–5	1963–5
A. *Institutional investment*				
Insurance companies				
Ordinary shares	93	112	7	10·5
Debentures/Loans	64	—	24	55
Preference shares	24	—	19	28
Other institutions				
Ordinary shares	—	250	7·5	13·4
Debentures/Loans	—	—	16	24·2
Preference shares	—	—	11	23·8
All institutions				
Ordinary shares	—	360	14·5	24
Debentures/Loans	—	—	40	79
Preference shares	—	—	30	42
B. *Total new shares issued*				
Ordinary	112	208	—	—
Debenture/Loan	85	165	—	—
Preference	26	20	—	—

Sources: E. V. Morgan, *Structure of Property Ownership in Great Britain* [Oxford University Press, London 1960].
J. G. Blease, *Institutional Investors and the Stock Exchange.*
The Times, 3 February 1967.

2. The composition of the top company board

The result of the considerations so far advanced is that the larger the company, the greater the proportion of directors there will tend to be on the board with outside connections from sitting on the boards of other industrial companies or on those of banks and insurance companies or on trade associations or government committees. On smaller company boards, by contrast, the members will be mainly the department or plant managers, a member of the founding family in the chair and a local stockbroker or accountant. This general statement is subject to wide variations in the actual composition of boards. We may distinguish four main types of board among the top companies:

(*a*) The few remaining boards that still consist almost entirely of members of the founding family—Cadburys on British Cocoa and Chocolate; Salmons and Glucksteins on J. Lyons; the Tates and Lyles; the Stewarts and Lloyds; and the family directors on the private companies of Pilkingtons and David Brown.

(*b*) The boards which are really only adjuncts to a dynamic tycoon like Wolfson or Clore, Fraser, Bedford or Thomson. Often the tycoons by skilful capital gains took over control of sleepy family companies.

(*c*) The boards that consist predominantly of co-ordinating controllers sitting on a whole range of banks, insurance and other companies, as in the case of Shell and B.P. and the Steel companies; S.C.O.W., United Steel, Vickers.

(*d*) The boards of some of the very largest companies, that consist entirely of managers of groups or divisions, who are the controllers of these groups, as in the case of Unilever, British-American Tobacco, Esso and Woolworths, although some of the foreign members of these boards may, in fact, be the equivalent of our co-ordinating controllers.

Most boards of the larger companies are made up of a mixture in various proportions of tycoon, founding family, co-ordinating controllers sitting on many boards, including banks and insurance companies, and of managers of divisions, plants or departments.

But we can nevertheless distinguish those that fall predominantly into three groups:

(*a*) Family- or tycoon-controlled.
(*b*) Controlled by co-ordinators with directorships outside.
(*c*) Management-controlled.

We are not concerned here with ultimate financial control but with *de facto* control by the board of directors.

Such a division makes it possible to attempt a distinction of objectives among the three groups and also to estimate the relative performance of each. If the Crosland thesis, now apparently adopted by Peter Shore, is correct, then the managerial group will be predominant or becoming so and will be distinguishable by motives more in line with those of the Labour movement. What we find by studying the top 120 home and overseas operating companies in 1954 and the partly different top 120 companies in 1966 may be summarized as follows.

From Table 7.7 we can see that while the managerial-controlled companies in the top 120 increased faster than the others over the years 1954–66, they did not yet, in 1966, make up a third of the total. The family- and tycoon-controlled companies who increased in number, all increased at the expense of the co-ordinator-controlled companies. Yet these remain the largest group. Their losses seem to be largely due to the decline in the proportion in the top 120 of companies in service industries and in manufacturing other than metals and engineering, and especially in those engaged in textiles and shipping. But they have more than held their own in the metal manufacturing and engineering group, which shows the biggest proportionate increase in the top 120 among the three industrial groups. This is of considerable significance because this group is the one from which the Government is hoping to see the major improvements in competitive performance in relation to foreign companies. For it is in the products of these groups—accounting for more than half of all U.K. exports—where imports have been rising in recent years so very much faster than exports (more than twice as fast between 1960 and 1966).

3. Comparative performance of companies with different types of board

A more detailed study is possible of the top companies whose assets, income and finance are surveyed by the Board of Trade (see Table 7.8). This survey excludes companies engaged in agriculture, shipping, shipbuilding, banking, finance, and in two of the periods, property and those operating wholly or mainly overseas. This should therefore give us some indication of any differences there may be between these mainly home manufacturing companies and the top 120 that included companies operating overseas. Dividing the largest 116 companies into those with predominantly tycoon- or family-controlled boards, those with co-ordinating controllers in the majority, and those with managers, we find thirty-four in the first group, forty-five in the second one and thirty-seven in the third. When analysis is made by type of company board, the family and tycoon companies, once again as in the 120 companies, had the highest rate of growth over the period 1957–63. Their income/assets ratio was not so high as that of the managerial-controlled companies. Their dependence on new capital was correspondingly much

Table 7.7 Top 120 Companies 1954 and 1966

By Type of Board, Industry and Growth

Type of board and year	Distribution by industry			Change in order among 120 by assets 1954–66					Total
	Services (incl. Brewing)	Metal/ Engineer- ing	Other mfg.	In	Up	Steady	Down	Out	
Family/Tycoon									
1954	19	4	13	12	9	7	10	10	36
1966	19	6	13						38
Co-ord. Controllers									
1954	16	19	18	11	9	11	16	17	54
1966	12	24	11						47
Managerial									
1954	5	11	14	9	11	7	8	5	31
1966	7	13	15						35
Totals									
1954	40	34	46	32	29	25	34	32	120
1966	38	43	39						120

Note: Since four companies in the top 120 of 1966—Wallpaper Mfg., Lewis' Investment Trust, Pressed Steel and Viyella—were taken over in that year, four others have been added to take their place. Wallpaper Mfg., and Lewis' Investment Trust had been in the first 120 in 1954; the other two had not.

Table 7.8. Assets, Income and Finance of Largest 116 Companies Analysed by Type of Company Board

No. of companies	Type of company board	Total assets 1957 £m	Total assets 1963 £m	Asset growth 1957–63 (1957 = 100)	New capital 1958–63 £m	Income/gross assets ratio 1960–3
34	A. Family/Tycoon	1,605	2,835	177	90·8	14·6
	29% of the 116	28	29	—	32	—
45	B. Co-ordinator Controlled	2,565	4,174	163	122·8	12·6
	39% of the 116	45	43	—	43	—
37	C. Managerial	1,570	2,716	172	71·4	15·3
	32% of the 116	27	28	—	25	—
116	Total	5,740	9,725	170	285[a]	14
	100% of the 116	100	100	—	100	—

[a] This is the gross figure of capital raised. Sales of capital in the period amounted to an annual £4 million by the 'A' group, £4·8 million by the 'B' Group and £0·9 million by the 'C' Group, totalling £9·7 million on average over the period.

greater, about as great as that of the large group of co-ordinator-controlled companies, who had however a much lower income/asset ratio than the other two groups. The implication is that the managerial-controlled companies among the top 116 at home were succeeding in maintaining a higher than average rate of return on their assets but not in getting any very much greater rate of growth than the average as a result.

There were evidently significant differences in the performance of companies with different types of boards over the twelve years under consideration. Of course, survival in the top division of the company league by increase in size of assets, though this must come either through merger, take-over or ploughing back of profits, is no necessary test of efficiency but only of fitness to survive in the modern jungle of capitalism. What is most obvious, however, is that the very companies upon which the Crosland thesis depends—those preferring growth rather than profit maximization—turn out to be the tycoon/family-controlled companies. For if a distinction can be made between growth and profit maximization it must be between growth by merger and take-over rather than by ploughing back of high profits. There never was any question of difference between paying out high dividends and ploughing profits back. All companies preferred up to a point to retain profits and so did the shareholders, since in this way they enjoyed untaxed capital gains rather than taxed unearned income.

Examination of the detailed tables shows that it is among tycoon- and co-ordinator-controlled companies that nearly all the mergers and take-overs occurred. The high rate of disappearances of such companies from the top 120 (as well as the growth of their rivals) is largely the result of merger and take-over (the other main cause is the dropping out of some overseas companies). Mergers and take-overs accounted for the disappearance of twenty-three out of the thirty-two companies lost by 1966 from the top 120 of 1954. Three of these were breweries, four were shipping companies and five were textile companies, of which no less than four were swallowed by Courtaulds (see Table 7.9). By contrast the rise of the managerial-controlled companies was evidently mainly the result of internal growth from ploughing back profits. It is not that they retained more of their profit than others; they just made more profit, as Table 7.8 shows.

The tendency of the managerial companies to move up inside the

Table 7.9. Top 120 Companies Taken Over 1954–66 by Type of Company Board

Company taken over	Company taking over Family/Tycoon	Co-ord. controller	Managerial
A. Family/Tycoon-Controlled			
Amalgamated Press	Int. Publishing Corp.		
Patons & Baldwins	J. & P. Coats		
Union Castle	Brit. Commonwealth Shipping		
Kemsley Press	Thomson Org.		
de Havillands		Hawker-Siddeley	
Walker Cain			Allied Breweries
Clan Lines	Brit. Commonwealth Shipping		
Mitchells & Butlers	Bass, Ratcliff		
Angells Brewery			Allied Breweries
B. Co-ordinator-Controlled			
British Celanese		Courtaulds	
Lewis' Investment Trust	Sears Holdings		
British Aluminium		Tube Investments	
United Molasses	Tate & Lyle		
Fine Spinners & Liner Holdings		Courtaulds	
		Ocean Steamship	
Lancashire Cotton Corp.		Courtaulds	
Royal Mail Lines		Furness Withy	
Staveley Coal	Stewarts & Lloyds		
British Nylon Spinners		Courtaulds	
Wallpaper Manufacturers			
Pressed Steel			B.M.C.
C. Managerial-Controlled			
Ruston & Hornsby		English Electric	
Viyella		Courtaulds	

top 120 and for the others—particularly the co-ordinator-controlled—to move down may be more significant than survival or non-survival in the top division of the league. The average rate of increase is significantly higher for these managerial companies than for the others, although the most rapid increases of all were enjoyed by the tycoons like Clore of Sears Holdings or Cecil King of International Publishing. What this implies for the managerial companies in the absence of take-overs is a high rate of profit. But this always was the contradiction in the Crosland thesis. . . . A firm that does not maximize profit will not grow and opens itself to being taken over. The contradiction is carried over into Crosland's own attitude of contempt for the 'so-called controllers' of British industry like Lord Chandos, who actually behaved in the way he recommended—'patron of the arts', with 'good work relations', etc. The 'appalling profit record' of A.E.I., which Crosland derided and claimed was the cause of Lord Chandos 'having little prestige in the business world', was the result of A.E.I. having taken precisely the 'long social view' about the development of nuclear power, and this just did not pay off. (Quotations are from *The Conservative Enemy*, pp. 88–9.)

4. The managerial company

It seems highly doubtful whether the new President of the Board of Trade or the new Minister of Economic Affairs will in the event feel so happy in their association with the managerial companies. Nearly a quarter of them, analysed in the top 120, are foreign-owned, five of them American. All but one of the motor-car companies are in this group and the exception (Rootes) is now American owned. They may find more congenial contact with the electrical engineering companies, which make up another quarter of the top managerial group. These are the companies where government contracts and research funds have provided an important source of finance. The corollary of high profits and a high rate of profit retention is of course small reliance on the Stock Exchange for new capital. It is a striking fact that, while nearly all companies having had rapid growth relied on raising new capital for their growth, the managerial-controlled companies have relied on this source the least. They have therefore of course needed the services of merchant bankers and city connections that much the less. In so far as they rely on government finance for their growth, their government connections become the more important. This does not, however, mean that they will necessarily fit in with Labour's plans. If they are powerfully placed they can dictate to the Government; if they are weak, then their attitudes will have little effect on the rest of British industry.

The fact seems to be that they are still relatively weak. We have seen only some foreign, motors and electrical firms as evidence of the managerial outlook upon which the new Minister of Economic Affairs hopes to build his future economic plans for a Labour Britain. We should not forget that the Government has now brought the steel companies under its control, and nine out of eleven of them figured in the family- or co-ordinator-controlled groups. Nevertheless, this still seems a somewhat narrow base for the exercise of government power. Of course the Minister could well argue that one should go down the list of the next 180 firms or more. But a glance down the list could not be wholly reassuring for him. Heinz, Hoover and Kodak appear near the top—three more American firms, and six others lower down. Then some companies have already disappeared in take-overs, like Rover, Jaguar and Ilford. Smaller aircraft firms are due to be nationalized. We may find Firth Brown, Reyrolle, Alfred Herbert, Birmid, B.S.A., Davy Ashmore, Dowty, Wilmot Breeden and G. & J. Weir in engineering; a scatter of electrical companies—Smiths, Birmid, Decca and Ever Ready; more breweries . . . and a mass of companies in building and building materials, stores and food-processing and services.

There are plenty of middle-sized firms moreover with family and banking directors who could not be regarded as managerially controlled. Several of them are revealed in Table 7.13. The fact is, however, that below the 150 giants, which control half of all the company assets, and over two-thirds in the case of manufacturing companies' assets, there is a long tail of companies, particularly in engineering, which are mainly sub-contractors to the larger firms.

No complete figures are available for the distribution of assets by company range for all the companies in different industries, but they are available for the 2,000 or so companies quoted on the Stock Exchange and surveyed in the Board of Trade Studies of Company Assets and Incomes (see Table 7.10). The most remarkable feature of these figures is that whereas in most industries representatives of the top 120 companies account for some two

Table 7.10. Net Assets of the Largest 116 Companies as a Proportion of all Quoted Company Assets by Industry 1957 and 1963

	2,020 companies net assets 1963 £m	116 companies net assets 1963 £m	116 as % of 2,020	2,020 companies Growth of net assets 1957–63	
				£m	Index 1957 = 100
Food, Drink, Tobacco	2,333	1,752	76	832	155
Chemicals and allied[a]	2,112	1,890	90	686	148
Metal manufacture	1,427	1,158	82	489	150
Vehicles	751	527	70	125	120
Engineering/Shipbuilding	1,725	375	22	1,260	177
Electrical engineering	1,149	865	75		
Textiles, Leather, Clothing	1,345	714	53	372	138
Other manufactures	2,530	1,265	50	960	161
All manufacturing	13,073	8,546		4,424	151
Transport and distribution	1,938	987	51	588	143
Construction and services	629	200	32	410	300
Property management	877	237	27	—	—
All non-manufacturing	3,444	1,424	42	—	—
excl. property	2,567	1,187	46	998	164
Total	16,517	9,970	53	—	—
excl. property	15,640	9,733	62	5,422	153

[a] *Notes:* 1. Chemicals and allied excludes Shell and B.P. since they operate mainly overseas.
2. Shipping, Agriculture, Banking and Finance are also excluded.
3. Between 1957 and 1963 the 116 companies raised their assets by 70% or £3,985 million. The remaining 1,900 non-property companies raised theirs by 33% or £1,437 million.

thirds of all assets, in engineering the proportion is only 25 per cent. Even in the top 300 companies list there would only be half the engineering assets. Only in building materials supply and some service industries are there similarly small proportions of assets in the larger companies. If the Minister of Economic Affairs is relying on this tail of medium to small engineering companies to see eye to eye with him, he is likely to be disappointed. Many of them are family firms and most tend to be precisely those which because of their small scale and unprofessional management are falling behind in a competitive world. Moreover we know from our earlier studies that the largest 116 companies were growing at about twice the rate of the rest of the quoted companies. It will be hard enough to bring the slower growing members of the 116 up to the growth rate of the faster growing members, let alone bringing the long tail up to the head.

5. Managerial functions

We need now to turn to another argument. It could be said—as Mr Crosland explained in *The Conservative Enemy* (p. 80)—that while some firms have a few bankers and financiers on the boards the real power lies with the inside managers, whether they have a majority or a minority on a particular board. However they get their finance, these men can be influenced by government, or so it is said. We need then to consider more precisely the different functions of management.

Any claim by workers to control over the firms and industries in which they work must start from a clear distinction of these different functions. They are basically of three kinds—those concerned with finance, with technical problems and with personnel. Failure to make this distinction has led to much of the lack of confidence among workers about their capacity to exercise managerial functions, since it is widely believed that these are mainly technical. It is the thesis of this paper that they are not; at the level of company boards they are mainly concerned with finance. It is thus on the control of company finance that this paper has chiefly concentrated; but a few words are required on the technical and personnel functions of management.

Technical problems and their solutions are of course fundamental to all decisions on investment policy and on employment policy, but the role of the technical expert is essentially advisory. It is rare to find more than one or two qualified scientists or engineers on company boards and many of the top companies have none. It is sometimes argued that the lack of technical expertise on company boards is precisely what is wrong with British industry. A Manchester University study in 1950–3 showed that less than half of the firms studied employed a science graduate, but where they did, a fair proportion of these men (14 per cent) sat on the board of directors. However, even in these firms there was no case of a man who had been employed solely on research or development being appointed to the board of his firm. All had in fact come to the board from their scientific training by way of involving themselves in the firms' general production or commercial activities. This may or may not be the best way of using scientists but it is evidently how they are mainly used in industry.

Some conclusions might be expected from comparing the performance of companies in the last ten years according to the presence or absence of scientists on their boards, but there appears to be no correlation of survival value with proportions of scientists or engineers on the boards, if we judge only by the initials printed after board directors' names.

It needs clearly to be emphasized here that technological choice is determined not so much by consideration of technical efficiency or cost saving as of marketing and price management. This is not to say that cost reduction is not a central driving force of modern industry—a force which has frightening implications for its effects on employment opportunities and income distribution as automation develops. Such effects, as Professor Meade has pointed out so lucidly on his little study on *Efficiency, Equality and the Ownership of Property*, follow because increased automation seems likely to create a situation where a small labour force works at high wages in highly productive automated factories while the rest provide services and sub-contracts at low pay to the automated sector. This is indeed a real danger which we can already see developing in the U.S.A. and Japan.

At the same time we can also see in the U.S.A., as Professor Galbraith has recently reminded us in his Reith lectures, that the choice of products and the balance between private goods and public services no longer depends upon how we spend our money in the market nor even upon technological innovation. Both our choices and technological choice are determined by the management of the market, both in respect of sales and prices, that it is the objective of every giant corporation to achieve. It is not only that many innovations are now merely gimmicks—the size or shape or colour of the container—designed to sell an old product. New technologies that are really new discoveries will not be used if they conflict with the marketing of the old or will be used in such a way as to minimize the conflict. Natural gas, to take but one example, is pushed into house warming where it will compete with electricity, not into industry where the conflict would be with oil, for the oil companies own also the process of gas supply.

The technologist, though he often reveals a certain arrogance both towards the workers below him and the financiers above him in a hierarchical system, knows in his heart that he is just as much the servant of the latter as are the workers. For the present the technologist identifies with the aims of his master, as indeed do many of the workers (and not only the better paid ones); but in time consciousness must grow among both that a hierarchical system based upon property relations can no longer develop man's technological capacities. New relations of co-operation must replace the hierarchies of exploitation. The movement for workers' control is but the first expression of this growing consciousness.

Technical expertise is not then apparently essential to board membership. What is more, workers themselves know of hundreds of cases where an ounce of practical knowledge is worth tons of theory, not of course at the stage of invention or innovation, but at the stage of practical application of new techniques to the production process. Many costly mistakes would have been avoided if workers had been consulted before new plant was introduced. Indeed this is becoming so obvious that shop stewards in large enterprises today spend much of their time discussing the effect of the introduction of new machinery on labour deployment, although generally too late for maximum effect. The experience at the Esso Fawley refinery was significant in this respect. When new techniques of production and payment were introduced some years ago, shop stewards increased their powers as leaders of their work groups even when many of their traditional negotiating rights were reduced. (A. Flanders, *The Fawley Productivity Agreement*, p. 202.)

The introduction of technical change of this sort is closely connected with personnel management. Again the experience at Fawley is significant. The separation of personnel and line management was found to create serious difficulties and indeed much of the 'labour relations' apparatus was found to be largely superfluous. (Op. cit. pp. 252–3.) It was the knowledge of the production managers and their assistants on the one hand and the leaders of the men on the job on the other that were required to solve both technical questions and questions of pay. Intermediaries were of little help.

It may well be that many of the production managers and technicians of British industry are in sympathy with the new President of the Board of Trade, the new Minister of Economic Affairs, and even with Labour's aims. They are all subject to the pressures of the corporation image and some may enjoy the corruption of corporate expense accounts and stock options. Many, however, are undoubtedly frustrated by a system that takes so much out of them, leaves them feeling less than fulfilled and contemplating emigration, while they ask why Britain is falling behind growth elsewhere. Some cling to a vision of the Common Market, stirring lethargic companies into action; others hope for more American thrust in the board room; few have any faith in nationalized enterprise. Large numbers could be won for a clear exposition of authoritative plans from government departments which showed a determined effort to carry them through. But the way for governments to reach their hearts will not be through the board rooms of their companies; that is where finance is talked and not technology. It will not, however, be easy for the new Ministers to make contact with allies beneath the boards and associations, the cartels and federations of industry. But workers on the shop floor considering the possibilities of workers' control should look for these allies among the technicians and production managers. They will find far more than they expect.

6. The work of the controllers

If this general analysis is correct, then we may divide the main work of the directors of the boards of a modern company into three parts:

(*a*) Examining plans for the timing, siting, scale and financing of new investment, including new subsidiaries, and for the writing off of old investment, considered in the light of technical

developments, competition (national and international), market research, government policies, etc. This must include a continuous examination of the prospect of mergers and take-overs.
(*b*) Controlling company finance, including cost control, pricing and depreciation policy, profit distribution between reserves and dividends, borrowing policy. This must include a watching eye over cartels and other price agreements and over the stock market price of shares in the companies concerned.
(*c*) General supervision of management appointments and policies, covering sales and market changes, production faults, cost rationalization, ordering of plant and materials, labour employment, advertising, public relations.

The larger the company the more the directors will be concentrating on (*a*) and (*b*). A small company's board may happily dispense with these questions for most of any year since they will be largely outside a small company's control, and they may concentrate almost entirely on (*c*). We may take the word of Lord Cole, Chairman of Unilever, in an *Observer* interview (6 January 1963) that the board's main task is 'making the broad decisions that determine the investment of capital and the placing of senior managers'.

The fact is that the greater part of the decisions under (*a*) and (*b*) above are really social decisions, often affecting a sizeable portion of the nation's capital and labour, and should be taken by some agency responsible to society as a whole, rather than by a group of directors who are in effect a self-perpetuating oligarchy, responsible to no one but themselves (shareholders do not in practice actually attend their company meetings). Workers' representation on the controlling boards might be one way of making them socially more responsible; but major social decisions about the priorities and location of investment would still need to be made socially as part of an overall social plan. Workers' control over management is equally if not more important in the field covered by (*c*) above, but it will evidently have to be combined with some measure of social control over (*a*) and (*b*)—at least as much as exists in relation to the nationalized industries.

The negotiation and finance of mergers and take-overs is controllers' business *par excellence*. But in addition to the power which a giant firm may exercise, many firms work closely together in associations and federations. Only a few companies are virtually monopolies like the Distillers Company in spirits or Imperial Tobacco, with its large shareholding in Gallahers and association with British–American Tobacco. In most industries there are three or four giants and between them there are cartels or price agreements and gentlemen's agreements to share the market. We may instance the big bulk steel producers, the oil companies, the cement and chocolate manufacturers. Agreements on price do not mean that they do not compete for markets. We need only look at the advertisements to know that; but they do not generally compete on price. They may also have international agreements about markets. A cartel is by its very nature an unstable arrangement, holding only until the next agreed revision of prices and markets. As the two chief authorities on the subject have written: 'The cartels provide a relatively stable framework within which conflicting interests may be reconciled by manoeuvre, bargain and compromise.' (G. W. Stocking and M. W. Watkins *Cartels in Action*, New York 1949.)

Most companies in Britain belong to their appropriate Trade Associations and Employers' Association, the one concerned with pricing policies and standards, the other with employment policies. Both join together for common action to influence the Government through the Confederation of British Industry. Much of a director's time and even more of our so-called controllers' time must be spent on work in such Associations. The steel companies in the last annual report of their Federation listed twelve Product Conferences and thirty-four committees in addition to their Council and Executive Committee, on which directors were chosen to sit. In such conferences and committees the big firms provide the leadership, and especially in the matter of prices, despite the criticisms levelled at several firms and industries by the Monopolies Commission and Restrictive Practices' Court.

Although such associations and federations may provide the necessary framework for effective oligopoly, it appears that actual interlocking of directorates is often still regarded as of value. This practice found its most extreme form in the case of the steel companies where prior to nationalization five of the major company chairmen all sat together on the board of United Steel and three directors of other major steel firms sat on the board of the Steel Company of Wales. Another example was A.E.I. which had directors of I.C.I., Vickers, Cammell Laird, B.P., Pilkingtons, Massey Harris, Courtaulds, Dalgety and many smaller firms on its board at one time. These are the companies which we have called co-ordinator-controlled, and most of such companies had a merchant banker on the board as well as directors of the big commercial banks and the big insurance companies. The reasons are not far to seek.

7. The special role of the merchant bankers

Any industrial company can be expected to do all its banking through one of the Big Eight commercial banks, and if it is a large company the chairman or other leading director may well be asked to sit on the board of the bank. At the same time, any company that wishes to issue shares on the Stock Exchange will do this through an issuing house (a merchant bank) which underwrites the issue and takes a commission, and may wish to take up some of the shares (at a premium), even if there is no difficulty in disposing of them on the market. A very large company which has a fair amount of issuing business will be regularly advised by the Issuing House of its choice, and a director of the Merchant Bank often sits on the industrial company's board. Indeed, these merchant bankers, who have private and trust capital to risk, are to be found on the boards of banks and insurance companies as well as on the industrial company boards. A study I made in 1958 revealed 120 merchant bankers with 250 seats on the boards of the Big Banks and major insurance and industrial companies, as well as many hundreds of seats on smaller companies, trusts, etc. They provided four directors of the Bank of England and about a third of the nearly 400 controllers I was able to identify (Table 7.11*a*). A check on these figures for the position in 1966 seems to show little change (Table 7.11*b*.)

The insurance companies, according to the Radcliffe Report of 1959, abide by an unwritten law that they will not hold more than 5 per cent of the equity of any one industrial company and that 'they avoid entanglement in management'. This does not prevent them from taking a great interest in the dividend that any company in which they have invested is likely to declare, nor from encouraging their directors to sit on the boards of the larger industrial companies. A happy solution is where a merchant banker sits on the

Table 7.11. (a) The Controllers and what they controlled in 1958

Major boards the controllers sat on	120 Merchant Bankers	168 others on the 'Big 8' banks	23 on other bank boards	67 others on 'Top 50' Co. Boards	378 total 'Controllers'
Bank of England	4	1	2	4	11
'Big 8' banks	29	168	—	—	197
20 other banks	37	49	23	—	109
Top 36 insurance companies	73	114	8	10	205
Top 120 home industrial	59	92	19	83	253
30 top overseas companies	39	44	11	14	108
7 government committees	6	9	2	5	22
Total major boards	247	477	65	22	903

Sources: Stock Exchange Year Book 1958. Who's Who 1958.
Directory of Directors 1959. N.I.E.S.R. Classified List of Large Companies.

Table 7.11. (b) Merchant Banker/Controllers in 1966 Directorships on Top Boards

Chief merchant bankers	Bank of England	'Big 8' banks	Other banks	Top 20 insurance companies	Top 150 home industries	Big overseas companies	Total major companies (excl. trusts)
146	3 plus two ex-Governors	28 incl. all 8 banks	55	49 incl. 12 different companies	60 incl. 45 different companies	43 incl. Shell (2) B.P. and P. & O. (4) RTZ (3) Hudson's Bay (2) Burmah Oil (3)	403

Sources: Stock Exchange Year Book 1966–7. Directory of Directors 1966.

boards of an associated commercial bank, an investing insurance company and one or more industrial company. Indeed it appears that there are groups of industrial companies connected by interlocking directorships with certain insurance companies, a big commercial bank and one of the merchant banks. Some of these connections are indicated in Table 7.12. Some of the recent mergers have, in fact, taken place inside such groupings, presumably with the advice and assistance of the merchant bank concerned.

Another recent development resulting directly from the effects of foreign competition on British industry is the huge increase in the outflow or capital from British firms to overseas subsidiaries and branches. This was stepped up after 1959 from a regular £200 million a year to a regular £350 million a year, with dire consequences for the balance of payments. Before 1914 most overseas British investment was in foreign government bonds and other government guaranteed stock like railways and utilities. In the 1920s the proportion in oil and other minerals and raw material production was greatly increased. In these earlier periods it could be argued that the City of London and especially the merchant bankers who floated these loans, were operating at the expense of investment in industry at home and were giving the defence of sterling priority over growth at home. We noted this earlier as one of the contradictions of modern capitalism.

The merchant bankers have from their very origins strong connections with overseas trade, and especially the financing of overseas investment, but they are today on balance more involved in floating shares for industry at home. At the same time, it is now British industrial companies themselves who are interested in overseas investment. Most investment abroad is now directly company investment, and two-thirds of this is in already developed industrial lands and mainly in manufacturing. This is true both for British and United States capital. Thus, a sort of cross investment has developed as the giant international companies fight to hold on to their place in each other's markets. We can see this not only in oil, motors and chemicals production, but in drugs, soft drinks and food manufactures. The giant industrial companies are just as interested, therefore, as the City of London in having a national balance of payments surplus adequate to allow of the ploughing back of their overseas earnings and sending new capital too, to expand their overseas holdings.

Table 7.12. Finance Capital Groups in Britain, 1960

Interlocking Directorships in Banking, Insurance, Industry and Commerce (only major companies included)

Group	Merchant banks	'Big 8' commercial banks	Other banks and trusts	Insurance companies	Home industrial companies	Companies operating overseas
1	Lazards de Steins	Lloyds	Cowdray Trust Whitehall Securities S. Pearson Merc. Credit B.O.L.S.A. Shield Unit	Royal Exchange Commercial Union	Gallaher Eng. Electric E.M.I. Rolls-Royce British Match Wm. Cory	P. & O. Dalgety
2	Rothschilds Sassoons (associated with Barclays)			Sun Alliance		De Beers Anglo-American R.T.Z. Rand British South Africa
3	Morgan Grenfell Yula Catto	National Provincial	Merc. Bank (of India)	Legal & General	Vickers Cammell Laird A.E.I. Reyrolle C. A. Parsons	
4	Kleinwort, Benson and Lonsdale (associated with Flemings)		National and Grindlays M. & S. Securities Lombard Bowmakers	North British	Schweppes House of Fraser	

5	Fleming	National Provincial	Coutts Ottoman Union Discount	Sun Alliance	Imp. Tobacco Gallahers Boots T.I.	British-American Tobacco Tanganyikan Concessions
6	Philip Hill, Higginsons, d'Erlangers Samuels	Midland	City Centre	Eagle Star	Associated Engineering Elliott Auto. Beecham Hawker-Siddeley Rank Org. Stone-Platt Rediffusion Utd. Drapery Brit. Elect. Traction Sears Holdings	Consolidated Goldfields Shell Autofagasta Channel Tunnel
7	Hambros		Union Corporation	Phoenix	I.C.I. E. Gomme	British West Africa Diamond Dev.
8	Schroeders Helbert Wagg	Lloyds	City Properties	Atlas Legal & General	Pressed Steel Babcock & Wilcox T. Tilling Tate & Lyle	
9	Jardine, Matheson	Martins	Hong Kong & Shanghai Chartered Commercial Bank of Australia	London Royal	Cunard Furness-Withy	Hudson's Bay B.P.
10		District		Liv., London & Globe	Lancs. Cotton Lancs. Steel	Turner & Newall

Table 7.12.—(contd.)

Group	Merchant banks	'Big 8' commercial banks	Other banks and trusts	Insurance companies	Home industrial companies	Companies operating overseas
11		Barclays	Barclays DCO U.D.T. Halifax B'dng Yorkshire Penny British Linen British Wagon	Norwich Union Phoenix	Barclay-Courage	
12	Inchcape Gray Dawes McNeill	Three Banks			Distillers	P. & O.
13	Gibbs Arbuthnot Latham	Westminster	Aust. & N.Z. Bank of N.S.W.			Australian Mercantile Land

Sources: S. Aaronovitch, *The Ruling Class* [Lawrence and Wishart, London 1961].
W. Mennell, *Take-over: Growth of Monopoly in Britain, 1951–61* [Lawrence and Wishart, London 1962].
Revised for 1966 by M.B.B. from Table 7.13.

The big industrialists need the merchant bankers more than ever now to help them with the complicated movements of their international currencies, including movements into and out of sterling, and to try to overcome the inherent conflict of their desire to avoid repatriating their foreign earnings, while preventing a run on sterling which would lead to government action to stop their growth at home. Their very actions in expanding output overseas, moreover, tend, as we saw, to reduce their direct exports and so to erode the national payments surplus from which their future overseas expansion must be financed. The conflict is not one between finance and industry or banking and trade, but one which we noted earlier is inherent in the system as a whole. Government measures to produce a payments surplus, by a check to imports of goods through deflation of demand, only weaken the industrial base at home. Yet more discriminating government controls on imports of goods and exports of capital, combined with government planning of foreign trade, would call into question the whole role of the merchant bankers as intermediaries in international transactions. Once again, the controllers are trying to supply some order and co-ordination in place of anarchy. No wonder that the connection between the controllers and the Government becomes closer and closer as merchant bankers move on to government planning bodies, or like Lord Melchett, into the organization of nationalized steel, and as ex-ministers, like Mr Maudling, move into the merchant banks and on to the boards of finance and industry. Table 7.13 gives details of the main company boards which some 150 merchant bankers bestride today.

8. The relations of government and industry

In war-time, when industry had to be controlled in the national interest, the leaders of the top companies moved directly into the Government—Sir Andrew Duncan from steel to the Ministry of Supply, Lord Chandos from metal engineering to the Ministry of Aircraft Production, Lord Woolton from retailing to the Ministry of Food, Lord Leathers from shipping to the Ministry of Transport, Sir John Anderson from Vickers to Economic Co-ordination. With the increasing degree of state intervention now required in a peace-time economy, a similar integration of industry and government develops. The problem remains: who is to control

Table 7.13. Merchant Bankers on the Top Boards, 1966

Merchant bank and banker	Banks and trusts ('Big 8' in italic)	Insurance companies (top 20 in italic)	Home industrials (top 150 in italic)	Overseas companies (largest in italic)
LAZARDS				
Lord Kindersley	*Bank of England* *Lloyds* B.O.L.S.A.	*Royal Ex.* Atlas	Rolls-Royce (Ch.) British Match	
Hon. R. H. M. Kindersley		*London* *Sun Alliance*	*Eng. Elect.* *S.C.O.W.*	
Lord Poole (Ch.)	S. Pearson Whitehall Sec.		Utd. Eng. Potteries	
Visct. Cowdray	Whitehall Sec.		Westminster Press	Mexican Eagle
A. D. Marris	*Barclays*	*Comm. Union*		*P. & O.*
C. P. Dawnay	*Martins*	*Guardian*	*E.M.I.*	*Wm. Cory* *Dalgety*
M. R. Norman	*Williams Deacon's*	Union Disc.	*Gallaher* (Ch.) *Wiggins Teape* *Staveley Inds.*	
E. W. Grazebrook	Mercantile Credit Trusts	*Comm. Union*		
D. Meinerzhagen	Mercantile Credit Alexanders Disct.	*Liverpool* *London Globe* *Royal*	*Rootes* Trollope & Colls.	
D. L. d'A. Willis		*Phoenix*		*Swedish Match* *Indust. Select.*
J. W. Hatch			Chloride Elect.	
from DE STEINS (now assoc. with Lazards)				
Sir Edward de Stein			*Gallaher* (Pres.) *E.M.I.*	
G. W. ff. Dawnay	*Barclays*	(ex Guardian)	(ex E.M.I.)	(ex Dalgety)

MORGAN GRENFELL				
Lord Bicester (Ch.)	(ex B. of Eng.)	*Yule Catto*	*Vickers* *A.E.I.* (V. Ch.)	*Shell* (ex B.O.A.C.)
Lord Rennell Visct. Harcourt	Nat. Bank Australasia	*Sun Life* (V. Ch.) *Legal & Gen.* (Ch.) Greshams (Ch.)		
Sir Geo. Erskine			*G.K.N.* (ex Harrods)	*British Commonwealth Shipping*
J. E. H. Collins		*Royal Ex.* Atlas	*Rank/Hovis*	*Hudson's Bay*
W. W. H. Hill-Wood	Anglo-American Secs.	*Comm. Union*	British Sugar Corpn. (ex. British Celanese)	
K. C. P. Barrington			Baker Perkins *Cerebos* United Biscuits	
D. A. Pease	Alexanders Disct.	Nat. Mutual Life	Truman Hanbury Helnan Group Tyne Tees T.V.	
YULE CATTO (now assoc. with Morgan Grenfell)				
Lord Catto	Lazards Merc. Bank (of India)		*G.E.C.*	
Sir J. H. S. Richardson Sir Alex. Sim	Chartered		(ex *Goodlass, Wall*) Cementation (D. Ch.) (ex W. T. Henley)	
Sir Ken Mealing	Merc. Bank (Ch.) Hong Kong & Shanghai	Eastern Ins. & Reinsurance	Ultramar	
D. F. Macmillan W. E. Catto	Trusts			*Assam. Cons. Tea*
HAMBROS				
J. O. Hambro (Ch.) C. S. A. Hambro Lord Glenconner	Bay Hall Trust Nat. Mortgage Bank of N.Z. (Ch.)	*Phoenix* (Ch.) *Royal Ex.* *Northern* (Ch.)	Taylor Woodrow *I.C.I.*	*Diamond Dev.*

Table 7.13.—(contd.)

Merchant bank and banker	Banks and trusts ('Big 8' in italic)	Insurance companies (top 20 in italic)	Home industrials (top 150 in italic)	Overseas companies (largest in italic)
HAMBROS—*(continued)*				
Hon. H. W. Astor	Winterbottom Trust	*Phoenix*	ex The Times	
			Hutchinson	
J. M. Clay			*Swan Hunter*	
			Consett Iron	
			Firth & Brown	
J. G. Cuckney			Standard Indust.	
			Spirella	
E. E. Mocatta	Mocatta & Goldsmith			
H. N. Sporborg		*Sun Alliance*	*British Match*	*British West Africa*
		Atlas	E. Gomme	
			Skefco	
ROTHSCHILDS (incl. Sassoons)				
Lord Rothschild				*Anglo-American*
				R.T.Z.
F. R. A. de Rothschild	Shield Unit	Northern Star		*de Beers*
F. L. de Rothschild		*Sun Alliance*	*Carreras*	
Leopold de Rothschild	*Nat. Provincial*			
N. C. J. de Rothschild	Shield Unit			
M. Bucks	Anglo-Israel		Cussons	
P. Shelbourne			*Delta Metal*	
			Enfield Rolling Mills	
			Seager Evans	
BRANDTS				
W. A. Brandt (Ch.)		London Ass. (D. Gov.)		
KLEINWORT, BENSON, LONSDALE (associated with Flemings—see below)				
E. G. Kleinwort (Ch.)				

C. H. Kleinwort		*North Brit. & Merc.* (Ch.) *Comm. Union* (V. Ch.) Fine Art & Gen (Ch.) Ocean Maine (Ch.)		
Lord Rockley	*Nat. Provincial*	Clerical, Med. & Gen.	*Schweppes* (D. Ch.) Ilford (D. Ch.)	
Sir Mark Turner	Merc. Credit (Ch.)	*Comm. Union* Fine Art & Gen.	*Calico Printers* Brit. Home Stores	*R.T.Z.* *Tanks*
R. F. Medlicott	Barclays D.C.O.		Birfield Sangamo Weston	Central Mining & Investment *Rhodesia–Katanga*
R. Maudling			*A.E.I.* *Dunlop*	
G. P. S. McPherson	Brit. & French	Standard Life		
D. L. P. Oppe		London & Manchester	Maple Cementation J. Bright	
I. M. L. Forde	Trusts			
GIBBS (associated with Arbuthnot Latham—see below)				
Lord Aldenham	*Westminster* (Ch.) Eng. Scot. & Aust.		*Brit. Match Corp.*	
Sir G. C. Gibbs (Ch.)	Barclays D.C.O. Australia & N.Z. Union Disct.		Morris Garages	
H. K. Goschen		*London Life* Mercantile & Gen.		Rubber Holdings
Earl of Ranfurley		Colonial Mutual Life		Overseas Holdings Ashanti Gold
C. J. J. Clay	Ottoman			
INCHCAPE (incl. Gray, Dawes & McNeill)				
Earl of Inchcape	*Nat. Provincial* Chartered	*Royal Ex.* Tanker Ins.		*B.P. Burmah* *P. & O.*

Table 7.13.—(contd.)

Merchant bank and banker	Banks and trusts ('Big 8' in italic)	Insurance companies (top 20 in italic)	Home industrials (top 150 in italic)	Overseas companies (largest in italic)
INCHCAPE (incl. Gray, Dawes & McNeill)—*continued*				
Sir Wm. Currie	*Williams Deacon's* (D. Ch.) *Royal Bank of Scotland*	Marine & Gen.	*Wm. Cory*	*P. & O.*
BALFOUR WILLIAMSON (now owned by B.O.L.S.A.)				
Sir Geo. Bolton (Ch.)	*Bank of Eng.* B.O.L.S.A.	Sun Life	Clugston	*Canadian Pacific*
SCHRODERS-HELBERT WAGG (ex Lionel Fraser of T. Tilling (Ch.))				
H. W. B. Schroder (Ch.)				
A. Abel Smith		Prov. Mutual Life	*Pressed Steel* (Ch.) Bryan Donkin (Ch.)	
G. W. H. Richardson	*Lloyds* (V. Ch.)	*Legal & Gen.*		
Earl of Perth	*Royal Bank of Scotland*		*Tate & Lyle*	International Holdings
Hon. A. L. Hood			*A.E.I.* Wimpey Blaw Knox	*Petrofina*
H. F. Tiarks	B.O.L.S.A.		*Joseph Lucas* *Pressed Steel* Securicor	*Antofagasta*
J. Backhouse		Nat. Prov. Inst. Reins. Corp.	*Lancs. Steel* Rover Car	*Sena Sugar*
C. H. Villiers	Banque Belge Standard Bank (S. Africa)	Sun	United Premium Oil & Cake	
A. Russell	*District* Alexanders Disct. Yorkshire	*Legal & Gen.*	United Molasses (*Tate & Lyle*) *Turner & Newall*	*I.B.M.* (U.K.)

A. C. G. Ponsonby		*Employers Liability*		
M. S. Verey	Rothschild Inv.	*Northern Assoc.* (D. Ch.)	*Boots*	*Australian Merc. Land*
CHARTERHOUSE AND THOMASSON (incl. S. Japhet)				
W. F. M. Ram (Ch.)			*Delta Metal* (D. Ch.) *Enfield Rolling Mills*	
Sir H. Nutcombe Hume	Metropolitan Estate & Propty. Charterhouse Inv. (Ch.)		Currys Slough Estates	
Sir A. Morse	Mercantile Bank Hong Kong & Shanghai Bowmakers Brit. Standard Bank of M.E.			
E. H. Owen	Nat. & Grindlays		Crittall	
C. M. Rait	National (D. Ch.)			N. African Mining W. African Dev. Co.
J. G. Vaughan			Cora Ltd. Geo. Kent (D. Ch.)	
S. G. WARBURG (subsidiary of Mercury Securities)				
S. G. Warburg (Ch.)	Anglo Israeli			
Sir Andrew MacFadyean				Rubber and Timber Cos. *R.T.Z.* (D. Ch.)
G. E. Coke	Mercury Secs.	U.K. Temperance & Gen.		
Sir J. Helmore	Brit. French		United Glass (Ch.) Thames Ply (Ch.)	
O. R. Guard			Assoc. British Eng. (D. Ch.) Southern Gas	Harrods (B.A.)
T. J. Fraser	Major Finance			
W. T. Straker Smith	Jessell Toynbee			
Lord Gladwyn				Rio Flour

Table 7.13.—(contd.)

Merchant bank and banker	Banks and trusts ('Big 8' in italic)	Insurance companies (top 20 in italic)	Home industrials (top 150 in italic)	Overseas companies (largest in italic)
MATHESONS (Jardine Matheson)				
W. H. J. Keswick	Bank of Eng.	*Sun Alliance* *London*		*B.P.* *Hudson's Bay* Hunnall Tea
J. H. Keswick	*Martins* (D. Ch.) Hong Kong & Shanghai Merc. Credit Yorkshire (D. Ch.)	Thistle		
Sir H. Trevelyan	Brit. Bank of M.E.		*Eng. Electric*	*B.P.* Ampal Tin Burma Mines
D. S. Middlewitch				
GUINNESS & MAHON				
H. E. Guinness (Ch.)			*Dunlop* W. & R. Jacob	
H. S. H. Guiness	Prov. Bank of Ireland			
Sir Geo. Mahon	Merc. Credit		Cerebos (Ireland)	
D. R. Scholey	Mercury Secs.	Sphere (Ch.) Orion (D. Ch.)		
J. E. A. R. Guiness		Provident Mutual Life Ins.		
J. H. Guiness	Bank of Ireland		Bostik (Ireland)	
Sir M. Wright				
ARBUTHNOT LATHAM (see Gibbs above)				
J. F. Prideaux	*Westminster* (D. Ch.) Bank of N.S.W.			*Australian Merc. Land* Commonwealth Dev. Corps. (D. Ch.)
H. R. C. Arbuthnot		*London Ass.*		

N. J. Robson	Ottoman			
H. H. T. Dawson	Dawson & Forbes			
HILL-SAMUEL (inc. Philip Hill, Higginson, d'Erlangers, Samuels)				
Lord Sherfield (Ch.)	Finance Corp.		(ex The Times)	
Hon. P. Samuel (D. Ch.)			British Field Products (Ch.)	*Shell*
K. A. Keith (D. Ch.)		*Eagle Star*	*Beechams*	*Consd. Trust*
			Utd. Draperies	
R. E. F. de Trafford	*Williams Deacon's*	*Royal Ex.*	*Elliott Auto*	
	Electronic Trust	Atlas	Berger-Jenson	
Visct. Bearsted	*Lloyds*	*Sun Alliance*		(ex Shell)
Lord Melchett	(ex Tanker Finance)	(ex Guardian)		(ex Anglo Norness L)
Hon. A. Maxwell Stamp			de la Rue	
			Triplex	
H. C. Drayton	*Midland*	*Eagle Star*	*British Elec. Traction*	*Antofagasta*
			B.I.C.C.	*Consd. Gold*
				Ashanti
Chas. Clore	City Centre (Ch.)		*Seers Holdings* (Ch.)	
K. H. Preston	*Midland*		*Stone Platt* (Ch.)	
			W. & T. Avery	
G. B. Huiskamp				*Shell*
				B. P. (Dutch)
A. O. Bluth			*Vickers*	
			Jack Olding (Ch.)	
G. H. M. Ross Goobey	City Centre		*Imp. Tobacco*	
H. R. Moore	Dev. Finance Corp.		*Assoc. Eng.* (Ch.)	
	Covent Gdn. Props			
J. R. Colville	Coutts	*Eagle Star*		(ex. R.T.)
	Ottoman			
D. E. Webb	Beaver Trust	*Phoenix*		
M. Menzier	Barclays D.C.O.	S. African Ins.		
F. R. Kirwan-Taylor	Covent Gdn. Props.		Lotus Cars	
			Godfrey Davis	

Table 7.13.—(contd.)

Merchant bank and banker	Banks and trusts ('Big 8' in italic)	Insurance companies (top 20 in italic)	Home industrials (top 150 in italic)	Overseas companies (largest in italic)
HILL-SAMUEL—*(continued)*				
Leo d'Erlanger		Prov. Mutual		Channel Tunnel (Ch.) (ex B.O.A.C.)
BARINGS				
Earl of Cromer	(ex Gov. Bank of England)			
J. F. H. Baring		*Royal*	Trafford Park Estates	
Lord Ashburton		*Sun Alliance*	*Pressed Steel*	
Lord Howick			*Swan, Hunter*	Colonial Dev. Corp.
J. C. Philimore		North British	W. H. Smith	Liebig
		Comm. Union		Brazilian Traction
		Fine Art & Gen.		
A. H. Cannwarth	Save & Prosper	Equity & Law Life Ins.		
		Law Reversionary		
Sir E. J. Reid	Hong Kong & Shanghai	Prov. & Mutual Life		British–Chinese Co.
A. W. Giles	Inchcape	Scottish Life	Outwich	
FLEMINGS (see Kleinwort, Benson & Lonsdale above)				
P. Fleming (Ch.)	Trusts	Scottish Amicable		
R. E. Fleming	*Barclays*	*London*		*Burmah Oil*
	Barclays D.C.O.	*Sun Alliance*		Commonwealth Dev. Corp.
	Save & Prosper			
M. F. Berry	*Westminster*	Metropolitan Life		British S. Africa
		London Life		
D. J. Robarts	*Nat. Provincial* (Ch.)	*Sun Alliance*	*I.C.I.*	
	Austral ia & N.Z.			
	Coutts			
	Yorkshire			

G. J. Jamieson	Union Disct.	*Sun*		*London Tin*
W. R. Merton				Channel Tunnel
Lord Wyfold	Bay Hall Trust			
COUTTS (owned by National Provincial Bank)				
S. J. L. Egerton (Ch.)	*National Prov.* Alexanders Disct.	*Phoenix*	(ex The Times)	
Lord Clitheroe	*National Prov.* Mercantile Invest.		*Tube Investments* *John Brown* Finance Corp. for Industry	*Borax* *Union Minière* *Tanks*
Lord Latymer	*National Prov.* Ottoman	U.K. Temp & Prov.		
Visct. Sandon	*National Prov.*	U.K. Temp. & Prov.		
Hon. D. A. Money-Coutts			*Imp. Tobacco*	
D. B. Coutts	National Disct.		*Rolls-Royce* Financial Times	
J. R. Colville	Ottoman			
J. L. E. Smith	Ottoman	*Royal Ex.*		
GRINDLAYS				
Lord Aldington	*Lloyds* National & Grindlays (Ch.) National Disc.	*Sun Alliance* London	*G.E.C.* John Brown Eng. China Clay	

Sources: Stock Exchange Year Book 1966–7.
Directory of Directors, 1966.

Table 7.13.—(contd.)

TOTALS. 146 Merchant Bankers on 400 Top Boards (excl. Trusts).

Banks & Trusts	Top 20 Insurance	Top 150 Home Industrials	Big Overseas Companies
83 (incl. 28 on the 'Big 8' and 3 Bank of England plus 2 ex.)	*49* (incl. 12 different companies)	*60* (incl. 45 different companies)	*43* (incl. Shell 2, B.P. 4, Hudson's Bay 2, P. & O. 3, R.T.Z. 3, Burmah Oil 3

the controllers themselves? Is it to be the People through Parliament and a National Plan, or Finance Capital through its self-appointed controllers?

It has always been a common practice for ex-Ministers to go on to the boards of banks, insurance and industrial companies, and for top company directors to join Conservative administrations. Of recent years we may note a number of chairmen of companies, often deeply involved with government contracts, who came straight from cabinet office, not only Lord Chandos of A.E.I., but also Lord Monckton of the Midland Bank, Visct. Amory of Hudson's Bay, Lord Kilmuir of Plessey, and with him an ex-Defence Minister, Lord Head. The names of ex-ministers on top boards are legion—Selwyn Lloyd on the Rank Organisation, Lord Shawcross (a Labour Minister!) on Ford Motors, Shell, A.E.I., Rank Hovis and MacDougall, Viscount Tenby (Major Lloyd George) on Rank and Associated Portland Cement, Lord Butler back to the family firm of Courtaulds with Lord Eccles, and most recently Mr Maudling on A.E.I. and Dunlop.

The most interesting recent development, however, is the large number of top civil servants who have gone to industry and finance at the highest levels—Sir Henry Wilson Smith to G.K.N., Mr Paul Chambers with Sir William Coates to I.C.I., Sir Maurice Bridgeman to B.P., Lord Plowden with Sir William Strath to Tube Investment, Sir Leslie Rowan to Vickers, Sir Edward Mayfair to I.C.I. and then Glaxo, Francis Cockfield to Boots—all of these chairmen or managing directors drawn from the Treasury or Inland Revenue Department.

Of course there is a movement in the opposite direction too. The Labour Government has brought in Sir Frank Kearton, Chairman of Courtaulds, to head up the N.E.D.C. with Sir Maurice Laing and other industrialists on the council, and Mr Dewdney, managing director of Esso Petroleum, Lord Campbell of Booker M'Connell and others to chair its subcommittees. These are all part-timers, but full-time appointments include Mr Fred Catherwood of British Aluminium, and Lord Brown of Glacier Metals and Associated Engineers. We could add to these lists a host of industrialists on the boards of nationalized industries, on the Regional Economic Councils and Government Committees everywhere. Perhaps the most fascinating was the most recent appointment of Sir Humphrey Trevelyan, one-time ambassador, then director of Jardine

Mathesons, the merchant bank, the British Bank of the Middle East, B.P. and English Electric, recalled by a Labour Government to negotiate with the nationalists in Aden.

No one should forget in this connection the common ties of background in kinship, schooling, universities and clubs of the high-ranking civil servants, the financiers and industrialists, not to mention the front bench of the Tory Party. A third of the 380 controllers in Table 7.11 went to Eton and the proportion among the merchant bankers in Table 7.13 is higher still.

8

THE RULING CLASS

S AARONOVITCH

By and large, government in Britain has been concerned with maintaining finance capital and its capitalist basis. It accepts it as axiomatic that the Big Five Banks, I.C.I. and the oil companies are vital to Britain and that their interests are basically the interests of the nation. . . .

The nationalization of coal, power, road and rail transport and steel was brought about by a compound of economic necessity and working-class pressure. Finance capital, however, was well able to adapt the newly nationalized industries to serve its interests, and then to mutilate them when it arrived at a position to make changes. A striking example of the interests of big finance-capitalist groups being fostered by State policy is given by the way in which the nationalized coal industry has been cut back, to the benefit of oil interests, and, again connected with this, by the atomic energy programme.

In the first years after the war there was a continual shortage of fuel. The National Coal Board's development programme was not yet bearing fruit, though the decline in the industry had been arrested and improvements in output per manshift and in recruitment were beginning to show. Even so, the Labour government's estimate of the future output of coal was extremely pessimistic, even while the Minister exhorted miners to put their backs into coal production. It was assumed that coal output would not rise beyond 200 million tons a year and would therefore inevitably fail to meet the needs of an expanding economy. The Conservative Party argued that, in any case, any real improvement in coal output demanded 'sanctions' against the miners. Into this climate entered the predicted increase in the demand for oil for transport, steel-making and the like. The outcome was the Labour government's full encouragement to the oil companies in setting up refineries in Britain. Mr Attlee was entirely justified in claiming that Stanlow, Fawley, Isle

First published in The Ruling Class *by S. Aaronovitch, Lawrence and Wishart*, 1961.

of Grain, Shellhaven and Coryton, representing the investment of hundreds of millions of pounds by the great Anglo-Dutch-American, oil monopolies, could not have come into being without the initiative and active participation of the government. This was a major success for the oil monopolies.

Once in being, these great refineries had to find outlets for *all* their products—not only for the highly refined motor fuels and lubricants that would otherwise have been imported, but also for the residues, including the bunker fuels that could replace only coal. Naturally enterprises as aggressive as the oil monopolies, having got a foot in the door, proceeded to kick it open. Oil was offered to fill any gap between supply and demand for home-produced fuels. A period of intensive pressure and negotiation led finally to the announcement in 1955 of the privately owned oil monopolies' victory over nationalized coal. The government and ministries, the National Coal Board and the Electricity Board were all involved in the decision to expand rapidly the use of oil at power stations, with the aim by 1960 of burning five and two-thirds million tons a year, equivalent in heating value to nine million tons of coal. On this basis the State considered the economy secure against fuel shortage and at the same time had a powerful means of pressure on the miners. The way began to be opened for a new assessment of the National Coal Board's development plans in purely big-business terms.

In 1956, the consequences of invading Egypt revealed overnight the flimsy basis for the government's policy, and the gap between supply and demand for fuel gaped wide open again. It became clear that the power stations could hardly secure annually more than four and a half million tons of oil, equivalent to seven million tons of coal. But though the supply of oil had turned out to be insecure, the nationalized coal industry had still no opportunity to flourish. Influential interests came forward with the promise of a new power source, safe from the strength of the miners or of Arab nationalists. Two significant events coincided with the crisis brought about by the invasion of Egypt. First, a year's successful operation of the Calder Hall installation showed that nuclear power was technically feasible; secondly, prospecting in Canada had been rewarded with the discovery of almost inexhaustible deposits of uranium ore. Supported by the Atomic Energy Authority's over-optimistic estimates of future costs, the government committed the Electricity

Authority to installing 5,000–6,000 megawatts of nuclear power by 1965.

The great electrical engineering and boiler-making firms were quick to see the prospects. Such a nuclear programme was going to be worth almost £1,000 million, or two to three times as much as an equal amount of coal-burning plant. Export possibilities looked encouraging too. Again the State machine played its part. The Atomic Energy Authority and the Ministry of Fuel and Power acted as marriage brokers to the giant combines who formed 'nuclear consortia' in order to build the atomic power stations. These groupings are:

1. Associated Electrical Industries with John Thompson. In 1960 A.E.I. entered into close connections with C. A. Parsons and A. Reyrolle, who had dominated a group called Nuclear Power Plant Company. It would be reasonable now to regard these as constituting a single grouping.
2. English-Electric/Babcock and Wilcox/Taylor, Woodrow.
3. General Electric Company with Simon-Carves.
4. Atomic Power Constructions, which brings together International Combustion Holdings with Richardsons Westgarth and Crompton Parkinson.

The Atomic Energy Authority itself was organized on the advice of top industrialists such as Lord Waverley, Sir John Woods and Sir Wallace Akers so as to give the maximum assistance to private capital; and this assistance has been given. Each of the consortia has been awarded contracts in such a way as to make even the *Economist* comment rather tartly that:

> . . . so far the atomic business has been conducted in this country on the principle of dealing out contracts among consortiums as if they were a deck of cards. Since the first round of tenders, when four groups bid for three orders, there has been no competition. Nor will there be in the future if the Minister of Power is to be taken literally at his word, because he has plainly stated that under the one-station-a-year policy all the teams will get enough work to keep them busy, as if their efforts were all of equal merit.

Since the original plan for nuclear energy was adopted, however, a drastic sea-change has taken place. Instead of a gap in the supply of fuels, great surpluses have appeared both in the coal and oil industries (where indeed there had been one for some time). At the same time as the price of these fuels came down, the export prospects for nuclear power units evaporated. In June 1960 the government announced that the 1957 plan would not be completed by 1965 but by 1968. (This latter facilitated the links between A.E.I.-Thompson and the Parsons–Reyrolle interests, and will undoubtedly lead to further mergers and take-overs.)

The general line of State policy has become clear. From the outset it has fostered fuel oil as a competitor with coal. It grossly miscalculated the costs of atomic energy, but organized its atomic energy programme so as to give the biggest opportunities to a tiny group of powerful combines without real concern as to the final cost to the consumer. And it has used both its oil and atomic energy programmes to undermine the existing structure of the National Coal Board and weaken the position of the miners.[1] The coal industry, as far as the picture went in mid-1960, was to undergo a steady contraction by 1965, with the closing or merging of 205 to 275 pits and a reduction in manpower from the 1958 level of 700,000 to around 600,000. The uranium producers, such as Rio Tinto, have valuable long-term contracts for the supply of uranium at very profitable prices to the Atomic Energy Authority which the A.E.A. will naturally be required to honour. The atomic power installations are being built at prices which have little to do with costs but will be reflected in the charges for electricity. The oil companies will be able to push forward in the knowledge that the government is out to contract the coal industry and weaken the bargaining strength of the miners.

The history of the government's fuel policy illustrates only too well that nationalized industries, whatever their size, are subordinated to the interests of the most powerful groups of finance capital—and are likely to continue so, unless popular pressure is strong enough to prevent or modify that policy. . . .

It is conceded nearly everywhere that the Cabinet has concentrated within itself the main powers of government decision. There is no need to pose the power of the Cabinet against the growth in influence of government departments. In every sense they are closely connected—the development of each expresses the nature of finance capital and the problems it gives rise to, though there is a certain division of labour between them.

[1] I am not arguing that the government also planned industrial stagnation, which was a vital factor in producing the coal surplus, though government policy undoubtedly assisted.

The Cabinet itself developed primarily out of the needs of war; its modern organization resulted from the work of the Committee of Imperial Defence set up in 1902.

Only a minority of the members of the government are in the Cabinet. And within the Cabinet itself a very small group exercises the major influence. There are also circles outside the government altogether who co-operate with the most important members of the Cabinet in determining policy.

The concentration of influence within a section of the Cabinet and its incorporation of the circles around it is linked with the system of Cabinet Committees. One recent writer on these matters states bluntly that:

> . . . we are governed, over a wide area . . . through a system of Cabinet Committees co-ordinating the executive functions of Departments. As the Departments in fact arose upon the foundation of Committees of the Council, so the Cabinet Committees have been called into existence by the growing multiplicity and range of the Departments. And it is the needs of defence and war, which, primarily and directly, have been responsible for this process.[1]

Most of the Ministers excluded from the Cabinet are those concerned with industry and production.

There is a great deal of secrecy about the Cabinet Committees, and those connected with them are prevented by the Official Secrets Act from saying much about them. (This secrecy was endorsed by Herbert Morrison in his book *Government and Parliament*. In the same book he lists approximately seventeen Standing Committees and four Temporary Committees apart from the Cabinet Secretariat. The Committees include: Defence Committeee; Economic Policy Committee; Committee on Manpower; Future Legislation Committee; Lord President's Committee, etc. The Committees and their personnel are, of course, subject to change.)

Some idea of how the system works is given in the following quotation.

> In 1950–51 a fourth phase began as a somewhat different technique than that of formal enquiry through the Government Organisation Committee was gradually introduced. It became the practice that the Ministers concerned should be advised on the more important problems coming within their own fields by informal committees of Permanent Secretaries under Treasury chairmanship. . . . Some major problems have been referred to outside Committees for advice. Thus the future responsibility for atomic energy was

---

[1] John Ehrman, *Cabinet Government and War, 1890–1940* (Cambridge University Press, London 1958), p. 4.

referred to a small committee under the chairmanship of Lord Waverley; Sir P. J. Grigg took the chair at a Committee which enquired into the responsibility for Department Records; and the organisation for the Management of Crown Lands was examined by a committee over which Sir Malcolm Trustram Eve presided. . . .[1]

The same source, referring to the Government Organization Committee, wrote that it has

taken the initiative in having review committees set up in a substantial number of the major departments. . . . These top-level reviews have been conducted by committees containing in all cases members from outside the Civil Service, sometimes with one of the outsiders as chairman. . . . Since 1950–51, therefore, normal practice has come to mean informal enquiry by Permanent Secretaries or eminent men of affairs working part-time in small groups. . . .[2]

The eminent men of affairs are those in command of big finance-capitalist groups or of their main components; they are neither the secretaries of powerful trade unions nor convenors of shop stewards (who, it should be remarked, display superb powers of organization).

We therefore have Cabinets and Cabinet Committees led by and composed of businessmen (apart from the Permanent Heads, to whom we shall refer in a moment) continuously drawing in their colleagues from finance and industry for consultation and decision-making.

The Cabinet and its Committees, including interdepartment committees of enquiry, may be said to represent the main forums (clubs and dinner parties aside) where finance capital can decide State policy, reconcile conflicting interests or win out over rivals.

This integration of finance capital with the machinery of State continues in the Department Advisory committees. K. C. Wheare writes:

Much government legislation has been discussed with the interests concerned before it is introduced. Committees to enquire and to advise, before which interested parties may have given evidence and upon which interests themselves may have been represented, perhaps considered the problem and made recommendations. Organised interests make representations direct to Ministries and propose or criticise legislation. They make representations too to members of Parliament while a bill is proceeding through the House. When standing committee stage is reached the representatives of these interests often

---

[1] *Organisation of Central Government 1914–56*, edited by Professor W. J. M. Mackenzie, p. 337.

[2] ibid., p. 338.

attend the sittings in the space reserved in the committee rooms for members of the public and are available to discuss matters with members.[1]

As another writer put it:

> The Advisory committee is the means by which the pressure group has been given a place in the formal structure of Government. (J. D. Stewart, *British Pressure Groups* [Oxford University Press, London] 1958, p. 8.)

If we were describing this process in detail we should need to consider the many other organized forms of consultation, the role of the Trade Associations and so forth. (For much additional information, in addition to the books by K. C. Wheare, J. D. Stewart, S. E. Finer, see also *The British Political System* by John Gollan [Lawrence and Wishart, London 1954], and *The British State* by James Harvey and Katherine Hood [Lawrence and Wishart, London 1958].)

'Quasi-government bodies'

But there is one extremely important part of the system of rule we have no yet considered—the so-called quasi-government bodies, of which one expert poetically stated: 'Like flowers in spring, they have grown as variously and profusely. . . .' (Sir Arthur Street, 'Quasi-Government Bodies since 1918', in *British Government Since 1918*, Allen and Unwin, London 1950, p. 160.)

If the direct organs of the British State machine are well insulated from public questioning, this is doubly true of the quasi-government bodies, of which the most important for our enquiry are such bodies as the Court of the Bank of England, the Atomic Energy Authority, the boards of the Nationalized Industries, the Marketing Boards and the Councils of the B.B.C. and I.T.A.[2]

From the standpoint of formation and execution of policy in the economic sphere, perhaps the most important and interesting is the Court of the Bank of England.

Under Montagu Norman's leadership, the Bank of England sought to build itself up as a powerful independent centre for international financial relations (e.g. with other Central Banks and with the Bank for International Settlements), responsible for the

[1] K. C. Wheare, *Government by Committee* (Oxford University Press, London 1955), p. 136.

[2] Is the Monarchy to be described as a quasi-government body? All experts on the constitution agree that the monarch is in many respects a member of the Cabinet.

government's financial business but able to take independent decisions and act as the main spokesman for finance capital as a whole. It was a saying of Lord Norman when Governor that 'my job is to think out what the government wants before it knows it'. (Quoted in *Minutes of Evidence to Radcliffe Committee*, Q. 4318.)

The 1957 Bank Rate Tribunal showed that under Norman's successors and in spite of nationalization, the Court of the Bank of England has continued this policy. The Governor of the Bank of England, speaking to the Tribunal, repudiated the notion that the Bank is 'a mere operating department under the Treasury'. He went on to say:

> The Bank of England is the banker, agent and confidential adviser to Government over a wide range of financial matters, domestic and international. The Bank has also a direct responsibility for market monetary management, which includes the fixing of Bank Rate and various other market operations. . . . The strength and the independence of thought of the Bank derive mainly from a Court constituted on present lines, taking an active and continuous part in forming policy.[1]

That this is no merely formal declaration was shown by the evidence of the Tribunal. The specific recommendation for an increase in the bank rate came from the Committee of Treasury of the Bank of England. The Governor consulted with the Chancellor of the Exchequer, and the Chancellor with the Prime Minister. The question and answers then went as follows:

> 10697 Were the Cabinet then informed that the Prime Minister had reached the conclusion that the Government should accept the view of the Bank of England that Bank Rate should be increased to 7 per cent. ?—That information was given to the Cabinet.
>
> 10698 Did the Cabinet express approval of that conclusion ?—They took note of it.

As Professor Devons has pointed out, the history of the discussions revealed the small role played by the Cabinet as a whole and by those ministers concerned with economic affairs, such as the Minister of Labour and the President of the Board of Trade.

On a later occasion, in evidence to the Radcliffe Committee, Mr Cobbold as Governor emphasized the responsibilities and relative independence of the Bank. In matters like the bank rate, interest rates and credit policy, he said that 'the initiative normally rests with the Bank of England . . . by and large we should regard the first responsibility about Bank Rate, monetary policy and so on as

[1] *Evidence*, p. 208.

lying with the Bank'. (Q. 260.) When asked if he equated his position with that of a leading Civil Servant he replied: 'Not at all. I am a servant of the Bank of England.' (Q. 762.) In further discussion before the Radcliffe Committee, the Governor argued that though the Chancellor of the Exchequer had power to direct the Bank of England, only the Bank of England could direct the commercial banks. And Sir Oliver Franks, chairman of Lloyds Bank and a member of the Radcliffe Committee, reinforced this point as follows:

> The impression in the clearing banks is that the clearing banks could be directed only if the then existing Court of the Bank of England so voted and decided that while all the broad facts about overriding power are as you [Mr Cobbold] say, it would formally be for the Bank, after listening to the Chancellor, to take its own decision.

If the matter were purely formal we may be sure there would not be this strong insistence on the initiative and independence of the Bank of England.

The meaning of this will be clearer if we indicate the personnel of the Committee of Treasury of the Bank of England. At the time of the Tribunal they were: C. F. Cobbold, Governor, related to the Hambro family of whom Sir Charles Hambro is a Director of the Bank (but not on the Committee of Treasury); H. C. B. Mynors, Deputy-Governor (whose brother was Temporary Principal H.M. Treasury in 1940, and who is related to the Brand family—of Lazards—and more distantly, to the Colvilles of Rothschilds); Sir G. L. Bolton, Executive Director at the time, who since then has become chairman of the Bank of London and South America, and a director of Consolidated Zinc Corporation, Sun Life Assurance Company of Canada and other concerns; G. C. Eley, chairman of British Drug Houses, British Bank of the Middle East, chairman of Richard Crittal, director of Equity and Law Life Assurance Company and others; Sir John Hanbury Williams, chairman of Courtaulds—into which family married the Hon. R. A. Butler; Basil Sanderson, chairman of Shaw, Saville and Albion Company and of the Aberdeen and Commonwealth Line, director of Ford Motor Company, Furness Withy, Dalgety & Company, etc., and Minister of War Transport, 1941–5; and finally Lord Bicester, head of Morgan Grenfell, director of Shell, Vickers, etc.[1]

[1] It has since been announced that on Mr Cobbold's retirement as Governor, his place would be taken by the Earl of Cromer, of Baring Bros. the merchant bankers.

Any hasty conclusion that this proves the comparative unimportance of the Cabinet should be resisted, since a closer analysis shows the extremely close personal relations—by marriage and business—that exist between the Committee of Treasury (and other Bank of England directors) and the members of any of the post-war Conservative Governments. (On this, see 'The Social Background and Connections of the "Top Decision Makers" ' in *The Manchester School*, January 1959.)[1]

But it is also an advantage that the Cabinet as a whole should not claim exclusive power over the operations of the Bank of England, both because that gives some room for manoeuvre to each body, and because differences of estimate can arise which may make it politically necessary for the Cabinet to take a different position—at least in public. The Bank is as it were a reserve instrument of finance capital.

In the case of the Atomic Energy Authority, the big businessmen who were asked by the government to decide its structure and powers carefully limited the sphere of the authority so as to give 'private enterprise' the maximum scope and benefit from the experience and research of the A.E.A.

It would be impossible in the space available to explore much further the role of the boards of the other nationalized industries. In nearly all cases they represent combinations of former top-brass administrators, top technical experts (as in the electricity authority), representatives of finance capital (especially in the Area Boards), and a few trade union officials of near-pensionable age. But while pressure is exerted on them continuously from sectional interests, the main lines of policy are decided on 'advice' from the Minister and his circle. By his circle we naturally include his normal business and family associates and also the Permanent Heads of the Civil Service.

Departments of State

It might well be true to say that more books have been written to expose the 'new despotism' and power of bureaucracy than have been devoted to exposing the economic and political power of finance capital. There does indeed exist what I might call the

[1] [See p. 185 of this book].

'bureaucratic delusion' that the country is really run by the Permanent Heads of the Civil Service in whom all power resides, while Ministers and Cabinet Ministers are like mere puppets. The complex and continuous process of forming and executing policy under modern conditions has, however, undoubtedly given the Departments of State great influence; and this influence is not, of course, exercised by the great mass of Civil Servants but by the very small number, a few hundred in all, who constitute the top group of the Administrative Class.

In a very real sense, as the Haldane Report of 1918 recognized, the Departments of State cannot be considered as 'extensions of the Ministers' private office', but 'exist in their own right as elements in the constitution'. (See Professor W. J. M. Mackenzie, 'The Structure of Central Administration in Great Britain since 1918', in *British Government Since 1918* [Allen and Unwin, London 1950], p. 83.) They acquire certain traditions, connections and momentum. There must be some logic and uniformity about their operations, so that they do not seem entirely arbitrary or the instruments of a system of spoils. But while they have in this sense a separate existence, viewed overall the Administrative Class and especially the Permanent Heads must be considered as part of the political and executive brain of the ruling class—their loyalty being guaranteed by training, selection and family background.

The bulk even of the Administrative Class in the Civil Service does not nevertheless come directly from the main families of finance capital (though a number do). They come mostly from the fringes of those families—the poor relations, one might say; and this is indicated by the difference in school and club to which the top civil servant belongs as compared with the directors, say, of the big banks, insurance companies, or Ministers of the Crown. The top civil servant, with some exceptions, was educated at a good but 'minor' public school, such as Tonbridge, Edinburgh Academy or Malvern. Over four-fifths did not go to the top six (Eton, Winchester, Harrow, Rugby, Charterhouse and Marlborough), whereas of present Bank of England directors, directors of the Big Five banks, and Cabinet Ministers—half went to the top six and of that half the majority to one school alone—Eton. The top civil servant (again with some important exceptions) does not dine as a member at Boodles or Whites or Bucks (and certainly not at the Carlton) but belongs predominantly to the Oxford or Cambridge or the

Athenaeum or Reform or United University. They share a common background with their superiors far more at the university stage, and perhaps in this the British Civil Service is more like the Continental Civil Service than some commentators suppose. However, it is not argued here that there is a caste barrier separating the Administrative Class and the direct representatives of finance capital. There is considerable overlapping in clubs and schools as well as universities. But there is undoubtedly a difference to be accounted for.

In part, of course, to build an administrative machine of this size and quality means absorbing the most 'suitable' of middle-class youth into a group that identifies itself with the *status quo*; for it is not a job suitable for the sons and daughters of the bankers and big industrialists. There is perhaps a deeper meaning, but before we examine it further we must note a certain gradation in State departments. The Permanent Heads of the Ministries of Fuel and Power, of Commonwealth Relations or of Education are not nearly so important as the Heads of the Foreign Office or the Treasury; and the Director-General of the Post Office is less important than any of these. It is the Foreign Office that shows the most marked difference in selection and personnel. The Foreign Service is markedly distinct from the Home Civil Service. (On this see Harvey and Hood, *The British State*, Chapters 7, 12 and 13.) It has its own system of recruitment and selection, and the proportion of its top personnel who were at Eton and belong to the 'bankers'' clubs is higher than in any other section of the Civil Service.

In my view, this is because in the Foreign Office the forming and carrying through of policy are closely combined. It is in the nature of Foreign Policy that the State is involved in all international agreements and manoeuvres more directly than in any other sphere; a vast number of important decisions must be taken directly by the leading personnel in the Department. As a result, even greater care is taken to ensure that the Foreign Service draws only upon the most devoted and loyal elements—those closest to the top circles of finance capital.

Lord Strang, former Permanent Secretary in the Foreign Office, underlines the growth in the policy-forming power of the Foreign Office: 'But must the Foreign Office itself, which is within hail of the elected makers of policy, trespass beyond the role of mere transmitting agent? As we have seen, it must; and the reason is simply that there is so much to do.' (*The Foreign Office* [Allen and Unwin, London], 1955, p. 151.) I suggest there are also stronger reasons.

A key position in the State is also occupied by the Treasury. In the course of time, this Department has come to control the spending of all government departments, plays an important part in the formation and carrying through of economic policy and is also in tight control of recruitment, selection and promotion in the entire Home Civil Service. The Treasury has, Janus-like, two heads. One is the Head of the Home Civil Service and secretary to the Cabinet; the other is specifically responsible for economic affairs. (It is only recently that these functions were separated in this way with the formal appointment of two Joint Permanent Secretaries.) This has been held to strengthen the Treasury position in forming economic policy at the expense of the professional economists who, mainly as a result of the war, had come to play quite an important advisory role. But however valiantly the London School of Economics buries its Fabian past, professional economists cannot be trusted to serve finance capital as well as the specially selected civil servants. Sir Roger Makins, who was the Joint Secretary responsible for economic affairs, was sired by Sir Ernest Makins, Tory M.P. for Knutsford from 1922–45, who left estate worth £403,202—the son being the main beneficiary. (See *Financial Times*, 29 June 1959.) Sir Roger Makins left the Treasury to become chairman of the Atomic Energy Authority, whose head Lord Plowden had alternated between business and the Treasury, moving from there to the Atomic Energy Corporation. Lord Plowden has now resumed his business interests as director of some very important companies, including Tube Investment, Commercial Union Insurance and others. Sir Leslie Rowan, a Second Secretary of the Treasury, retired from the Service in 1958 and became director first of Vickers—as director of finance—and later of Barclays Bank.

The top men of the Treasury move in and out of the City freely; their policies are well known to suit finance capital, and their subsequent careers show where their affinity lies.

The so-called exchange said to take place between the top civil service and 'business' is largely a misnomer. The road is normally 'one way only'—on to the boards of big business. Of those members of the Administrative Class with salaries above £500 who left to accept outside posts between 1920 and 1930, over half of those whose destination became known went into business. There is no reason to believe that the proportion is now lower.

Whether we consider the Cabinet and its committees, or the so-called quasi-government bodies, or the government departments, all the evidence points to the conclusion that these policy-making and administrative organs of the State are not 'independent' bodies. They are manned and controlled by finance capital. Finance capital is not some 'lobby' outside the political system, but is built into its foundations. The finance capitalists are in truth the ruling class.

9

THE BUSINESS BACKGROUND OF MPs

A ROTH

. . . [During the past few years] one might have thought that there would be a substantial decrease in the total number of Chairmanships, Deputy Chairmanships and directorships held by MPs. In fact, the fall has been slight. There has been a rather minor drop in the number of 'top brass' posts in industry—those of the order of Chairman, Deputy Chairman or Managing Director; from 355 such posts, present or past, in the 1964–6 Parliament, it fell to a total of 324, a decline of 9 per cent. Of these, 290 or almost 90 per cent are held by Conservatives, 32 by such Labour MPs as Robert Maxwell, and two by Liberal MPs.

There has been a similar minor drop in the total of present and past directorships held by MPs. In the 1964–6 Parliament the total held was 770. In the House elected in March 1966 we have discovered a total of 693, a fall of 10 per cent. Of these 693 directorships, 601 or 86 per cent are held by Conservative MPs, 70 or just under 10 per cent by Labour MPs and 22 are the possessions of the dozen Liberal MPs.

Two fairly strong reasons suggest that this fall in economic representation will soon be eliminated. First there is the tendency toward what might be described as 'the inheritance of acquired directorships' or the 'political Lysenkoism of the Tories'. This means that when a Tory MP leaves the House he passes on directorships in politically-conscious companies to a colleague. Thus, Quintin Hogg became a director of the Wellman Smith Owen Engineering Corporation when its Chairman, Sir Peter Roberts Bt., was planning to retire from the House and politics. Similarly, Hugh Fraser, Tory MP for Stafford and Stone, became a director of Steel Barrel Scammels and Associated Engineers Ltd in succession to the late Sir Herbert Butcher Bt. When Sir Richard Thompson Bt. was defeated at Croydon South, Daniel Awdry, Conservative MP for Chippenham, followed him on the board of the B.E.T.

First published in Parliamentary Profile Services, *1967.*

Omnibus company. Somewhat more distantly, Sir John Foster became in 1967 successively a director and Chairman of Sir Isaac Pitman & Sons Ltd, the publishers, in succession to Sir James Pitman, Conservative MP for Bath until 1964.

The second reason for expecting the gap to be made up is the fear among Conservative MPs that they may be in opposition until perhaps 1974. Therefore there is a rather strong urge to find the outside jobs to absorb the energies and provide the additional incomes that might have come by way of Ministerial appointments. The increase in MPs' pay from £1,750–3,250 which came by joint agreement in 1964 was not enough to make most Conservative MPs full-timers. It did have this effect on most Labour and some Liberal MPs like Eric Lubbock who immediately gave up most of his directorships.

The Conservative MP's reluctance to become a full-time MP is indicated by the fact that, of the 253 Tory MPs elected in 1966, it is only possible to discover a dozen for whom we cannot pinpoint a remunerative current outside post in business, the professions or commercial agriculture. And of these dozen full-timers three have retired from their businesses or professions and two, at least, have inherited wealth. This fact, that less than 5 per cent of Conservative MPs are full-timers, helps explain their negative attitude toward morning sessions.

The vital statistics

A glance at our chart, 'A Comparative Table of Economic Backgrounds' [Table 9.1], gives some useful indications of how and where Conservative vital statistics have altered as the representation has slimmed on the Commons benches. These statistics are suggestive rather than definitive because it is very difficult to compare like absolutely with like. Thus, as one Conservative magnate volunteered, he would happily trade in his substantial property chairmanship for a director's seat on the I.C.I. board. Similarly, a directorship on the board of Chartered Bank, such as has been acquired by Anthony Barber, is worth much more than one on an obscure bank on the Channel Islands. In some cases a directorship in a family firm, when it is allied to a substantial shareholding by the MP or his wife or children, is a form of ownership designed to minimize tax liability. In other cases a directorship is a way of lending the prestige of the House of Commons in exchange for as little as £100 a year. In such cases the company simply wants the name of an MP on its board and on its notepaper.

Even allowing for such variations it is worth while looking at the statistics which emerge if one analyses the Parliaments of 1962–3, 1964–5 and 1966–7. For one thing it transpires that, despite the retirement of outstanding 'top' people in the last two General Elections, the best connected have done relatively well. Thus, although the number of Tory MPs dropped from 363 to 253 (a fall of 30 per cent) as a result of the two General Elections, the number of 'top brass' posts held by them went down only from 332 to 290 (a drop of 12·5 per cent). There was a more proportional fall in the number of directorships, which dropped from 845 in 1962–3 to 601 in 1966–7, a fall of 28 per cent. (In all of these cases we have used both the current and previous directorships of MPs in order to equalize the backgrounds of those out of Government with those in Government, who are expected to drop their formal links.)

One of the fields in which a decline in economic representation has kept well up with the drop in Conservative MPs has been that of agricultural land. In the 1962–3 House, Conservatives sat while holding 642,430 acres according to our calculations. By 1966–7 this land represented had fallen to 446,107 acres, a drop of 30·5 per cent.

Little can be generalized about the halving of the number of Tory MPs with a background of manual labour, since the number dropped from four to two.

Table 9.1. A Comparative Table of Economic Backgrounds

Professions and trades	1962–3			1964–5			1966–7		
Party No. of MPs	Con. (363)	Lib. (7)	Lab. (260)	Con. (303)	Lib. (9)	Lab. (318)	Con. (253)	Lib. (12)	Lab. (363)
Chairmen, etc.	332	1	33	326	4	25	290	2	32
Directors	845	5	61	683	17	70	601	22	70
Executives	61	2	9	84	5	40	64	9	40
Manual Workers	3	0	80	4	0	112	2	0	123
Distribution:									
Banks	13	0	1	22	0	4	19	1	5
Investment Trusts, etc.	52	0	3	55	1	5	53	1	6
Insurance	55[a]	0	7[a]	45	0	10	38	1	12
Economic Associations	67[a]	0	6[a]	67	1	10	64	1	12
Manufacture	95[a]	1	12[a]	76	1	16	62	2	20
Construction and Engineering	28[a]	1	1[a]	27	1	4	27	1	8
Property	50[a]	0	5[a]	54	0	13	59	2	14
Agriculture (acreage)	642,430	0	5,270	521,460	1,200	4,737	446,107	1,125	3,387
Overseas Investment	33[a]	0	4[a]	22	0	6	26	0	5
Investment from Overseas	18	0	4	21	1	4	14	1	4
Export-Import	28[a]	0	8[a]	18	0	9	16	0	12
Mining	20	0	1 + 39[b]	10	0	35[b]	10	0	3 + 38[b]
Food and Drink	30[a]	0	0	25	1	3	24	0	5
Transport and Distribution	59[a]	0	9[a]	40	0	17	32	1	25
Retail	33	0	11[a]	26	0	17	23	0	17
Service Trades and Professions	36[a]	1	9[a]	32	3	13	25	4	31

Newspapers/Periodicals/Books	43	0	8[a]	31	1	16	30	2	22
Advertising/Public Relations	29	1	4	28	1	7	21	2	13
Entertainment	23[a]	0	11[a]	31	1	33	34	4	42
Charities and Co-operatives	12[a]	0	2[a]	17	0	17	14	2	21
Barristers/Solicitors	63/14	4/1	26/8	68/16	4/0	31/13	56/15	3/0	38/17
Doctors	3	0	6	3	0	8	2	1	9
Teachers	17	0	62	40	2	55	16	1	99
Journalists/Writers	42	1	52	40	2	54	42	2	74
Technocrats	4	1	2	3	1	6	3	1	9
Organizers	5	0	76	7	2	72	8	2	80
Sponsored Candidates	1	0	10	1	0	151	1	0	154

[a] Adjusted at a later date. [b] Ex-miners.

10

THE POWER OF LABOUR AND THE CAPITALIST ENTERPRISE

RALPH MILIBAND

In the light of the strategic position which capitalist enterprise enjoys in its dealings with governments, simply by virtue of its control of economic resources, the notion, which is basic to pluralist theory, that here is but one of the many 'veto groups' in capitalist society, on a par with other 'veto groups', must appear as a resolute escape from reality.

Of these other groups, it is labour, as an 'interest' in society, whose power is most often assumed to equal (when it is not claimed to surpass) the power of capital. But this is to treat as an accomplished fact what is only an unrealized potentiality, whose realization is beset with immense difficulties.

For labour has nothing of the power of capital in the day-to-day economic decision-making of capitalist enterprise. What a firm produces; whether it exports or does not export; whether it invests, in what, and for what purpose; whether it absorbs or is absorbed by other firms—these and many other such decisions are matters over which labour has at best an indirect degree of influence and more generally no influence at all. In this sense, labour lacks a firm basis of economic power, and has consequently that much less pressure potential *vis-à-vis* the state. This is also one reason why governments are so much less concerned to obtain the 'confidence' of labour than of business.

Moreover, labour does not have anything, by way of exercising pressure, which corresponds to the foreign influences which are readily marshalled on behalf of capital. There are no labour 'gnomes' of Zurich, no labour equivalent of the World Bank, the International Monetary Fund, or the OECD, to ensure that governments desist from taking measures detrimental to wage-earners and favourable to business, or to press for policies which are of advantage to 'lower income groups' and which are opposed to

First published as 'The Capitalist State' in New Left Review, *no. 29, 1970.*

the interests of economic élites. For wage-earners in the capitalist world, international solidarity is part of a hallowed rhetoric which seldom manifests itself concretely and effectively; for business, it is a permanent reality.

The one important weapon which labour, as an 'interest', does have is the strike; and where it has been used with real determination its effectiveness as a means of pressure has often been clearly demonstrated. Again and again, employers and governments have been forced to make concessions to labour because of the latter's resolute use of the strike weapon, or even because of the credible threat of its use. On innumerable occasions, demands which, the unions and the workers were told, could not conceivably be granted since they must inevitably mean ruin for a firm or industry or inflict irreparable damage on the national economy, have somehow become acceptable when organized labour has shown in practice that it would not desist.

Determination, however, is the problem. For labour, as a pressure group, is extremely vulnerable to many internal and external influences calculated to erode its will and persistence. Because of the effectiveness of these influences, governments have generally found it unnecessary to treat labour with anything like the deference which they have accorded to business. They have sometimes trod on the latter's toes, but never as heavily as they have trod on the toes of labour—as Mr Wilson's Labour government, for instance, has done in pursuit of an 'incomes policy'.

One important weakness which affects labour as a pressure group, as compared to business, is that the latter's national organizations are able to speak with considerably more authority than can their labour counterparts.

There are a number of reasons for this. One of them is that business organizations can truly claim to 'speak for business', either because they include a very high percentage of individual business units or because the firms which they do represent are responsible for a crucial part of economic activity. The equivalent labour organizations on the other hand nowhere include a majority of wage-earners, and mostly include far less. Business associations, in this sense, are much more representative than trade unions.

Secondly, and more important, business is nowhere as divided as labour. The point has been made before that business is neither an economic nor an ideological monolith, speaking always or even normally with one single voice on all issues. Indeed, its separate interests find everywhere expression in the different national associations which represent different sectors of the 'business community'. These divisions, notably the division between large-scale enterprise and medium or small business, are by no means negligible, either in specific or in general terms. But they do not prevent a basic ideological consensus, which is of fundamental importance in the representation and impact of business. Thus the policies advocated by the Diet of German Industry and Commerce may well be more 'moderate and liberal' than those of the Federation of German Industry;[1] and similar shades of difference may also be found among national business associations in other countries. But these differences obviously occur within a fairly narrow *conservative* spectrum of agreement which precludes major conflict. Business, it could be said, is tactically divided but strategically cohesive; over most of the larger issues of economic policy and over other large national issues as well, it may be expected to present a reasonably united front.

This is certainly not the case for trade union movements anywhere. *Their* outstanding characteristic, in fact, is division, not unity; and the divisions from which they suffer, far from being tactical and superficial, are more often than not deep and fundamental.

Trade unions have of course always been divided from each other (and often, indeed, within themselves) in terms of the particular functions and skills of their members, sometimes by geography, often by religious, ethnic or racial factors. But, whether because of these factors or for other reasons, they are above all divided by ideology and attitudes from each other and within themselves.

In some countries, for instance France and Italy, these divisions find institutional expression in the existence of separate, distinct and often bitterly antagonistic federations—Communist, social-democratic and Christian, whose conflicts are a profoundly inhibiting factor in their encounter both with employers and with the state, and in their effectiveness as pressure groups. Nowhere does business suffer anything remotely comparable to these divisions.

Moreover, even in countries where ideological cleavages have not

[1] Braunthal [G.], *The Federation of German Industry in Politics* [Cornell University Press, 1965], p. 27.

found institutional expression, trade union movements have still been subject to profound divisions, which may be contained within one organization, but which are scarcely less debilitating.

This, for instance, has always been the case for the trade union movement in Britain, where the divisions have often been based on functional differences between the unions, upon which have also, often coincidentally, been superimposed differences and conflicts between more militant and less militant unions; and this latter difference has also regularly occurred inside individual unions, with a more militant and left-wing element at odds with a generally more 'moderate' and 'responsible' leadership and following.

This division between leaders and members is also one which has not usually affected business associations. The basic cause of that division, from which Communist unions have by no means been immune, lies in the profoundly ambiguous role which trade union leaders tend to assume in capitalist societies. For on the one hand, these leaders are expected to defend the 'sectional' interests of their members with the utmost determination, both against employers and, where occasion arises, as it often does, against the state; but on the other hand, they are also expected by 'public opinion', and often required by the state, to act 'responsibly', in the 'national interest', which generally means that they should curb and subdue their members' demands rather than defend and advance them.

This is particularly true in regard to strike action. As Dr V. L. Allen has noted,

> Strikes take place within a hostile environment even though they are a common every-day phenomenon. They are conventionally described as industrially subversive, irresponsible, unfair, against the interests of the community, contrary to the workers' best interests, wasteful of resources, crudely aggressive, inconsistent with democracy and, in any event, unnecessary.[1]

But what is important about this is that trade union leaders, particularly 'reformist' ones, are themselves deeply influenced by these notions. As Dr Allen also notes,

> Union officials are particularly prone to the anti-strike environmental influences because they are frequently made out to be responsible for the behaviour of their members. . . . Once they are committed to a strike call, union officials tend to become defensive, apologetic and concerned about

---

[1] V. L. Allen, *Militant Trade Unionism* [Merlin Press, London 1966], p. 27.

taking avoiding action. When they are actually engaged in a strike, they are frequently motivated by a desire to end it quickly irrespective of the merits of the issue.[1]

These 'environmental influences' are indeed formidable. They include not only the mass media, which may be relied on, almost unanimously, to blast the 'irresponsibility' of any major (or even minor) strike, whatever the merits of the case, and similarly to condemn those who lead it; they also include the government which may equally be expected, whatever its political label, to use every available means of influence and power at its command to erode the will and purpose of the strikers, and particularly of their trade union leaders.[2] This may not always be successful; but it is at least always tried.

Nor is it only 'environmental influences' of this sort which tend to cause union leaders to be chary of sustained militant action for the advancement of their members' interests. Such action is likely to involve a serious drain of union resources. It is also likely to strengthen the hand of militant elements inside the unions whose challenge to their authority trade union leaders are naturally concerned to resist. Moreover, the fear of failure, despite great sacrifices, always looms large, and is enhanced by an unnerving awareness of the strength of the forces arrayed against labour. And while the success of militant action must often depend upon the solidarity and support of other unions, this is seldom easy to obtain; even when it is obtained, it is not at all guaranteed to last the necessary length of time.

Some of these weaknesses are inherent in the position of trade unions in capitalist society. But in this instance too, structural constraints may be more compelling, or less; and this is at least in part determined by the ideology and outlook which trade union leaders bring to their task.

With the exception of France and Italy where the largest trade union movements are run by Communists and other Marxist socialists, the trade union movements in the countries of advanced capitalism are led and dominated by men who call themselves

[1] ibid., p. 27.

[2] For a notable recent example, involving the Labour government, see P. Foot, 'The Seamen's Struggle', in Robin Blackburn and Alexander Cockburn (eds.), *The Incompatibles* [Penguin, Harmondsworth 1967: see Chapter 1 of this book].

socialists, or social-democrats, or Christian democrats, or, as in the case of the United States, mainly plain Democrats. These different labels obviously betoken substantial differences in attitudes towards the capitalist system. Where some trade union leaders, notably in the United States, accept that system as given, and do so very gladly, others tend to subscribe to a belief in the ultimate achievement of an altogether different social order. And where American trade union leaders generally believe and proclaim that there exists a fundamental identity of interests between capitalist management and labour,[1] most trade union leaders in other capitalist countries are on the whole less apt to believe this, or at least to proclaim it.

On the other hand, the practical importance of the ideological differences between American and the vast majority of non-Communist trade union leaders and officials in other capitalist countries can easily be exaggerated.[2] For while American trade union leaders explicitly accept capitalist structures as beyond challenge, their counterparts in other countries have tended, *in practice*, to act on the same view, and to treat as irrelevant to trade union strategy whatever commitment they may have to another social order.

This has greatly eased the relations of trade union leaders with employers and governments and provided a firm basis for a process of collaboration between them which has turned these leaders into junior partners of capitalist enterprise. That process has now assumed a much more official character than in the past: trade unions are now regularly 'consulted' by their governments, and their representatives are also to be found in various organisms of the state system. Trade union leaders have found it easy to believe that, because they have been recognized as a necessary element in the operation of capitalism, they have also achieved parity with business in the determination of policy. In fact, their incorporation into the official life of their countries has mainly served to saddle

[1] Thus, even a trade union leader like Walther Reuther, who is often thought of as being to 'the left' of most other American trade union leaders, is apt to proclaim that 'we must shape policies in the knowledge that free labor and free management are less antagonistic than partners, that they have more in common than in conflict. We need to broaden areas of understanding and minimise areas of conflict' (Quoted in Henry S. Kariel, *The Decline of American Pluralism* [Stanford University Press 1961], p. 63).

[2] Indeed, it can easily be exaggerated, as far as their trade union activities are concerned, in regard to many Communist trade union leaders as well.

them with responsibilities which have further weakened their bargaining position, and which has helped to reduce their effectiveness.

There are, however, other and more specific reasons for dismissing as altogether unrealistic the view of labour as an interest group comparable in strength to business.

Serious pressure group activity, it is generally agreed, now occurs much more at executive and administrative, rather than at legislative, level. As the state has increasingly come to assume greater powers in all fields of economic and social activity, so have the major 'interests' in society also naturally come to direct their pressure activities towards government and administration. This as will be seen presently, does not mean that legislatures are of no consequence in this respect. But it does mean that the most significant part of pressure group activity must now bear on the executive power; it is now only the weakest groups which seek to wield influence primarily through legislatures, precisely because they have little or no hold over the executive. The major 'interests' use both means, with the greater emphasis on the government and the administration.

But as has already been argued at length, business enters this competition on extremely favourable terms in comparison with labour or any other 'interest'. For businessmen and their representatives normally have a *rapport* with ministers, civil servants and other members of the state élite which is very different from that of labour and *its* representatives. Given the influences which affect political office-holders and administrators . . .—social provenance, personal ties and connections,[1] class situation, self-interest, ideological inclinations, conceptions of the 'national interest'—business pressure groups may reasonably expect that their views and demands will meet with an *initial* degree of comprehension, sympathy or at least respect of a kind entirely different from that accorded to their labour equivalents; and this is just as likely to be the case when 'left-wing' governments are in office as when labour has to deal with conservative administration.

[1] One Japanese writer recalls the rather charming fact that 'shortly after he took office late in 1954, Prime Minister Hatoyama Ichiro issued an order to all government agencies forbidding civil servants to play golf and mahjong with businessmen' (N. Ike, *Japanese Politics*, Eyre and Spotiswoode, London, 1958, p. 160). For the closeness of the relations of civil servants to business in Japan, see ibid., pp. 161 ff.

An additional and important reason for this difference is that labour, as a pressure group, always *appears* as a very much more 'sectional' interest than business. Its demands, however worthy in themselves, are easily capable of being construed as detrimental to economic and financial viability, as inflationary, as inimical to the efficient conduct of industrial or other affairs, as dangerous to the maintenance of 'confidence', not least abroad, as certain to imperil the competitiveness of home enterprise, as 'selfish' or 'unrealistic' or 'unsound'—in short, as clearly against the 'national interest'.

The demands of business, in contrast, are *always* claimed to be in the 'national interest'. For one thing, business opposition to labour demands which can be, and are, characterized in the terms just noted is, by definition, congruent with that interest. For another, business demands which are designed to strengthen the position of individual firms or of particular industries, or of capitalist enterprise at large, can always be presented, with a high degree of plausibility, given the capitalist context in which they are made, as congruent with the 'national interest'.

This may not always achieve the desired results, and it is obviously not the case that all business pressure is always successful and labour pressure always in vain. It is rather that governments and civil servants are very likely to feel that in endorsing the former, they are in all conscience furthering the 'national interest'; and equally likely to feel that this is not the case, or is very much less likely to be the case, in relation to labour's demands.[1]

This likelihood is further increased by the vast resources which business interests are able to marshall in the advancement of their cause. Government departments and regulatory agencies which are concerned with matters and policies affecting the major interests are strongly influenced by the information and evidence presented to

[1] A French writer notes, in this connection, that 'top civil servants prefer to deal with the top men of industry and finance rather than with the representatives of small or medium enterprises, or vine or beet growers. To the failings of the former, the latter add a complete lack of understanding of economic life and an all too evidently exclusive concern for their particular interests. Moreover, the interests of large employers are interlinked with the national interest. This creates a community of language between these employers and officials; and though officials are aware of a certain ambiguity in the situation, they appreciate the knowledge these men have, and the fact that they are able to give to their demands the polish of general ideas.' (Brindillac, *Les Hauts Fonctionnaires*, p. 871).

them by these interests, and indeed often rely, in the determination of their policies, upon it. Moreover, they are highly susceptible to the weight and intensity of the pressures which interests are able to generate. From this point of view, business is infinitely better placed than labour, or any other interest, given its vastly superior resources. Moreover, the largest and most powerful firms do not need to rely on any intermediate body to speak to governments and present their case on their behalf—they do so for themselves, with the confidence born of their power. As Professor Meynaud also notes, 'Siemens, Rhône-Poulenc, Montecatini, Courtaulds, General Motors, need no intermediary to deal with the authorities'.[1] But these intermediaries are all the same of no mean importance in the presentation of industry's demands, in the pressures they are able to generate, and in the degree to which they are able, by the deployment of their resources, to help shape the official mind, and also 'public opinion'. As Professor Ehrmann has observed for France, 'the large, well-organized economic interests in the nation, especially when they are represented by competently staffed peak associations, such as the National Employers' Council, are in almost constant consultation with the Ministry's tax section' (i.e. the Ministry of Finance).[2] No interest other than business, anywhere, has the same ease of access to the most important organs of executive power, and none enjoys the same familiarity with its agents. Nor is any other interest able to wage, when required, the kind of pressure campaign which business interests can undertake. Thus, the Labour-Management Relations Act of 1947, better known as the Taft-Hartley Act, was profoundly detrimental to American trade union interests, and they fought hard against it; but their struggle was as nothing to the campaign which the National Association of Manufacturers was able to wage for its promulgation. In a different context, it is very difficult to think that any interest other than business could muster the kind of resources and sympathies which were mobilized in Britain to persuade the government to establish

[1] Meynaud [J.], *Nouvelles Etudes sur les Groupes de Pression en France* [Colin, 1962], p. 27. An American study also notes that among the 200 largest manufacturing concerns in the United States, 'Washington representatives are the rule rather than the exception, particularly among companies making "hard goods" for the government' (P. W. Cherrington and R. L. Gillen, *The Business Representative in Washington*, 1962, p. 1).

[2] H. W. Ehrmann, 'French Bureaucracy and Organised Interests', in *Administrative Science Quarterly*, 1961, vol. 5, no. 4, p. 541.

commercial television;[1] and it is equally difficult to believe that a trade union, or any other interest, would be able to command the resources required to wage for their own purposes the anti-nationalization campaigns which British firms have waged at one time or another since the war.[2] One American writer has said, in regard to the United States, that 'the flaw in the pluralist heaven is that the heavenly chorus sings with a strong upper-class accent . . . the system is skewed, loaded and unbalanced in favour of a fraction of a minority'.[3] This is also true for other capitalist countries.

The argument, it may be worth stressing yet again, is not that this imbalance automatically ensures that business interests always achieve their purposes and necessarily impose their will upon the state in regard to their every demand. Nor is it to suggest that other organized groups of every sort have not often waged highly successful campaigns, sometimes even against strong business opposition. Had business predominance been absolute, it would be absurd to speak of competition at all. There *is* competition, and defeats for powerful capitalist interests as well as victories. After all, David did overcome Goliath. But the point of the story is that David *was* smaller than Goliath and that the odds *were* heavily against him.

[1] For which see H. H. Wilson, *Pressure Group: The Campaign for Commercial Television in England*, Secker, London, 1961.

[2] See, e.g. H. H. Wilson, 'Techniques of Pressure', in *The Public Opinion Quarterly*, 1951, vol. 15.

[3] E. E. Schattschneider, *The Semi-Sovereign People*, Holt-Rinehart, New York, 1960, p. 31. Some thirty years ago Professor Schattschneider made the point in terms which remain singularly apposite: 'Business men collectively constitute the most class-conscious group in American society. As a class they are more highly organised, more easily mobilised, have more facilities for communication, are more like-minded, and are more accustomed to stand together in defence of their privileges than any other group.' (E. E. Schattschneider, *Politics, Pressures and the Tariff*, 1935, p. 287).

11

NATIONALIZATION AND THE PRIVATE SECTOR

JOHN HUGHES

Discussion on *The Insiders:* nationalization

How much more public ownership and/or control is desirable? For what objectives would it be proposed? Do we accept control of the large firms by a board of directors which is either self-perpetuating or shareholder-controlled—do we exclude consumers and workers from participation in general policy-making of the firm? Naturally, *Industry and Society* is silent on these matters, as it stands not any longer even for gradualism, but for the abandonment of the socialist objective. But has *The Insiders* taken us any further forward?

The Insiders attempts to fill this gap by a mere review—not even a critical assessment—of some of the Trade Union programmes purporting to deal with the extension of public ownership, such as those on engineering and on building. This is unhelpful, as these are confused documents, badly composed, to a varying degree out of date, based on inadequate analysis, and making only the haziest of proposals. It is a sad commentary on the work of socialists in connection with Trade Unions that so little of the necessary work of analysis, and discussion of ideas, at the level of each industry has been done. Socialists in the labour movement have still got to do their homework. I was never more shocked than when I realized how little thinking about steel nationalization had taken place or was going on at *any* level within the labour movement. That is not unique. It may be argued that it is idle to prepare blueprints. But it is not idle to attempt to understand the organization, technical and market problems, trends in development, of major industries; it is not idle to be able to criticize and expose the policies adopted by private ownership, and to exploit their deficiencies by publicizing alternative policies. *The Insiders* might have done better to try to assess what are the priorities here, rather than acting as if the

First published in Universities and Left Review, *no. 4, 1958.*

pitifully small amount of research material and programme proposals thrown up by the Trade Unions provided an adequate basis for moving forward.

The Insiders, however, is at its weakest in assessing the role of the state sector, and particularly the nationalized industries, in the mixed economy. For the socialist, interested in the transition to a predominantly socialist economy, it is not only the *size* of the state sector but its present *function* that matters. Is it a servant of the private sector—and if so, in what ways is this subordination achieved—or is it a challenge to the private sector? I think Clive Jenkins, in *The Insiders*, loses his way in a mass of detail about only one or two aspects of this relationship between the public and the private sector. Clive Jenkins deals particularly with compensation, and with the composition of the boards (the Acton Society Trust study *The Men on the Boards* had made the general situation in this respect obvious some years ago). But his facts are not fitted into any comprehensive analysis, nor is it very clear in what way the role of the nationalized industries should change. Yet this question of the *way* in which the nationalized industries are used in relation to the private sector is decisive. The state sector is already large—it accounts for nearly half of investment spending, some 30 per cent of employment income, a quarter of the national product. The extensions of public ownership intended by the Labour Party, particularly steel, still do not transform the role of the nationalized industries in the economy, but they would make a transformation of that role even more far-reaching. This question of changing the relation of the nationalized sector to the private sector from one of subordination to that of a challenge, a lever for the further extension of community control over industry, has to be clearly understood by socialists.

What are the main features of the existing relationship between nationalized industries and private sector? The nationalized industries are subordinated to the economic needs of private industry, and in fact provide the system's most important political and economic stabilizer. This is revealed in a number of ways. Take first the transfer of income to rentier groups and to private industry profits. In seeing only the question of compensation Clive Jenkins missed seeing the total situation. In 1949 interest payments by public corporations—mainly compensation—were £86 million. By the middle 1950s I estimate that the *annual addition to rentier incomes and private profits* directly due to the operation of the nationalized industries was at least £400 million before tax, apart from the direct subsidization of the private sector by about £50 million per annum due to selling nationalized industry products below real cost of production. This has somewhat staggering implications in a period in which wage claims for workers in nationalized industries are rejected because of alleged 'inability to pay'. The London bus strike is fought out over a sum of less than £1 million per annum, but £400 million is added to rentier and profit incomes. How?

First, the interest payments to rentiers. These are now running at over £160 million per annum. (Some of these are payments to the Treasury, but the Treasury lends money borrowed from private individuals and institutions—the national debt is increased.) The reason interest payments have risen and will continue to rise is that the nationalized industries borrow not only to finance 'net investment' *but even to replace a large part of their existing capital equipment*. At present the nationalized industries are adding to their indebtedness at the rate of over £400 million per annum. Given the continuation of current price and investment policies over £4,000 million of additional debt will be incurred by the middle 1960s, and by then interest payments to rentiers might well be double the present enormous load. This occurs because the pricing policies pursued by the nationalized industries involve them in doing no more than 'break even' after allowing for depreciation of capital equipment at historical cost—not the cost of replacement. Thus, in the case of the N.C.B., the annual reduction in *capacity* of the pits has been some 4 million tons a year according to the N.C.B.'s economic adviser (see article by Schumacher in 'N.C.B.—The First Ten Years'), costing some £40 million per annum to replace, but very little of this has been covered by the current price of coal. In the case of electricity the Herbert Report (Chapter 15) argued that the accounting rules followed understated the depreciation provision required by some £17 million in 1954–5. The National Income Blue Book data, although not sufficiently precise, shows what is happening: the amount borrowed each year by public corporations consistently exceeds the estimated 'net investment' (i.e. addition to capital equipment). The additional indebtedness attributable to each year is made up of state loans plus net stock issued minus net acquisition of financial assets (i.e. loans or stock not yet used for capital spending).

Table 11.1. Public Corporations: Annual Borrowing and Net Capital Formation (in £ millions)

Year	1948	1949	1950	1951	1952	1953	1954	1955	1956	Total
Amount borrowed	130	166	173	266	268	253	255	425	411	2,347
Net capital form[a]	39	88	97	130	137	192	233	254	254	1,424
Replacement of existing capital financed by borrowing	91	78	76	136	131	61	22	171	157	923

Source: N.I. Blue Book 1957. Tables 33 and 55.
[a] *Fixed capital.*

Thus, since 1948, the public corporations have accumulated over £900 million of outstanding debts not offset by increases in the fixed capital equipment of these industries. The low figures for 'replacement of existing capital financed by borrowing' in 1953 and 1954 in the table above are only apparent exceptions as in both these years the value of 'stocks and work in progress' was reduced whereas in a normal year this item increases. To put the situation another way, the public corporations have failed to cover, from the prices they charged, their costs of production and replacement of capital equipment. On average this deficit has been about £100 million per annum. The National Income input-output table shows that about half of this has directly benefited private trade and industry, a subsidy of some £50 million per annum.

So much for the size and rapid increase of the transfers to rentiers. These spring from the pricing policies pursued. But when the nationalized industries are purchasing from the private sector they are confronted with prices fixed in order to cover not only the costs of production of private firms, but also to finance most of their capital expansion. These prices are often the result of deliberate price fixing by cartels—the Monopoly Commission 'Report on the Supply and Exports of Electrical and Allied Machinery and Plant' is an interesting study in this respect. The nationalized industries, which have to borrow to finance their own expansion, are themselves having to bear most of the burden—through the prices they pay—of financing the expansion of the private firms they purchase from. The capital gains of course accrue to the private sector.

Electrical manufacturers

For instance, in the Monopoly Commission investigation of the electrical machinery and plant manufacturers it was found that these firms were fixing common prices despite variations in cost of production—in other words, profits even for the inefficient, and very high profit margins for the efficient. The firms justified this in terms of the high cost of the capital investment they were making. In this case, Central Electricity Authority orders accounted for 80 per cent of home market trade in major generating equipment. The Report showed that profit rates on cost, for members of this cartel, on large motors and alternators sold in the home market had been 9·3 per cent in the boom year 1937, but were 26·4 per cent in 1951, and 25·1 per cent in 1952. Capital gains for the producers of generating equipment, increasing indebtedness for the nationalized industries, and yet one recalls that the T.U.C.'s interim report on 'Public Ownership' was still justifying nationalization in terms of redistribution of wealth. It makes strange reading: 'Interest on compensation stock and on new capital, being guaranteed by the Government, will generally be less than it would have been had the industries remained under private ownership.' Alas, that was not the whole story!

The importance of nationalized orders to the private sector is very great. They are particularly concentrated upon certain sections of manufacturing and upon construction. The annual total of purchases by the public corporations from the private sector is approximately £1,500 million. 'Gross capital formation' accounts for nearly £600 million per annum[1] (in 1955, £562 million, in 1956, £590 million), and purchases of goods and services from the private sector for current production about £900 million per annum (see N.I. Blue Book, Table 31). In manufacturing, gross profits have been running at about 20 per cent of gross output, and if this figure can be applied to the purchases by nationalized industries it suggests that gross profits of the order of £300 million were realized in the private sector. This would result in net profits (i.e. after depreciation allowances) *after* tax of somewhere between £160 and £200

[1] There are no National Income figures to indicate how much of this capital investment was carried out by the public corporations themselves instead of by contractors, but the bulk of it was certainly carried out by private firms—for instance the C.E.A. did not produce its own generating plant.

million. It is worth remembering that these figures only deal with the public corporations; when central and local government purchases and borrowing are considered as well, the direct creation of rentier and profits incomes by the entire state sector is very much higher than that for the nationalized industries alone.

The subordination of the nationalized industries to the needs of the private sector is revealed in many other ways. Clive Jenkins illustrates one part of this by his examination in *The Insiders* of the composition of the Boards. It is revealed too in the general policy of modelling their organization and industrial relations policies on the pattern of large-scale private firms. We seem to have come full circle. The socialists thought of national ownership as creating a new industrial system, but the nationalized industries are told to act as would a large commercial concern, except that profit maximization is excluded—as this would strike at the interests of the private sector.

For instance, the Fleck Report on the N.C.B. declared:

> There is nothing in the legislation which created the N.C.B. that prevents the industry being managed in accordance with the best commercial practice. Nor is there any conflict between a commercial approach on the Board's part and the Board's being a good employer. On the contrary, many large commercial organizations in Great Britain have proved to be most advanced in their concept of the responsibilities of employers. (Page 7.)

This is, of course, the philosophy of very big business, of I.C.I., not that of socialists. But it is the point of departure for the nationalized industries today. The Herbert Report on Electricity Supply echoes the same ideas, the nationalized industries are to follow the practice of private business. . . .

> It should be conducted as a commercial concern . . . the industry should so conduct itself that in the service to its customers and the well-being of its staff it would stand comparison with the best to be found in private industry. . . . We could see nothing in the Act which required the industry to . . . conduct itself in such a way that it would have to face higher costs than a private business would face in similar circumstances. (Page 7.)

Again, in the B.T.C.'s 'Proposals for the Railways', we read:

> Today the British Transport Commission much more resemble in organization, purpose and status a large-scale commercial corporation. The Government are satisfied that this kind of structure is the right one. . . . (Page 4.)

The Conservative Government is 'satisfied' with such an approach to the functions of the nationalized industries, but are socialists satisfied?

There are two other important ways in which the nationalized industries are subordinated to the needs of a predominantly capitalist economy. One is their use as a stabilizer to offset the fluctuations of the private sector. This has been particularly clear both in the field of investment policy and of pricing since 1955. In the absence of effective controls over the rate of investment in the private sector, nationalized industry plans have been 're-phased'. The destabilizing of the public corporations has still, however, not been carried so far as in the case of local authority house-building, where a vital social need is shamelessly sacrificed to offsetting the inherent instability of profit-making industry.

The other way in which the nationalized industries are used is as servants of the Conservative Government's attempts to impose a wages standstill on the Trade Unions. Governmental influence over nationalized industries policies on pricing and industrial relations is very great, and it is not surprising that this is the chosen sector. *Apparently* there is no question of the Trade Unions asking for a share in profits, as there are no profits. What has been said earlier about the transfer of over £400 million a year to rent and profit incomes as a result of the operation of the nationalized industries is apt enough comment on this 'inability to pay' argument. However, the Government knows that the newspapers and other 'mass media' will stress the argument that higher wages 'must' mean higher prices—the workers are appealed to in their capacity as consumers to oppose the claims of the workers in the public sector. The beauty of this is that if such policies lead to worsened industrial relations, to strikes, to problems of inter-Union relations, the blame does not attach to a system of private profit-making industry. The criticism centres on the publicly owned industries, but the benefits from a 'tougher' industrial relations policy accrue to the private sector. It is true that the Government, even so, does not feel capable of fighting more than one Union at a time—it could not handle both a rail strike and a London bus strike, but it was prepared to face one or the other. And it was a Cabinet decision that bought off the railwaymen, the Cabinet made the 'final offer', not the Transport Commission—subordination was complete and obvious. Thus, the Government, private industry, and the mass media, use the nationalized industries as both an economic and a political support for the system of private ownership. We have reached the stage where, if the labour movement does not learn to use the nationalized sector as a lever to transform capitalism, it will find the nationalized industries used as a weapon against the interests of the workers. This is the new dress of exploitation.

12

OCCUPATIONAL BACKGROUND OF MEMBERS OF PRINCIPAL PUBLIC CORPORATION BOARDS

CLIVE JENKINS

Table 12.1. Occupational Background of Full-time and Part-time Members of Principal Public Corporation Boards (As at March 1956)

Corporation board	Total of Members	Company Directors	Regular Officers	Senior Central or Local Govt. Officers	Representative of Labour Party, Trade Union or Co-operative Movements	Technicians or Professional Managers	Land-owners or Farmers	Universities, Voluntary Organizations etc.
BRITISH TRANSPORT COMMISSION	13	7[a]	1		1	4		
LONDON TRANSPORT EXECUTIVE	7				2	5		
B.T.C. Area (Railways) Boards (excl. Chairmen who are Members of the B.T.C. and other B.T.C. Members)								
Eastern Area	5	4			1			
North-Eastern Area	4	2			1			1
Scottish Area	6	4			1			1
Southern Area (including non-B.T.C. Chairman)	6	5			1			
Western Area (including non-B.T.C. Chairman)	6	5			1			
London Midland Area	6	3	1		2			

[a] One also ex-senior civil servant.

First published in Power at the Top *by Clive Jenkins, MacGibbon and Kee, 1959.*

Table 12.1.—(contd.)

Corporation board	Total of Members	Company Directors	Regular Officers	Senior Central or Local Govt. Officers	Representative of Labour Party, Trade Union or Co-operative Movements	Technicians or Professional Managers	Land-owners or Farmers	Universities, Voluntary Organizations etc.
CENTRAL ELECTRICITY AUTHORITY	5			1	1	2		1
London Area Board (including Chairman)	7	3		1		2		1
South-East Area Board (including Chairman)	6	1			1	2	1	1[a]
South Area Board (including Chairman)	7	1			1	3	1	1
South-West Area Board (including Chairman)	7	1			1	3	1	1
East Area Board (including Chairman)	7	1	1	1	1	2	1	
East Midlands Area Board	7	3			1	2		1
Midland Area Board	8	4			3	1		
South Wales Area Board	8	4			1	2		1
Merseyside and North Wales Area Board	7	4				1	2	
Yorkshire Area Board	6	1			2	1	1	1
North-East Area Board	7	3			1	2	1	
North-West Area Board	8	3			1	2	1	1
GAS COUNCIL (Other Members are Chairmen of Area Boards)	2	2[b]						
Scottish Board	7	2			2	3		
Northern Board	8	2		1	1	3		1
North-West Board	7	6			1			
North-East Board	7	2			2	2		1
East Midlands Board	7	3			1	3		
West Midlands Board	7	3[c]			2	1		1
Wales Board	8	2		2	2	2		
Eastern Board	7	1		1	1	4		
North Thames Board	7	3		1	1	1		1

[a] Former Conservative Member of Parliament.
[b] Also 'Technicians'. [c] One also civil servant-Technician.

Table 12.1.—(contd.)

Corporation board	Total of Members	Company Directors	Regular Officers	Senior Central or Local Govt. Officers	Representative of Labour Party, Trade Union or Co-operative Movements	Technicians or Professional Managers	Land-owners or Farmers	Universities, Voluntary Organizations etc.
GAS COUNCIL—(*contd.*)								
South-Eastern Board	8	3		2	1	1		1
Southern Board	8	5[a]			1	1		1
South-West Board	8	3			1	2		2[b]
BRITISH OVERSEAS AIRWAYS CORPORATION	10	4		1	2[c]	3		
BRITISH EUROPEAN AIRWAYS CORPORATION	8	4	1[d]	1	2[e]			
NATIONAL COAL BOARD	11	1		2	3	5[f]		
National Coal Board Divisional Chairmen	9	1	1	1		6[g]		
TOTALS	272	106	5	15	47	71	9	19

[a] One also Labour member of Local Authority.
[b] One is chairman of an employers' organization.
[c] Also Chairman of Gas Board.
[d] Also member of Parliamentary Labour Party.
[e] Also 'Company Director'. [f] One also civil servant.
[g] Almost all held positions of trust and responsibility with previous coal-owners.

NOTE

1. Accountants are classified as 'Company Directors' if they currently hold directorships. Otherwise shown as 'others' unless history identifies them as Managers.
2. Technicians who may have held company directorships prior to nationalization are not listed as such unless it seems clear that they had become primarily administrative.
3. Those 'technicians' previously employed by Local Authorities are classified as such and not as 'local government officers'.
4. Those listed as 'Senior Central or Local Government Officers' are administrative or executive, i.e. Town or County Council Clerks.
5. 'Representative of Labour Party, Trade Union or Co-operative Movements' are those persons appointed because of their experience in trade unions, the Co-operative Movement or the Labour Party.

13
AMERICAN INVESTMENT IN BRITAIN
MICHAEL HUGHES

Introduction

In response to the rapidly changing market conditions at home and overseas (1) the corporations in advanced industrial nations have developed increasingly more sophisticated organizational frameworks to promote greater specialization in the process of capital accumulation. Perhaps the most dramatic changes have been in America, where corporate administrative structures have developed, during this century, from the national corporation (around 1900), to the multidivisional (from the 1920s) to the multinational corporation of today (2).

These large corporations are a condition for and a consequence of economic growth and development in the advanced industrial nations of the capitalist world. It is these organizations which are, along with the State, one of the most prevalent sources of capital investment, and provide frameworks for employing skill and expertise, technology, product innovation and distribution. The trend is for these corporations to become increasingly more economically powerful as their world role and global functioning extends, along with their size and financial independence.

The phenomenon of an internationally operating company is not entirely new to the British economy: they have existed since the formation of the chartered companies during the expansion of Europe from the sixteenth century onwards—for example, the British East India Company (from 1600 to the 1880s) and the Royal Niger Chartered Company (from 1886), which traded with a monopoly charter and established imperial and territorial domains, where they performed most of the functions of a nation-state (3). What is a new experience for the British (and European) economy is the massive expansion of American firms into advanced industrial nations, whereby the economic power of a foreign nation is felt at home (4). Is the metropolitan power challenged?

It is the most important feature of the multinationals that they invest directly into the economy of a foreign nation, rather than exporting goods produced at home. The foreign operations of the multi-national corporations are becoming a substitute for normal import/export activities (5). Since these activities transcend nation-state boundaries, this raises important questions about the host nation's control over its economy, for now we have a situation where the relationship between economic and political systems is no longer a purely internal one, where the external relations are between nation-states. Rather, there is a territorial non-coincidence between control of capital and the nation-state (6). This decreases the power of a nation-state and presents it with problems arising from the interface between the foreign multinational corporations and the domestic economy. Consequently, we cannot presume to identify the interests of the multinationals with the future of nationalistically evaluated economies, particularly when the situation is one where these corporations can be seen as agents of neo-imperialism (7).

It is in this context that I shall consider the American multinational corporations and the concern expressed over their role in Europe and Britain. I shall begin with a discussion of Servan-Schreiber's thesis (8), and a recent alternative to it.

Europe and American corporations

In 1967, Jean-Jacques Servan-Schreiber documented the massive expansion of American firms in Europe (9). This American challenge came in the form of large-scale direct corporate investment into European companies, particularly in the manufacturing and allied industries, and represented the bulk of American private investment abroad. More recently, Robert Rowthorn (10), although not sharing Servan-Schreiber's fear of the large U.S. multinationals, regards this American expansion as '. . . one of the most striking features of the capitalist world during the last quarter century . . .'. Therefore, I think that it is important to outline the main features of this perceived threat by the multinationals, briefly and, of course, in a much simplified fashion.

Essentially, the argument turns on the notion that modern technology requires large corporations which can function in an international system of production and marketing, i.e., they will develop a global strategy. The corporations are the only type which can attain a sufficient concentration and allocation of capital necessary for growth and progress. Furthermore, it is argued that countries which cannot generate these multinational firms with a geocentric technology will become colonies of those countries having such firms. More specifically, the penetration of American capital into European countries is very extensive and will lead to a loss of control by European countries over their industrial resources, and will involve a weakening of a nation's capacity to determine its own future. Unless there is a rapid response and a concerted effort by European governments and industry to create and encourage the formation of further large, strong multinational corporations of their own, expand research and development facilities and institute better management training, then the prospects of a European community are very dim. Instead, the next largest industrial force outside the U.S.A. and the U.S.S.R. will be American corporations and affiliates in Europe (11).

According to this type of argument (12), one of the most significant features of the multinational corporation is its enormous size. Many American firms tend to be much larger than non-American ones, and this is taken as the most crucial factor which makes their innovative and growth capability generally superior to that of European firms and, consequently, a threat to the future of non-American industrial enterprise. Furthermore, the American multinationals usually concentrate upon those sectors of the economy most technologically advanced, most adaptable to change and with the highest growth rates. In addition to this the American subsidiaries overseas have access to and benefit greatly from the vast amount of research and development undertaken by the parent company in the United States, especially that financed from the U.S. Government's defence programmes, for example, in armaments and aerospace, which makes for considerable 'spin-off' to be exploited by the contractors in the large and adventurous American consumer market. Finally, we are shown how the American multinationals are more productive, and are more efficiently controlled by better-trained management, having skills superior to those of their European counterparts (13).

Although these arguments can be penetrating and illuminating, the stress placed upon the size of the American firms, their efficiency, productivity and growth potential, may not be wholly justified. Rowthorn's study (14) of a sample of European and American firms shows that there is no systematic relationship between the size and average growth rate, although the American firms do exhibit more steady growth, and that the profit rates are not higher but tend to display less variability than those of the European firms. This study suggests that the European companies are holding their own in competition with the American corporations and that they are narrowing the gap in industrial productivity between the two systems.

Hymer and Rowthorn (15) see the notion of the American challenge as a myth based upon exaggerated claims for the prowess of American multinationals. It is a myth which provides a basis for an argument for a policy of protectionism, an argument which serves the interests of the large European firms but not necessarily the public interest. The success of certain sectors of private enterprise is being raised almost to the status of a national goal in a competition which is not necessarily in the long-term interests of the public as a whole. It is unlikely that the American multinationals can be beaten at their own game, and if European companies do attempt to go mutinational, in an all-out bid to rival the Americans, then it may help the U.S. corporate strategy, because going multinational means weakening the ties between the firm and the nation, leaving the national economy in a weaker position in relation to the American-dominated international economic system. The European firms taking the road to multinational operations would swell the ranks of the existing footloose corporations roaming the world in search of greater rationalization of their production and leave the domestic economy with diminished economic resources to be used in the nations' interests. This strategy could well lead to the American 'colonization' of Europe, although it set out with precisely the opposite intentions. The power of the large multinationals can erode the restraints of individual national economic policies by employing a global strategy formulated to exploit the differences between capitalist nations.

Both of the above arguments have as a crux of their alternative to the surrender of Europe to the neo-imperialist aspirations of American business, the 'better' use of capital and co-ordination of trade and industrial production. The major difference between them is that on the one hand government and industry are advised to join forces and build a European counter-offensive to the

American penetration into Europe, based on the assumption that only multinationals can produce the necessary conditions for progress, and freedom from American economic and political power, whereas on the other hand the solution rests in the hands of the nation-state, which must bring the economic resources under closer control by the political system, and thereby gain sufficient strength to resist the process of rationalization by the American multinationals. Of course, Britain and other European countries have multinationals already and are also encouraging industry to reorganize in an attempt to create more viable economies. However, information as to the effectiveness of either strategy, and the consequences for the future of the societies of Britain and Europe, is sparse (16). The situation in Europe is characterized by a steady flow of mergers within and across national boundaries and various other moves to consolidate industry in the face of the ever-increasing side of American investment, which can be seen as a series of thrusts and counter-thrusts between the European Economic Community and America.

The penetration of American capital into Europe

After Canada, which in 1960 had 43 per cent of its mining and manufacturing industry owned by American subsidiaries (17), Europe is the most penetrated by U.S. capital, in which the largest share of the direct corporate investment goes to Britain.

Table 13.1. U.S. Direct Investment Abroad, 1967 (selected countries)

Country	Value of assets in $(000,000)
Canada	18,069
U.K.	6,101
W. Germany	3,487
France	1,904
Italy	1,242
Netherlands	917

Source: U.S. Department of Commerce *Survey of Current Business*, October 1968.

So substantial is this flow of investment that the main channel of economic transaction between America and Europe has become not exports but corporate investment (18). Moreover, during the last ten years American investment has been increasing twice as fast in Europe as in Canada. It appears that the U.S. multinationals regard Europe, and especially the prospects of an even larger Common Market, to be the biggest market growth area in the near future, and have sought to increase their investment stake accordingly. Goods produced by U.S. subsidiaries in European countries earn profits for their parent companies in America by taking advantage of the E.E.C. trade agreements, a strategy which successfully circumvents trade barriers. For instance, from 1950 to 1967 investment by U.S. corporations in European manufacturing and mining industries rose more than tenfold: from $1,358m to $14,185m; whereas investment in Canada during the same period rose only by five times: from $2,315m to $11,902m (19).

This rapid increase of American investment activity in Europe has involved 3,000 U.S. companies since 1958, and accounts for about one-third of all their foreign investment (20). This investment is concentrated in the more technologically advanced industries, primarily in four main groups: vehicles, chemicals, mechanical and electrical engineering, which take 85 per cent of the total investment (21). Consequently, by the mid-1960s American subsidiaries were producing 75 per cent of all the computers sold in Europe, led by the giant I.B.M., which manufactures 65 per cent of all the computers in the non-communist world (22). By 1968, General Motors, Ford and Chrysler controlled 30 per cent of the European motor-car market, and American oil companies refined and distributed over 25 per cent of the petroleum (23). A small number of large American multinationals are responsible for the largest proportion of the U.S. investment: General Motors, Ford and Standard Oil (New Jersey) represent 40 per cent of the American direct corporate investment in Britain, Germany and France (24). Chorafas has estimated that, on present performance, American subsidiaries could own 75 per cent of the science-based industry in Europe by the late 1970s (25).

This American control over important areas of European industry has considerable significance for social and political life as well as the economic system. Servan-Schreiber's remark that 'we see a foreign challenge breaking down the political and psychological framework of our societies' (26) may be unduly pessimistic, and rather sweeping, and perhaps more a symptom of the political and economic struggles between American and European oligopolies. However, when countries encourage closer trading links with each other, as in the E.E.C., in an attempt to rationalize their own industrial resources, then as it is becoming clear in the closing stages of Britain's negotiating for entry into the E.E.C., major changes in the domestic economy become issues the significance of which extend beyond the decision-makers of the economic system to the political parties, trade unions and other interested groups (and to the 'man in the street').

Similarly, but less overtly, when relations with America take on the more concrete form of direct ownership and control of industrial assets by the U.S. rather than just diplomatic exchanges, then, since it involves industries operating within the economic and political framework of Britain and Europe, the transfer of many economic and political influences is much quicker and far more effective. When an American firm manufacturing in Britain makes a decision based on the interests of the parent company in the United States or upon the U.S. Government's economic or foreign policy there is potential conflict with the British Government's plans for industry, and it will diminish the power which trade unions and government would otherwise be able to wield. The global strategy and deployment of assets used by the multinationals provides a wider choice of responses when confronted by other power groups than would be the case with a nation firm, and are therefore more difficult to control or influence.

American multinationals in Britain

The initial surge of investment by American firms into the British economy began about a century ago. A few of these firms soon established themselves in a wide range of industries and in several important and new expanding fields of technology such as photography and the electrical industry. By the early 1900s American capital had penetrated the economy to an even greater extent and controlled interests in technologically advanced industries (27) which today absorb most of the American investment in Britain. During the 1920s the U.S. became one of the major capital-exporting countries and British economic policies, restricting the imports of manufactured goods, further encouraged American companies to invest capital in Britain and set up factories to produce the goods directly in the market, which they found more difficult to penetrate by the more conventional method of exporting (28). Consequently, by 1940, there were 600 American subsidiaries and affiliates operating in Britain, with assets worth $530m (29).

After World War II, the Bretton Woods Agreement and the General Agreement on Tariffs and Trade made way for a second and more intensive wave of trade and investment from the United States throughout Europe. Britain received her share of this investment, whereby American firms could increase their share of the British consumer market despite limitations placed upon imports from the U.S. Between 1945 and 1950, 100 new American subsidiaries were set up and the already established ones grew considerably. It enabled these U.S. corporations to grow in a period when domestic expansion was limited. An important effect of this for Europe and Britain was that the U.S. had a potentially larger share of the world market without having to face so many tariff barriers. The greatest flow of capital investment into Europe from America occurred between 1950 and 1957, when the book value of this investment rose by tenfold, from $1,358m to $14,185m. This meant that the American firms were going to enter Europe in a more extensive role and try to repeat the success they had experienced in Britain. This is borne out by the figures for 1957–66, when the U.S. subsidiary expenditure on plant and equipment in the U.K. rose by 2½ times, while it increased 8 times in the EEC. Therefore, in 1967 investment by American companies in Britain amounted to $6,010m; this amount of U.S. investment in a foreign economy is topped only by Canada, at $18,069m (30).

This investment represents the stake of 1,600 American subsidiaries and Anglo-American-financed firms in the British economy (31). It is almost two-thirds of all the U.S. corporate direct investment in manufacturing and petroleum industries in Europe (32). As a result, over the last ten years American subsidiaries have financed between 6 and 7 per cent of the corporate capital formation in the U.K. and have earned 8 to 9 per cent of the profits. More importantly, American firms now employ about 6 per cent of the labour force in the manufacturing industries, supply 10 per cent of the total goods made in British factories, and contribute 17·5 per cent of the visible exports. Much of the investment is in the technologically advanced sectors of the economy which show fast growth rates. Consequently U.S. companies produce half the petrol sold in the British market, half the pharmaceuticals sold to the National Health Service, and I.B.M. provide 40 per cent of the computers. If this investment trend continues American subsidiaries and affiliates could control 20–25 per cent of British industry by 1980.

An important aspect of the American involvement is that the prospective investors are encouraged by Government incentives to locate new projects in regions which suffer from under-employment and a low rate of capital investment. It is often easier for the multinational corporation to take advantage of this opportunity than for the national firms. The multinational's choice of location is not necessarily restricted by existing investment elsewhere in the country, and it can be integrated with an international strategy of product and market development. Also these firms can exploit a monopolistic position over local resources. Between 1945 and 1965 30 per cent of all foreign-owned firms (predominantly American) invested in Scotland, particularly those firms in the electronics industry (33). Regional development has been encouraged by Government cash incentives which in 1969–70 amounted to £350m (34), and has helped to create the second largest electronics industrial complex outside California. The American involvement has led to a situation where nearly one in ten people employed in manufacturing industries in Scotland are in American subsidiaries and more than 15 per cent of the new jobs in Northern Ireland since 1966 have been created by U.S.-controlled firms. Similar encouragement is given by many other European countries, which are eager to develop ailing areas of their economy where there is no tradition of manufacturing industry. However, the multinationals have a considerable amount of power, especially in this situation, since they control much-in-demand capital and can bring employment to depressed areas. Therefore governments are faced with important decisions concerning shifts in the power structure of certain sectors of the economy and the future of the labour market in various regions of the country (35).

The multinationals and the nation-state

The presence of such a large amount of American capital investment in Britain and Europe is part of the multinational corporations' global strategy to rationalize their production. It is only one element in the international division of labour towards which the American multinationals lead the industrial corporations of the other advanced nations of the capitalist world.

This strategy is characterized by international management, marketing and product integration whereby the multinationals co-ordinate production and assembly between several countries in which they will sell the range, or part, of the finished product (36). The operations are controlled from the parent company offices in America. It is this type of involvement in and control of subsidiaries in foreign nations which appears to threaten the host nation's control of the multinationals by the political and economic policies at their disposal.

Obviously, the corporations need to be sensitive to certain local interests and permit a degree of autonomy in their subsidiaries to accommodate local conditions and to bargain with governments for the best investment terms and incentives. However, the list of priorities upon which the firm's decisions are based is headed by the growth or profitability of the parent company. This often necessitates initial periods of unprofitable investment in order to secure political good will (especially in the low-income nations) but is calculated to provide enormous growth prospects and profits in the long term.

Since most foreign countries encourage the multinationals to invest and build factories in their economy (notably in the under-developed sectors and regions) for the perceived benefits that it will bring, the recipients are placed in a position where they cannot enforce very harsh constraints on the multinationals because other countries are competing for the same investment opportunities. It often matters little to the multinationals where they invest within certain areas of Europe, e.g., to expand Ford's plant at Dagenham or a plant in Germany (37). Consequently, trade-union pressure and Government intervention has limited effect since the multinational can still pursue its policy of product rationalization by moving out from or running down operations in a hostile environment and going to a nearby and more co-operative one.

Despite the limitations of existing investment and entry conditions which it can obtain in another country, the multinationals still possess considerable flexibility, and therefore more power than the host nations in terms of the way in which the firm can manoeuvre its resources when its plans conflict with the interests of the nation. Companies which are not just manufacturers and processors but producers of raw materials are confined by certain geographical conditions as well, but this is merely one more reason to become a multinational when the nature of the enterprise means that it is necessary to operate outside the domestic environment, for example in the case of oil and mineral extraction. However, as we will see, there are perhaps more risks to be taken in and a greater degree of dependence upon the host nations in these industries.

Let us now consider some of the reasons why a corporation moves abroad, and some of the more important consequences for the donor and the recipient of the investment.

The reasons for becoming an international company can be usefully placed into two categories, aggressive and defensive (38). Firstly, those strategies employed as defensive measures. Some multinationals become so since they seek access to and control of raw materials, which are not always abundant, or are perhaps scarce, in their own country. This is particularly important for the American economy since it depends upon overseas sources, especially the Third World, for the supply of many vital raw materials necessary for the more technologically advanced industries. By 1960 America was importing 32 per cent of its iron ore, 98 per cent of its bauxite, 35 per cent of its lead, 46 per cent of its copper and 60 per cent of its zinc, which means it had to import over half of the required metals, and is increasingly facing competition from Europe for these resources (39). Therefore, in order to maintain its position as the foremost processor of primary resources (in 1960 America consumed slightly over one quarter of the total world output of the above minerals), large amounts of capital have been invested in Latin America and elsewhere. The multinationals can then provide the necessary technology, perhaps not possessed by the recipient nation, and control the flow of exports to America.

However, much of the investment is situated in politically unstable countries, or where a popular government may re-exert control over the nation's assets (40). Although the amounts involved in any one of the countries are not large, for instance the American Oil Corporation's investment in Venezuela is 10 per cent of the total U.S. investment in oil, the supply of the vital resources for American industry is very much threatened when alternative supplies are also jeopardized by the increasing level of economic nationalism present in Latin America (e.g. Peru, Bolivia, Chile) and the Middle East (e.g. Libya), and the introduction of stronger consortia of oil producers (41). Moreover, this problem is likely to become more serious since many of the known reserves of the most vital minerals for the development of the technologically advanced industries are located in areas which are outside the sphere of the multinationals at present, and will involve the U.S. in further problems of foreign policy (42). Even if the supplies are not restricted in quantity, political factors may well prevent the import of these minerals from U.S. multinationals and mean that American industries will have to deal with foreign-controlled sources at considerably greater cost, which will further weaken America's position in relation to Europe and the U.S.S.R (43).

Even where the multinationals are successfully established there is increasing pressure from local interests for a higher percentage of local ownership. Then there is still no guarantee that the assets will not be expropriated after a short period of time when the political situation may be more volatile (44). Perhaps this degree of interdependence between the multinationals and low-income nations (with potentially unstable political systems), resulting from such a sophisticated global strategy and creating an extremely intricate economic and technological framework, will prove to be an inhibitive factor for American economic growth.

Another defensive aspect of the multinationals arises from the need to maintain the share of the market for their products. This is precisely the sort of strategy employed in Britain and Europe. This corporate investment in the British economy and takeovers by American firms enables them either to capture new markets for their products or to expand by taking over the existing markets established by the national firm, at the same time bringing the competition into a more oligopolistic structure. An added attraction to potential investors is that they will be able to manufacture, trade within and reap the benefits from larger markets created by free-trade areas (45). The U.S. subsidiaries are able to manufacture *in situ* and circumvent tariff barriers, while taking advantage of the other sorts of incentives to trade arranged between the various countries in the trade associations. Furthermore, the multinationals are able to pursue product integration by co-ordinating the manufacture of components for a large market within the trade area itself (46).

This interpenetration of individual national economies leads to a degree of interdependence which may well threaten the multinational strategy, as in the case of investments in low-income nations. When production is co-ordinated across several countries, government and trade-union action in one is likely to affect operations in the others, giving rise to political as well as economic problems within and between the countries if significant sectors of the economy are disrupted (47). Consequently, despite the multinationals' sensitivity to these problems and their efforts to minimize the negative effects upon their relations with governments and unions (48), the host nations are becoming more aware of these problems and the need to formulate international agreements and regulations between governments and unions in order to confront the multinationals; for example, on issues like parity of wages between workers in the various countries and the flow of capital from subsidiary to parent company. This could seriously damage the basis upon which the multinationals operate.

It is not only the host nation's economy which can experience problems when the multinationals are making decisions about the location of investment, based upon the exploitation of the differences between the various national economies and incentives. The corporation's domestic economy, especially the labour force, also experiences negative effects because the global operations of multinational firms enable them to overcome high domestic-factor costs by expansion elsewhere. Thus they can become 'runaway' industries, i.e., the firms will move out of their domestic economy to produce goods in lower-income nations, where they can still employ the same technology but more cheaply. This means that high-income nations like America face problems with their labour force when jobs are being removed to other countries like Britain (49). This is another problem which is likely to become more serious for the multinationals as the other advanced industrial nations catch up with American levels of productivity.

Let us now consider some of the more aggressive reasons for a firm to extend operations across national frontiers. One of the most important of the several interdependent reasons is the multinationals' capacity to exploit the superiority of their technology over that of some of the foreign national industries. Much of this knowledge has been gained from small, dynamic 'spin-off' firms which sprang up around the large, well-financed research institutes like the Massachusetts Institute of Technology. Often it is these initially small firms, for example Texas Instruments, which engage in technological and product innovation, and then grow into large corporations which can develop and market their products and those of the new 'spin-off' firms. This process is also made more easy by the greater willingness of American financial institutions to back the 'risk' venture and help to maintain a lead over the less risky and more cautious research and development system in Europe. The American consumer market is also much more affluent, and this enables the U.S. firms to gain valuable development and marketing experience in the domestic economy before introducing the product or technology into areas like Europe (50). This is the 'trickle-down' effect whereby it is the products rather than the technological expertise that are introduced by the U.S. subsidiaries. Therefore at least one of the potential benefits that the host nation might expect is not necessarily realized (51).

A second reason is the more profitable use of capital by the multinationals in lower-cost nations. By investing overseas a parent company can produce in and export from manufacturing subsidiaries, and thereby supply not only foreign markets but also the domestic one from these cheaper internationally integrated subsidiaries (52). Furthermore, this investment strategy enables the corporation to achieve economies of scale which may not be possible in the domestic economy where growth is restricted by competition from other strong corporations in an oligopolistic market structure (53). There is, however, some doubt as to whether it is really necessary to move abroad, in the case of many American firms, in order to obtain certain economies of scale, since these can often be attained by smaller nationally based corporations (54).

Thirdly, a firm can gain important and more relevant information about local markets and resources by manufacturing directly in that country or having interests in national firms, and therefore produce goods most suited to the locality. Also, American multinationals find that a greater familiarity with local conditions is necessary for work on or when in competition for contracts on tied-aid programmes from the U.S. Government, and that it furthers their case when tendering for overseas contracts (55).

This outward expansion of the American multinationals has been successful as a rational pursuit of industrial growth and profits, exploiting new resources and raw materials from the low-income nations and capital, talent and technology, in the more advanced nations of Europe. Some have made several errors in the process by underestimating the problems involved when their investment in foreign nations means that they employ increasing numbers of the country's labour force, control significant areas of the country's technology, and contribute to its balance of payments. Although these corporations run the long-term risks of creating an increasing degree of interdependence with the nations in which they invest and rely upon for the provision and processing of materials, it would seem that the problems so far have been short-term ones. The conflicts arising from the differences of interests between nation-state and multinational enterprise are likely to intensify as the nation's political boundaries and economic controls continue to be transcended by the increasing number of multinationals and involvement by them in Britain and Europe, and America itself. I shall return to this point again, but perhaps it would now be useful to consider briefly some of the advantages and disadvantages for the nation when it receives foreign investment, particularly from American multinationals.

Firstly, when a multinational invests capital in a new manufacturing plant it creates employment for the local labour force, and this can be particularly welcome by the host government and labour. This is especially so when the factory is situated in an area of unemployment or underdevelopment where investment is not otherwise forthcoming. It also means that the subsidiary's personnel will be trained in modern technological and management skills which can then diffuse into the economy when these employees move into the firms of national competitors, or when these advanced techniques stimulate other firms to maintain their position in the market after experiencing the effects of the multinational's superiority (56). The multinationals also mobilize capital and inject it into the economy from outside the country, adding to real output and more especially to exports. Finally, the firm will also bring, with its international package, wide export markets, to which the host economy may not have access, and an increasing demand for local components and resources from its own national and foreign affiliates.

Therefore it can be argued that countries like Britain do benefit from investment from the American multinationals. However, there are disadvantages, and we shall now consider some of them.

Perhaps the problem with the most serious long-term potential is that key decisions made by the parent company in relation to the subsidiary are those which have the company's interests in mind and may not be in harmony with the host nation's interests. The U.S. multinational's global strategy involves the manipulation of markets and resources, which means that product ranges change, and more importantly that the rationalization of labour resources and capital expenditure can lead to redundancies and dismissals of large numbers of employees. Furthermore, it is possible that American foreign economic and political policy may cause friction with the host nation, especially when this involves changes in export policy or restrictions upon mergers, which may be encouraged by the host nation but not by the U.S. Government. For the subsidiaries are still part of the American industrial system and become instruments of it, as well as part of the geocentric organization of the parent company. A second fear is that far from mobilizing capital from outside the country the subsidiaries in fact attract and absorb scarce domestic capital, which has a negative effect upon the competitive position of national firms. American firms only finance about one-third of their investments from their own profits or the American market, the majority of the capital coming from the host nation and the Eurodollar market (57). Similarly, the subsidiaries attract scarce domestic skills and contribute to the 'brain drain' to America. Thirdly, the multinationals invest in and control key sectors of the economy and depend upon research and development into advanced technology carried out in the United States. This curtails the advantages which the host research and development programmes could receive and means that the diffusion of technical and managerial skills into the economy is not immediately beneficial (58). Finally, the subsidiaries seek to minimize their tax burden by various techniques such as arbitrary transfer pricing, allocation of administrative costs and service fees. More importantly, it is possible to disguise large amounts of repatriated earnings and thereby contribute to capital outflows from the host economy. As well as manipulating international tax differences by using 'tax havens' for their headquarters or by setting arbitrary prices on goods passing between subsidiaries, according to the taxation levels for declared earning, the multinationals can take advantage of the fluctuations in exchange rates of the currencies in which the companies deal. By advancing or withholding payments between subsidiaries, or by requesting payment in particular currencies, the multinational can gain further financial benefit at the expense of the national economy and may aggravate a crisis situation by their speculations (59).

Conclusion

The above discussion turns on two important things: (i) a particular stage in the evolution of the structure of capitalist production methods and organization (60); and, perhaps more importantly in the context of this book, (ii) the concentration of economic power manifested in the multinational corporations in the American economic system, which is rapidly extending into Europe.

I have been considering power in several forms, but have not had the space in which to develop a clear conceptual framework. However, very simply, I have tried to discuss both the horizontal and vertical dimensions of the power relationship between the United States and its multinationals, and a nation-state, like Britain. One can see the enormous economic assets and resources of America (61) generating economic and political relationships with advanced industrial and low-income nations in which it is, or seeks to become, the dominant or more powerful partner (62). This is characterized by the multinationals which sponsor and exploit economic and technological developments in the pursuit of greater sophistication and mastery of the processes of capital accumulation—notably interterritorial units of production. The situation is one where there are clashes between traditional nationally oriented economic and political systems, and international business.

It is along these axes that we can trace the activities of the multinationals and the various host nations, in terms of rival economic and political interests stemming from the corporate paradigm of macro-unity (63). Although the development of the multinational's power seems incompatible with 'effective' nation-state boundaries (e.g. in Europe and the E.E.C.) this is not to support the view that the state, although under pressure, is likely to crumble (64), since the futures of capitalist nations need the State to remain if only partially to fulfil social control and welfare functions (65). Furthermore, the nation-state can still introduce measures to counter the power of the multinationals and their pursuit of product rationalization (66).

Perhaps the move toward multinationalism by the large corporations is a self-arresting process, since it involves contradictions in both its domestic economy (especially runaway industries and a dependence relationship with its hosts) and the host nation, notably economic nationalism in the low-income nations, and protectionist action and the challenges from increasing productivity in the advanced nations.

NOTES

(1) Especially changes in low-income nation-states which have meant that they are sufficiently advanced to become markets for more technologically advanced goods and can engage in international trade and capital exchange.

(2) 'Multinational' corporations are those involved in operations (typically manufacturing, mining and allied industries) situated in a number of economies, other than their domestic one, which are considered as a single market within an increasingly more integrated corporate, global, strategy.

The development of the various types of corporation mentioned is traced by A. D. Chandler, *Strategy and Structure* (Doubleday & Co., New York 1961).

Alternative terms to 'multinational' are commonly employed by other authors. For example, the 'international' corporation: R. B. Robinson, *International Business Policy* (Holt, Rinehart and Winston, New York 1966); and 'geocentric' organizations: M. V. Perlmutter, 'L'entreprise Internationale—Trois conceptions' *Revue Economique et Sociale* May 1965, 23, no. 2, pp. 157–65.

(3) For a comparison of this type of operation and the development of modern multinational firms, see G. Modelski, 'The Corporations in World Society', *Year Book of World Affairs*, vol. 22, 1968, pp. 64–79.

Also see R. Jenkins, *Exploitation* (MacGibbon and Kee, London 1970).

(4) The economy is opened up and made less stable since American capital invested in and extending into Britain and Europe is politically opportunist at an international level.

(5) See S. Hymer, 'The Efficiency (Contradictions) of Multinational Corporations', *American Economic Review* May 1970.

It is an alternative to the market whereby corporations initiate rational plans of action to exploit opportunities available for economic advantage and growth by controlling areas of a foreign economy.

(6) When this non-coincidence attains global proportions the problem is more intense since the corporations become more flexible, with respect to capital manipulation and product integration, and thereby keep ahead of counter-strategies by protectionist-oriented economies. This seems to be an argument based upon the notion of conflict between economic nationalism and geocentric technology. However, it could be argued that the distinction between them is irrelevant since the interests of corporations and governments in capitalist countries are so close.

For a fuller treatment of this point see R. Murray, 'The Internationalisation of Capital and the Nation-state', *New Left Review* No. 67, May–June 1971; also D. Horowitz (ed.) 'Corporations and the Cold War', *Monthly Review Press* 1969.

(7) Control or partial control of a foreign economy is increasingly important for multinational oligopolies and advanced capitalist nations. See R. D. Wolff, 'Modern Imperialism: The View from the Metropolis', *American Economic Review* May 1970, and R. Murray, op. cit. (1971). See also K. Nkrumah, *Neo-Colonialism: the Last Stage of Capitalism* (Nelson, London 1965).
(8) J. J. Servan-Schreiber, *The American Challenge* (Hamish Hamilton, London 1968).
(9) ibid.
(10) R. Rowthorn, *International Big Business 1957–67*, University of Cambridge Department of Applied Economics, Occasional Paper 24 (Cambridge University Press, London 1971): an econometric analysis of the 500 largest industrial companies in the world, which investigates the crucial features of Servan-Schreiber's thesis.
(11) See Servan-Schreiber, op. cit.; also R. J. Barber, *The American Corporation: its power, its money, its politics* (MacGibbon and Kee, London 1970). By 1980, 300 large corporations could be in control of 75 per cent of all the world's manufacturing assets. See also E. Mandel, *Europe vs. America? Contradictions of Imperialism* (New Left Books, London 1970). 200 of the above corporations may be American-owned.
(12) For example see, C. Layton, *European Advanced Technology* (George Allen and Unwin, London 1969), and *Trans-Atlantic Investments* (International Publications Service, New York 1967).
(13) See J. H. Dunning, 'U.S. Subsidiaries in Britain and their U.K. Competitors: a case study in business ratios', *Business Ratios*, Autumn 1966, pp. 5–18.
(14) R. Rowthorn op. cit. (note 10). Small to medium-sized American firms appear to grow faster than the large ones; percentage growth rate is not an increasing function of size. Among the large firms (sales above $500m a year), the Americans did not have a lead over European firms in the period 1962–7.
(15) Stephen Hymer and Robert Rowthorn, 'Multinational Corporations and International Oligopoly: The Non-American Challenge' in C. P. Kindleberger (ed.), *The International Corporation: a Symposium* (M.I.T. Press 1970).
(16) See J. H. Dunning, *The Role of American Investment in the British Economy*, P.E.P. Broadsheet No. 507. He argues that the recipient gains from American investment, providing Government controls are effective, but that there is insufficient evidence to draw any firm conclusions about the long-term effects.
(17) L. Turner, *Politics and the Multinational Company*, Fabian Research Series 279 (Fabian Society, London 1969).
(18) In 1966 U.S. exports were $24 bil., whereas overseas subsidiary production amounted to $110 bil. See L. Turner, *Invisible Empires: Multinational Companies and the Modern World* (Hamish Hamilton, London 1970). See also S. Rolfe, 'Updating Adam Smith', *Interplay* November 1968, pp. 15–19.
(19) See R. Rowthorn, op. cit. (note 10).
(20) See J. J. Servan-Schreiber, op. cit. (note 8).
(21) See N. Faith, *Sunday Times*, 11 October 1970, and J. H. Dunning, op. cit. (note 16).

U.S. firms also produce 95 per cent of Europe's integrated circuits. See C. Layton, *Transatlantic Investment* (The Atlantic Institute, Paris 1967).

(22) It is only in Britain and Japan where I.B.M. has less than 50 per cent of the computer market.
(23) See E. Mandel, op. cit. (note 11).
(24) See L. Turner, op. cit. (note 17).
(25) D. N. Chorafas, *The Knowledge Revolution* (Allen and Unwin, London 1968). It is worth noting that American subsidiaries already produce over 15 per cent of Europe's consumer goods.
(26) J. J. Servan-Schreiber, op. cit. (note 8).
(27) i.e., the four main areas: vehicles, chemicals, mechanical and electrical engineering. See also M. Simon and D. E. Novack, 'Some Dimensions of the American Commercial Invasion of Europe, 1871–1914: An Introductory Essay', *Journal of Economic History*, December 1964, vol. 24, no. 4, pp. 591–605.
(28) For more detailed accounts of economic developments, see H. J. Habakkuk and M. Postan (eds.) *The Cambridge Economic History of Europe* (Cambridge University Press, London 1965); H. Heaton *Economic History of Europe*, Rev. edn (Harper and Row, London 1963); F. A. Southards, *American Industry in Europe* (Houghton Mifflin, Boston 1931).
(29) See J. H. Dunning, op. cit. (note 16).
(30) Investment figures calculated from U.S. Department of Commerce, *Survey of Current Business*, and *National Income Blue Book*, for the respective years. See also, A. Scaperlanda, 'The E.E.C. and U.S. Foreign Investment: Some Empirical Evidence', *The Economic Journal*, March 1967.
(31) Following statistics quoted from J. H. Dunning, op. cit. (note 16), unless otherwise stated.
(32) U.S. Department of Commerce, *Survey of Current Business* 1968.
(33) The Scottish Council, *Investment in Scotland* (1967).
(34) See, L. Turner *Invisible Empires: Multinational Companies and the Modern World* (Hamish Hamilton, London 1970).
(35) De Gaulle tried to resist the advances of American multinationals planning to invest in north-east France, but when they threatened to build the factory just across the border, in Germany or Belgium, he was forced to recant.
(36) e.g., Ford's Pinto engines are made in the U.K. and W. Germany for use in Canadian and American cars assembled in N. America. General Motors (Vauxhalls) produce their trucks (outside the U.S.) in Britain. Thus corporations like I.B.M. have seventeen plants in thirteen nations; Ford and G.M. manufacture in twenty countries.
(37) R. Eglin, 'When Fords says Jump', *Observer*, 21 March 1971, p. 15.
The power of the multinationals is felt when their decisions adversely affect employment, exports and capital investment.
(38) See M. Z. Brooke, *The Strategy of Multinational Enterprise* (Longmans, London 1970) for a fuller account of these defensive and aggressive strategies.
(39) G. Kolko, *The Roots of American Foreign Policy; an analysis of Power and Purpose* (Beacon Press, Boston 1969). This situation will deteriorate seriously in the not too distant future: see H. H. Landsberg *et al.*, *Resources in America's Future: Patterns of Requirements and Availabilities, 1960–2000* (Johns Hopkins, Baltimore 1963), and R. Veron, 'The future of the Multinational Enterprise', in *The International Corporation* ed. C. Kindleberger (M.I.T. Press, 1970).
(40) e.g., Chile nationalized Anaconda's copper mines; Cuba has liberated over $1,000m. of U.S. fixed assets.
(41) See A. Breton, 'The economics of nationalism', *Journal of Political*

Economy, 72, no. 4, August 1964, pp. 376–86; S. M. Miller *et al.*, 'Does America's economy require Imperialism?' *New Society*, 5 November 1970; J. P. Morray, *The Second Revolution in Cuba* (Monthly Review Press, New York 1962); H. O'Connor, *World Crisis in Oil* (Elek, London 1962); P. Odell, *Oil and World Power* (Penguin, London 1970); J. Petras and N. Rimensnyder, 'What is happening in Peru?' *Monthly Review*, February 1970.

(42) Over half the known world reserves of manganese are in Russia and China, and most of the rest is in Brazil, India, Gabon and S. Africa. Over two-thirds of the tungsten is in China and Chile, Rhodesia; Congo and Peru have over two-thirds of the foreign copper reserves. Cuba and New Caledonia have half the nickel. Only zinc and lead seem to be in politically stable regions from the American standpoint. See G. Kolko, op. cit. (note 39).

For further figures see H. H. Landsberg *et al.*, op. cit. (note 39).

(43) Also in relation to Japan, although most of her trade and industrial growth has been conducted through exports and imports from foreign-owned sources and not via direct investment, relying instead upon other economy factors. Therefore, although the multinationals' involvement in gaining access to and control of important sources of raw materials has been a most valuable strategy, this is one area in which the future reliance upon the efficiency of the multinationals is in some doubt.

(44) The use of military strength by the U.S. Government to ensure a stable political environment for its overseas economic interests is perhaps a less potent force in these cases; it was not used to protect investments in Peru, Bolivia, Zambia and Libya. However, see H. Magdoff; 'Militarism and Imperialism', *American Economic Review*, May 1970, D. Horowitz (ed.), op. cit. (note 6), and J. Gerassi, *The Great Fear in Latin America* (Collier, New York 1965).

(45) e.g. Latin America Free Trade Association, Central American Common Market, Central African Economic and Customs Union, European Economic Community, European Free Trade Association.

(46) A certain degree of product standardization is also possible, especially in Europe: e.g. motor cars, office machinery, agricultural equipment.

(47) e.g. the possibility of a large number of redundancies when a subsidiary is run down in favour of a lower-wage country, or more generous government incentives, or when a strike in one country leads to workers in another being laid off owing to lack of necessary components.

(48) e.g. having more than one source of supply for essential components, introducing progressive wage agreements like the Esso plant at Fawley.

(49) See E. Jager, 'Multinationalism and Labour: For whose benefit?' *Columbia Journal of World Business* Jan–Feb. 1970. See also F. Decoster, 'Labour dispute in an International Company', *Bulletin of International Metal Workers Federation* (Geneva) March 1969, and M. Warner, 'Towards trans-national trade-unions?' *New Society*, 15 October 1970.

(50) Therefore, the American subsidiary has a vast fund of research and development experience on which to draw and exploit when in competition with national firms, perhaps having only one-third of the R. and D. capacity: see A. T. Knoppers, 'American Interests in Europe', in E. Moonman (ed.) *Science and Technology in Europe* (Penguin, Harmondsworth 1968).

(51) Unless the multinationals can gain by hiring 'local' brains at less cost, or need a certain amount of development work on products to accommodate them to a market which is slightly different from America.

(52) The amount of subsidiary imports from the parent company (and foreign affiliates) can be used as a measure of the degree of dependence of that industry (or economy) upon America. See M. T. Bradshaw, 'U.S. exports to Foreign Affiliates of U.S. firms', U.S. Department of Commerce: *Survey of Current Business* May 1969.

(53) See C. Kaysen and D. F. Turner, *Anti-Trust Policy* (Harvard University Press 1959); R. Vernon, 'Antitrusts and International Business', *Harvard Business Review,* vol. 46, no. 5, Sept.–Oct. 1968, pp. 78–87; R. Mikesell, 'Decisive factors in the flow of American Direct investment to Europe', *Economia Internazionale* August 1967. Smaller firms in the American economy may well need to move abroad in order to survive, or grow, when the market is dominated at home by large corporations.

(54) S. Hymer and R. Rowthorn, op. cit. (note 15).

(55) The large corporations still need to take note of different consumer tastes in their international markets despite the move towards product standardization. Several multinationals have discovered to their cost that it is unwise to assume that other countries will accept products which have been successful in the domestic economy.

(56) See J. N. Behrman, 'Foreign Investment and the transfer of knowledge and skills, in R. F. Mikesell (ed.) *U.S. Private and Government Investment Abroad* (Eugene Oregon 1962); J. H. Dunning, 'Technology, United States Investment and European Economic Growth' in C. P. Kindleberger (ed.) *The International Corporation* (M.I.T. Press 1970); J. B. Quinn, 'Technology Transfer by Multinational Companies' *Harvard Business Review* Nov.–Dec. 1969, pp. 147–61.

(57) The percentages are: 40 per cent financed from own operations abroad; 35 per cent from external sources abroad; and 25 per cent capital transfer from U.S. See R. Murray, op. cit. (note 6). In 1966 U.S. firms used $450–500 m. from the Eurodollar market. See J. J. Servan-Schreiber, op. cit. (note 8).

(58) See W. Gruber, D. Mehta and R. Vernon, 'The R. and D. factor in international trade and international investment of United States Industries', *Journal of Political Economy* Feb. 1967, vol. 75, pp. 20–37; C. Freeman, 'Research and development in electronic capital goods' National Institute for Economic Research No. 34, Nov. 1965, pp. 40–9.

(59) For more detail see: K. Hamada, 'Strategic Aspects of Taxation in Foreign Investments Income', *Quarterly Journal of Economics* vol. 80, no. 3, August 1966, pp. 361–75; S. Hymer, 'The International operations of National Firms: A Study of Direct Investment': doctoral dissertation, Cambridge, Mass. (M.I.T. 1960); R. W. Jones, 'International Capital Movements and the Theory of Tariffs and Trade', *Quarterly Journal of Economics,* vol. 81, Feb. 1967, pp. 1–38. J. A. Shulman, 'Transfer Pricing in Multinational Business': doctoral dissertation, Cambridge, Mass. (Harvard Graduate School of Business Administration, August 1966).

(60) For a more detailed analysis of the development of the multinational corporation in terms of the structure of capitalist production, see C. Palloix, 'Firmes Multinationales et Analyse du Capitalisme Contemporain' Université des Sciences Sociales de Grenoble, Institut de Recherche Economique et de Planification, Département d'Industrialisation et de Développement, February 1971 (Mimeograph. Paper given at the Conference on Imperialism, Institute for Peace and Conflict Research, Copenhagen, April 1971).

(61) America has half the world's realized wealth. See R. Jenkins, op. cit. (note 3).

(62) This involves the whole world, except perhaps China; see R. Jenkins, ibid.

(63) Despite the universality of ideology between business and the polity at the national level, conflicts arise between them at an international level, since the multinationals represent an external threat to which the nation is vulnerable.

(64) As to whether the nation-state will become, or is already, totally ineffective and will wither away in future capitalist society, see: G. Ball, 'The Promise of the Multinational Corporation', *Fortune*, vol. 75, no. 6, July 1967; C. P. Kindleberger, *American Business Abroad* (Yale University Press, 1969); R. Vernon, *Sovereignty at Bay: The Multinational Spread of U.S. Enterprises* (Basic Books, New York 1971).

(65) Multinationals could take on many state functions, as did the trading companies during the colonial era of the eighteenth and nineteenth centuries. See G. Modelski, op. cit. (note 3).

(66) e.g. introduction of trade tariffs and legislation (Monopolies and Mergers Act 1965, in Britain) to interfere with the rationalization of the production by the multinationals. For the case in Canada, see W. L. Gordon, *A Choice for Canada: Independence or Colonial Status* (McClelland and Steward, Toronto 1966); D. Russel (ed.), *Nationalism in Canada* (McGraw Hill, Scarborough, Ontario 1966); A Safarian, *Foreign Ownership of Canadian Industry* (McGraw Hill 1966).

C

THE WORKINGS OF ECONOMIC AND POLITICAL POWER

INTRODUCTION

One crucial consideration in the study of the workings of political and economic power is the character of the educational system. Thus in this section we have selected extracts which show the extent to which the prominent power-holders in British society have shared the same education at a small number of exclusive schools and universities. This is shown to be so in the case of cabinet ministers, Conservative MPs, senior personnel officers in all three armed services; senior civil servants, diplomats, and chairmen of government Committees of Inquiry and Royal Commissions; Governors of the Bank of England, directors of the Big Five banks, City firms, major insurance companies, directors and managers of major companies; the judiciary; Church of England bishops; BBC Governors; senior academics and senior medical staff. Two particular issues arise here. The first is that while a close relationship can be shown between holding positions of power and attendance at a small number of schools—and in certain cases at the two ancient universities (the relationship between which is also shown to be close by Glennerster and Pryke and *The Public Schools Commission*), the exact nature of the relationship between a public-school education and the attainment of a powerful position in British society is certainly complex and not easily examined. Power-holders have generally been to public school, and as one of the tables from *The Public Schools Commission* shows, these schools are attended almost exclusively by the sons and daughters of the professional and managerial classes and the armed forces, but what still remains problematic is the extent to which the schools themselves contribute to the distinguished careers of their past pupils. On the other hand the *ethic* of the public school and Oxbridge, with its emphasis upon the common bond of shared experience, means that there is some degree of consciousness, coherence and conspiracy among them, as mentioned in the *Introduction*.

Some evidence of the manner in which economic decisions are made was examined in a now classic article by Lupton and Wilson (Chapter 14). In this they analysed some of the networks of relationships between decision-makers giving evidence to a tribunal inquiring into an alleged Bank Rate leak. They suggest that the basis for this informality is often a shared social background which promotes a common belief and confidence in customary procedures. Over and above ties of friendship and common interest (partially exemplified by common club membership) the authors describe in some detail connections of kinship and of affinity between top decision-makers in a number of spheres.[1] The three diagrams from Guttsman illustrate the significance of the 'pluralists of power', those who exert influence through their membership of several powerful bodies. Tables from *The Public Schools Commission* indicate the important cumulative advantage in obtaining a place in the administrative class of the Civil Service, and of attendance at both a public or direct-grant school and Oxbridge (thus, the success ratio is three times as great compared with those from maintained schools graduating at other universities).

[1] Some further additions have been made by Anthony Sampson in *Anatomy of Britain* (Hodder and Stoughton, London 1962), and *The New Anatomy of Britain* (Hodder and Stoughton, London 1971).

14

THE SOCIAL BACKGROUND AND CONNECTIONS OF 'TOP DECISION MAKERS'

TOM LUPTON AND
C SHIRLEY WILSON

Our interests as sociologists have led us to make use of the Parker Tribunal evidence as a convenient starting point for the analysis of some social connections between persons prominent in banking, insurance, politics and public administration. Our choice of persons and categories was influenced by our starting point, and our enquiries were limited by considerations of time and space, and by gaps in the published sources of data. For these reasons our results are not statistically significant. But they will be of interest to sociologists, as representing the beginnings of an analysis of the social origins and interconnections of what we shall call the 'top decision-makers'[1] in British society. We think that economists and political scientists will also be interested. To our knowledge, no such analysis has previously been made. Haxey[2] traced some family and business connections of Conservative MPs, but this was to support a political argument. Bloomfield made a study of certain aristocratic and middle-class families.[3] But neither of these was part of a scientific investigation. To us, as sociologists, and as members of a Department of Social Anthropology, it was a natural first step to enquire whether the persons whose names appeared in the Tribunal evidence were linked to each other by relationships of friendship, kinship, affinity, common membership of associations, and so on.

[1] The term 'top decision-makers' is used as a makeshift. We are aware that not all the persons we consider are of equal prestige and authority. There are difficult problems of definition raised by this kind of investigation but we think it wise to postpone consideration of these. We shall presently state whom we have included in the category of 'top decision makers' for the purpose of this paper.

[2] S. Haxey, *Tory MP* (Victor Gollancz, London 1940).

[3] Paul Bloomfield, *Uncommon People, a Study of England's Élite* (Hamish Hamilton, London 1955).

First published in The Manchester School *vol 27, no. 1, January 1959.*

And the descriptions of behaviour given by witnesses in evidence revealed that some persons were so related. Reference to published sources revealed many more such relationships.

In attempting to interpret the behaviour they observe, sociologists look first at these 'networks' of relationships, and at the kind of training people receive to occupy positions within them. It seemed to us likely that there would be a 'structural' explanation for some of the behaviour described by witnesses at the Tribunal. This article is an attempt to map out some parts of the social structure of 'top decision-makers'.

II

Bagehot wrote: '. . . all "city" people make their money by investments, for which there are often good argumentative reasons, but they would hardly ever be able, if required before a Parliamentary committee, to state these reasons'.[1] The statements from several witnesses at the Parker Tribunal justified this forecast. At one point, after varying attempts to explain how Lazard's came to a decision to sell gilt-edged securities, Lord Kindersley interrupted counsel to say: 'I have had a feeling—I have been here listening to the evidence in the last day or two—that there is some lack of understanding as to the way my firm works.'[2] The evidence of Lord Kindersley and others revealed that some important decisions were taken and others accepted because colleagues knew about, and relied upon, each other's beliefs and special aptitudes. Lengthy analyses were not a necessary prelude to decision-making. This is not surprising. When decisions have to be made quickly most persons have to act according to precedent and 'hunch' and not in the light of detailed analysis of the current situation. The consequences of this process for economic decisions such as those which were described by Tribunal witnesses are the concern of the economist. As sociologists we were particularly interested *inter alia* in the influence of custom and precedent in defining roles and activities in the decision-making process. That influences of this kind were at work was indicated by persons appearing before the Tribunal. In

[1] Walter Bagehot, *Lombard Street* (Kegan Paul, Trubner and Co., London 1892).

[2] *Proceedings of the Tribunal appointed to inquire into allegations that information about the raising of the Bank Rate was improperly disclosed* (H.M.S.O., London 1957), p. 187: Q.7326.

his opening speech, the Attorney General, Sir Reginald Manningham-Buller, referred to 'the time-honoured fashion' of announcing changes in the Bank Rate. He also stated that: 'It would be a great departure from precedent and custom if the Chancellor of the Exchequer were to announce a change in the Bank Rate.'[1] When the Governor of the Bank of England, Mr Cameron Fromanteel Cobbold, was examined by the Attorney General, he explained his 'normal practice' when considering 'a specific proposal'. He said that, depending upon the nature of the proposal, he would consult others in addition to the 'recognized sub-committee of the Court for that purpose'.[2]

In addition to the influence of custom and precedent in decision-making, informality in relationships between decision-makers came out clearly in the evidence. A good example of this came out during the examination of Lord Kindersley by the Attorney General. The Attorney General was asking Lord Kindersley why he, and not Mr Cobbold, had gone to see Lord Bicester about the possible effect of the Bank Rate rise on the Vickers issue and on relations between the 'City' and the Bank of England. Lord Kindersley replied: 'I consider it perfectly natural that I should be allowed to go and talk to a colleague on the Bank of England . . . I do not think that Lord Bicester would find it in the least surprising that I should come to him and say to him: "Look here, Rufie, is it too late to stop this business or not?" '; and: 'I have discussed this with Jim—with the Governor and I am coming on to see you.'[3] The same kind of informality was seen in the activities of directors of some City merchant houses as described before the Tribunal.[4]

The basis of informality in social relationships is often a shared social background, which promotes shared beliefs and confidence in customary procedures. It was this evidence of informality and custom which led us to look for common social background, and links between persons other than those arising from the formal needs of business life. There were pointers in the evidence itself and elsewhere that we might find connections of kinship and of affinity.[5]

[1] *Proceedings*, p. 6.
[2] *Proceedings*, p. 198: Q. 7733.
[3] *Proceedings*, p. 191: Q. 7459 and 7462.
[4] See, for example, the evidence of the Keswick brothers. *Proceedings*, pp. 94, 100, 103, 108.
[5] Intermarriage amongst banking families has often been referred to. See for example: L. S. Pressnell, *Country Banking in the Industrial Revolution* (Oxford

Ties of friendship and common interest were revealed by the description of a shooting party at which members of the Keswick family were joined by Mr Nigel Birch and others; and by the meetings of Messrs. J. M. Stevens and D. McLachlan.[1]

Since it was clear that many of the 'top decision-makers' whom the evidence mentions were interlinked in sets of relationships other than those directly arising out of business arrangements, we wondered whether the same kind of affiliations would be found in a wider sample of such persons, i.e., whether such affiliations tended to be typical of the social milieu of this particular set of 'top decision-makers'. Our choice of a wider sample was influenced by our starting point, and the reader will find that it is biased. But we have included enough persons to make our findings of some sociological, if not statistical, significance.

III

The following are the six categories of 'top decision-makers' we have chosen to study:

(A) Cabinet Ministers and other Ministers of the Crown;
(B) Senior Civil Servants;
(C) Directors of the Bank of England;
(D) Directors of the 'Big Five' banks;
(E) Directors of 'City' firms;
(F) Directors of insurance companies.

Category (A) includes all the persons named.[2] Category (B) includes the twelve senior members of the Treasury Staff, and the Permanent Secretaries and their immediate deputies of twenty-one other ministries. Category (C) includes all directors of the Bank of England (as listed by Mr Cobbold before the Tribunal). Category

---

University Press, London 1956); R. J. Truptil, *British Banks and the London Money Market* (Jonathan Cape, London 1936), p. 262; H. Clay, *Lord Norman* (Macmillan, London 1957); E. Adlard (ed.), *Robert Holland Martin* (Frederick Muller, London 1947), p. 18.

[1] See the evidence of Mr J. M. Stevens—*Proceedings*, p. 222; and Mr D. McLachlan—*Proceedings*, pp. 16 and 17.

[2] *Her Majesty's Ministers and Heads of Public Departments* No. 60 (H.M.S.O., London July 1958).

(D) comprises all directors of the 'Big Five'. Category (E) includes the directors of fourteen merchant banks or discount houses, several of which were mentioned before the Tribunal. Some of these are private banks, others public companies, but all have an authorized capital of £2m or more. We have taken the directors of only eight insurance companies, all with an authorized capital of over £3m, to make up category (F). The selection of these eight out of all insurance companies with authorized capital of over £3m was not entirely random.[1] We made sure that the two large companies mentioned in the evidence were included. The analysis of the education, club membership, and connections of kinship and affinity, is based entirely on published data.[2]

Table 14.1 summarizes the data on schools attended by members of the six categories. We have lumped together under the heading of 'other public and grammar schools' a large number of schools of diverse size and character. No single one of them had educated enough of the persons in our categories to justify being named separately. The table shows that between one-quarter and one-third of the persons in each category except category (B) went to Eton College. Two-thirds of the Bank of England directors and a half of the Ministers went to the six named public schools, and in all categories except (B) nearly half were educated at these schools. Only three persons from all categories attended State elementary school only. The data on school education shows that the majority of persons in all categories shared the same kind of school education, with the exception of category (B).[3] We have not attempted to make anything of the totals in the right-hand column since they are distorted by the fact that many persons are members of more than one category, and this applies especially to categories (C), (D), (E) and (F). We have 529 names, but not 529 persons.

This last remark applies also to Table 14.2, which summarizes the information on college and university education. A feature of Table 14.2 is the predominance of Oxford and Cambridge. Over 70

[1] The main reference was *The Stock Exchange Year Book*, vol. 1, 1958 (Thomas Skinner and Co. Ltd, London).

[2] *Who's Who 1958* (Adam and Charles Black, London); *Burke's Landed Gentry 1952* (Burke's Peerage Ltd; London); *Burke's Peerage, Baronetage, and Knightage 1956* (Burke's Peerage Ltd, London); *Debrett's Peerage, Baronetage, Knightage, and Companionage 1957* (Odham's Press Ltd, London).

[3] It is interesting that category (B) is the only one of the six to which entrance is by competitive examination.

per cent of all Ministers went either to Oxford or Cambridge, and nearly 70 per cent of all senior civil servants, 50 per cent of Bank of England Directors, 50 per cent of directors of the 'Big Five'. The financial categories (C), (D), (E) and (F) show the greatest proportion of persons with no university education.[1] It will be noted that in Table 14.2, as in Table 14.1, large numbers of category (D), (E) and (F) members are to be found under 'no data'. If our information were complete the picture might possibly be significantly different. Like Table 14.1, Table 14.2 shows that, for those persons in our six categories for which we have data, the majority shared the same kind of post-school education, although there are some differences in this regard between the first three and the last three categories. Similarity of educational background forms a link between many members of our six categories both within categories and across their boundaries. And there are also many shared directorships in the last four categories.

The only systematic information we have been able to collect about the leisure-time activities of members of this sample concerned club affiliations. This is summarized in Table 14.3. Table 14.3 is less complete than Tables 14.1 and 14.2 because club membership was not always listed in the references we used. But many persons are members of more than one club. The totals at the bottom of the table represent a count of all the clubs listed in published sources. Below this in brackets is given the number of persons for whom information was available, and the number of persons in the category. The clubs named in the list are those most frequently mentioned. Others have been counted under headings such as 'sports clubs (various)' which includes polo, fishing and golf clubs. Yacht clubs have been named separately, and also the M.C.C. The various university clubs have been collected under one heading, and so have the various Services clubs, with the exception of the Guards and Cavalry clubs; these are separately named. A striking feature of the table is that the Civil Servants' club membership is confined largely to the Reform Club and to university clubs. There are few members of the other categories in these clubs. Amongst the other categories the clubs most frequently represented are the Carlton, Brooks's, White's and the Athenaeum. The information we have shows that none of the Senior Civil Servants in

[1] Reflecting perhaps a tendency for persons to enter banking and finance as young men, and to forego a university education.

Table 14.1. Schools

	Category						
	A	B	C	D	E	F	Total
Eton	11 (32·4%)	3 (4·1%)	6 (33·3%)	44 (29·7%)	35 (32·7%)	46 (30·9%)	145
Winchester	3	3	2	9	4	7	28
Harrow	1	1	0	8	4	7	21
Rugby	0	5	2	3	2	4	16
Charterhouse	0	1	0	4	0	6	11
Marlborough	2	1	2	3	1	0	9
Total	17 (50%)	14 (19·2%)	12 (66·6%)	71 (48%)	46 (43%)	70 (47%)	230
Other Public and Grammar Schools	15	54	4	53	13	26	165
State Elementary School only	1	0	1	1	0	0	3
No data	1	5	1	23	48	53	131
Total	34	73	18	148	107	149	529

Table 14.2. College and University

	Category						
	A	B	C	D	E	F	Total
Oxford	18	30	2	46	24	30	150
Cambridge	7	20	7	28	13	27	102
Total	25 (71·5%)	50 (68·5%)	9 (50%)	74 (50%)	37 (34·6%)	57 (38·3%)	252
London	2	5	0	1	1	2	11
Other Universities	1	10	2	10	2	8	33
Sandhurst	1	0	1	5	3	6	16
Dartmouth	1	0	0	1	1	5	8
Woolwich	0	0	0	1	1	1	3
None	4	9	7	36	13	21	90
No data	1	3	1	23	51	55	134
Total	35	77	20	151	109	155	547
No. in category	34	73	18	148	107	149	529

Table 14.3. Club Membership

	A	B	C	D	E	F
Athenaeum	4	8	2	14	4	8
Bath	0	2	1	11	4	6
Beefsteak	2	0	1	3	5	8
Boodle's	0	2	1	4	2	8
Brooks's	4	4	2	24	11	20
Buck's	2	0	0	3	3	8
Carlton	18	0	1	23	8	16
Cavalry	0	0	1	5	4	4
City of London	0	0	1	13	8	5
Guards	0	0	1	5	1	3
M.C.C.	2	1	1	8	5	20
New (Edinburgh)	2	1	0	4	3	3
Oriental	0	0	1	6	3	2
Pratt's	5	1	0	7	4	5
Reform	1	15	0	6	0	2
Services (various)	2	1	0	5	3	5
Sports (various)	1	4	0	11	1	18
St. James's	0	3	1	5	0	4
Traveller's	0	3	0	7	2	8
Turf	5	1	2	6	7	11
University (various)	0	15	2	6	0	3
White's	6	0	2	13	13	23
Yacht clubs	3	2	1	20	5	8
Other clubs	11	22	3	67	5	28
Total clubs	68	85	24	276	101	226
Number for whom data was collected	(31)	(63)	(14)	(119)	(53)	(90)
Number in category	(34)	(73)	(18)	(148)	(107)	(149)

category (B) belong to the Carlton club, or White's.[1] Again, in Table 14.3, a good number of the members of our six categories are shown to be linked by the sharing of a common activity, in this case club membership.

[1] We do not know how to assess the relative prestige or exclusiveness of the various clubs, but it is probable that the traditional impartiality of the Civil Service precludes its members from joining the Carlton, a club so clearly associated with one political party. Petrie says: '. . . the great names in the Tory hierarchy down the centuries have always been found, and are still to be found, in the list of members of the Carlton.' (*The Carlton Club*, Eyre and Spottiswoode, London 1955, p. 15.)

IV

The evidence we shall assemble in this section is of a different order to that we have so far studied, and we shall say something to introduce it. It might occur to some readers that the most important feature of the diagrams we present below is the recurrence of certain long-established family names, and they might wish to read significance into this in the light of other knowledge and interests, or of preconceived ideas. Others might argue that the diagrams mean nothing because they do not include certain prominent families, or because they are incomplete and biased; and so on. That is why we want to make it clear at the outset that, for this analysis, the diagrams are only intended to show the connections of kinship and affinity of some persons who are members of our six categories of decision-makers. We used the following procedure: we began by taking persons who were prominent in the Tribunal proceedings, for example Lord Kindersley and Mr Cameron Cobbold. We traced the names of parents, siblings, spouses and children, and constructed a small 'family tree'. By following up the names of paternal and maternal kin it often proved possible to join the 'family trees' together into a kinship diagram.[1]

We have not been able to trace the kinship connections of all persons in the six categories; and it is only possible to present a limited amount of the material so far gathered. To include all connections of kinship and affinity for even a few dozen people would clearly require a great deal of space and demand greater resources of time and personnel than those available. There may be no kin connections between a great many of the people we have selected; and there are persons represented on the diagrams who belong to none of the six categories. This has partly arisen because we had already the kin and affinal connections of some people referred to at the Tribunal before we extended the scope of enquiry.

For ease of exposition the material is presented in a series of small abridged diagrams. The names of some persons who link one diagram with another are enclosed in heavy black rectangles with numbers of linked diagrams in small circles attached. Persons who

[1] Properly speaking, a diagram of both kinship and affinity. Triangles represent males, and circles females. Unshaded signs represent living people. The equals sign signifies a marriage connection and the asterisk, a former marriage connection.

are members of one or more of the six categories have the appropriate group letter or letters below their names.[1] The names of some persons who are directors of other concerns, industrial or financial and commercial, are indicated, where appropriate, with the letters 'G' and 'H'.[2]

We now trace some of the connections illustrated, indicating links between diagrams, links which would make one chart in reality. It would take too long to trace every connection on all the diagrams; the reader is invited to complete this task for himself.

Diagram 1 shows some of the connections of Mr C. F. Cobbold, Governor of the Bank of England, and a member of a family of landed gentry. He is related on his father's side to the late Lt. Col. John Cobbold, who married a daughter of the 9th Duke of Devonshire. Lt. Col. Cobbold's sister married Sir Charles Hambro, a Director of the Bank of England. Lt. Col. H. E. Hambro married the widow of the 5th Earl of Cadogan, whose grandson married a daughter of Lt. Col. Cobbold (*see* diagram 9).

Diagram 2 traces links established by the marriage of Sir Everard Hambro with a relative of Lord Norman, who was formerly Governor of the Bank of England. A cousin of Lord Norman married an uncle of the present Home Secretary, the Rt. Hon. R. A. Butler. A daughter of this marriage married Sir George Abell, a Director of the Bank of England, whose brother-in-law, Mr Nicholas Norman Butler, married into the Hambro family.

Diagram 3 illustrates the marriages of other daughters of the 9th Duke of Devonshire, among them that of Lady Dorothy, wife of the Prime Minister and sister-in-law to Lt. Col. John Cobbold. One of her cousins (father's brother's daughter) married the 28th Earl of Crawford, whose son, Lord Balniel, is Parliamentary Private Secretary to the Minister of Housing and Local Government (late P.P.S. to the Financial Secretary to the Treasury). The Earl is brother-in-law to the Attorney-General (*see* diagram 15), and also to the Marquess of Salisbury. This name takes us to the next diagram—No. 4—which shows marriages of sons of Lord Eustace Cecil. One son married a daughter of the 10th Duke of Leeds, father-in-law of Lord Chandos, Chairman of A.E.I. (*see* diagram

[1] For reasons of space we have had to shorten some names and titles; we trust no one will take offence at this.

[2] The source used for this information was *The Directory of Directors, 1958* (Thomas Skinner & Co. Ltd, London).

12). Another son was Baron Rockley; his son, the present Baron, and Mr M. J. Babington Smith (a Director of the Bank of England and of A.E.I.) married daughters of Admiral Hon. Sir Hubert Meade Fetherstonhaugh, who is connected by marriage to the Glyn banking family (*see* diagram 21).

The 4th Marquess of Salisbury connects diagrams 4 and 5. His daughter, sister of the present Marquess, married Baron Harlech, the father of the Minister of State for Foreign Affairs, and father-in-law of the Prime Minister's son. Diagram 5 also connects with diagram 1, through the late Lt.-Col. John Cobbold; he was related on his mother's side to the 7th Earl of Dunmore, whose grand-daughter married Mr D. A. Stirling, a 'Big Five' director. Her brother, the late Viscount Fincastle, brings us to diagram 7. He married a daughter of the 2nd Baron Wyfold; another daughter is married to a son of Sir George Schuster, the brother-in-law of the Chairman of the Tribunal, Lord Chief Justice Parker.

Diagram 6 traces some of the connections of the Prime Minister's nephew by marriage, the 11th Duke of Devonshire, a brother-in-law of the writer Nancy Mitford; she married a son of Lord Rennell. Lord Rennell's wife is a sister of Lord Bicester, a senior director of Morgan Grenfell and Co. and a Director of the Bank of England. Lord Bicester, a witness at the Tribunal, was the 'Rufie' mentioned in the evidence. Lord Rennell links diagrams 6 and 22, for one of Nancy Mitford's sisters was married to Lord Moyne, grandson of the 1st Earl of Iveagh. Diagram 16 shows that Lord Rennell is also connected to the Keswick family by the marriage of his sister to a brother-in-law of J. H. Keswick. Mr W. J. Keswick, Director of the Bank of England, is related through his wife to Lord Lovat, brother-in-law of two Conservative Members of Parliament.

Diagrams 8 and 10 are joined by the name of the wife of Mr M. R. Hely-Hutchinson, whose brother is father-in-law to Mr J. M. Stevens, a Director of the Bank of England, who gave evidence at the Tribunal. Her father's family was linked by marriage to Baron Ashcombe, whose brother married a niece of Lord Norman. (Her later marriage is shown on Diagram 19.) Baron Norman's brother's wife was a daughter of the 4th Earl of Bradford, whose grandson, the 6th Earl, is a Crown Estate Commissioner. Another daughter of the Earl of Bradford married the 7th Duke of Buccleuch, brother-in-law to the 3rd Viscount Hampden. Viscount Hampden's son

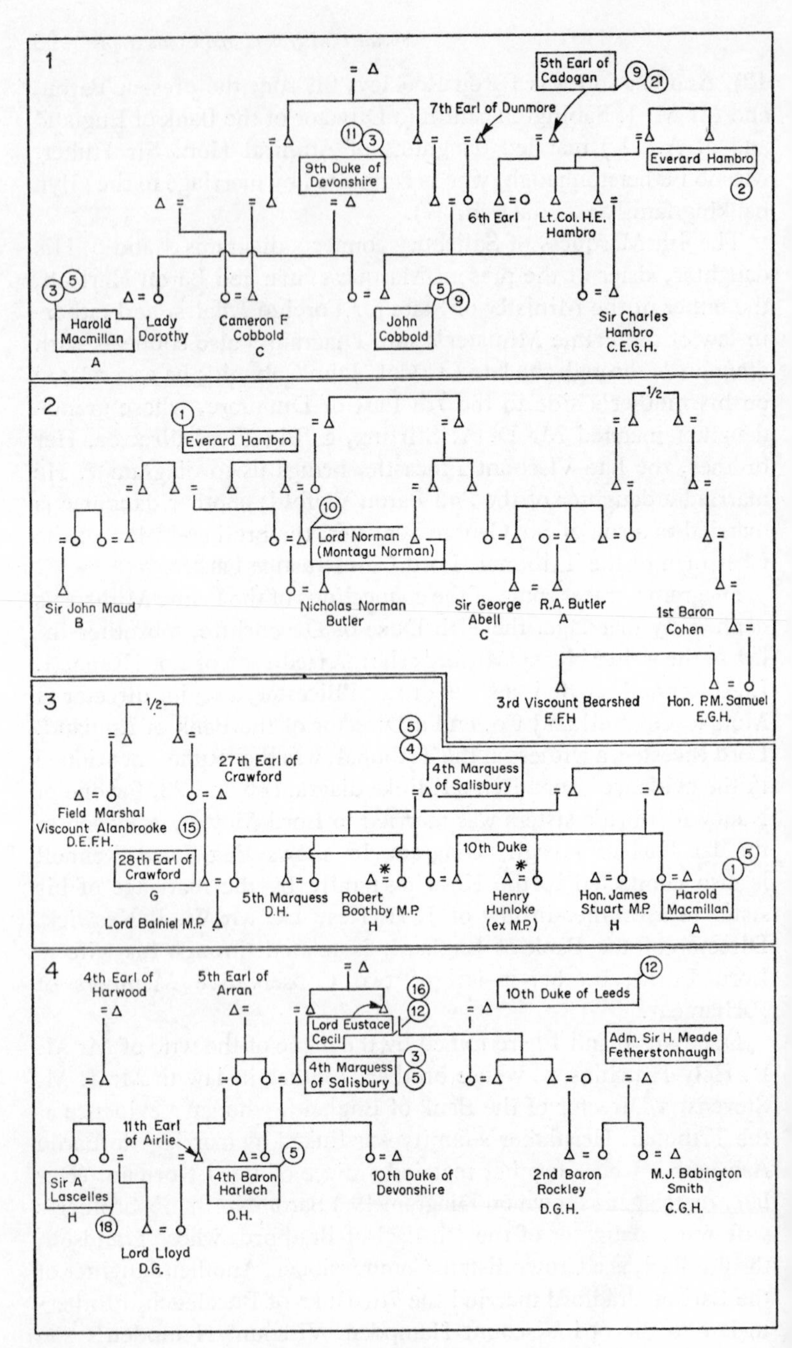
1
5th Earl of Cadogan
9
21
7th Earl of Dunmore
11
3
9th Duke of Devonshire
Everard Hambro
2
6th Earl
Lt. Col. H.E. Hambro
3
5
Harold Macmillan
A
Lady Dorothy
Cameron F Cobbold
C
5
9
John Cobbold
Sir Charles Hambro
C.E.G.H.
2
1
Everard Hambro
1/2
10
Lord Norman
(Montagu Norman)
Sir John Maud
B
Nicholas Norman Butler
Sir George Abell
C
R.A. Butler
A
1st Baron Cohen
3rd Viscount Bearshed
E.F.H
Hon. P.M. Samuel
E.G.H.
3
1/2
5
4
27th Earl of Crawford
4th Marquess of Salisbury
Field Marshal Viscount Alanbrooke
D.E.F.H.
15
28th Earl of Crawford
G
10th Duke
5th Marquess
D.H.
Robert Boothby M.P.
H
Henry Hunloke
(ex M.P.)
Hon. James Stuart M.P.
H
5
1
Harold Macmillan
A
Lord Balniel M.P.
4
4th Earl of Harwood
5th Earl of Arran
16
12
10th Duke of Leeds
12
Lord Eustace Cecil
Adm. Sir H. Meade Fetherstonhaugh
4th Marquess of Salisbury
3
5
11th Earl of Airlie
5
Sir A Lascelles
H
18
4th Baron Harlech
D.H.
10th Duke of Devonshire
2nd Baron Rockley
D.G.H.
M.J. Babington Smith
C.G.H.
Lord Lloyd
D.G.

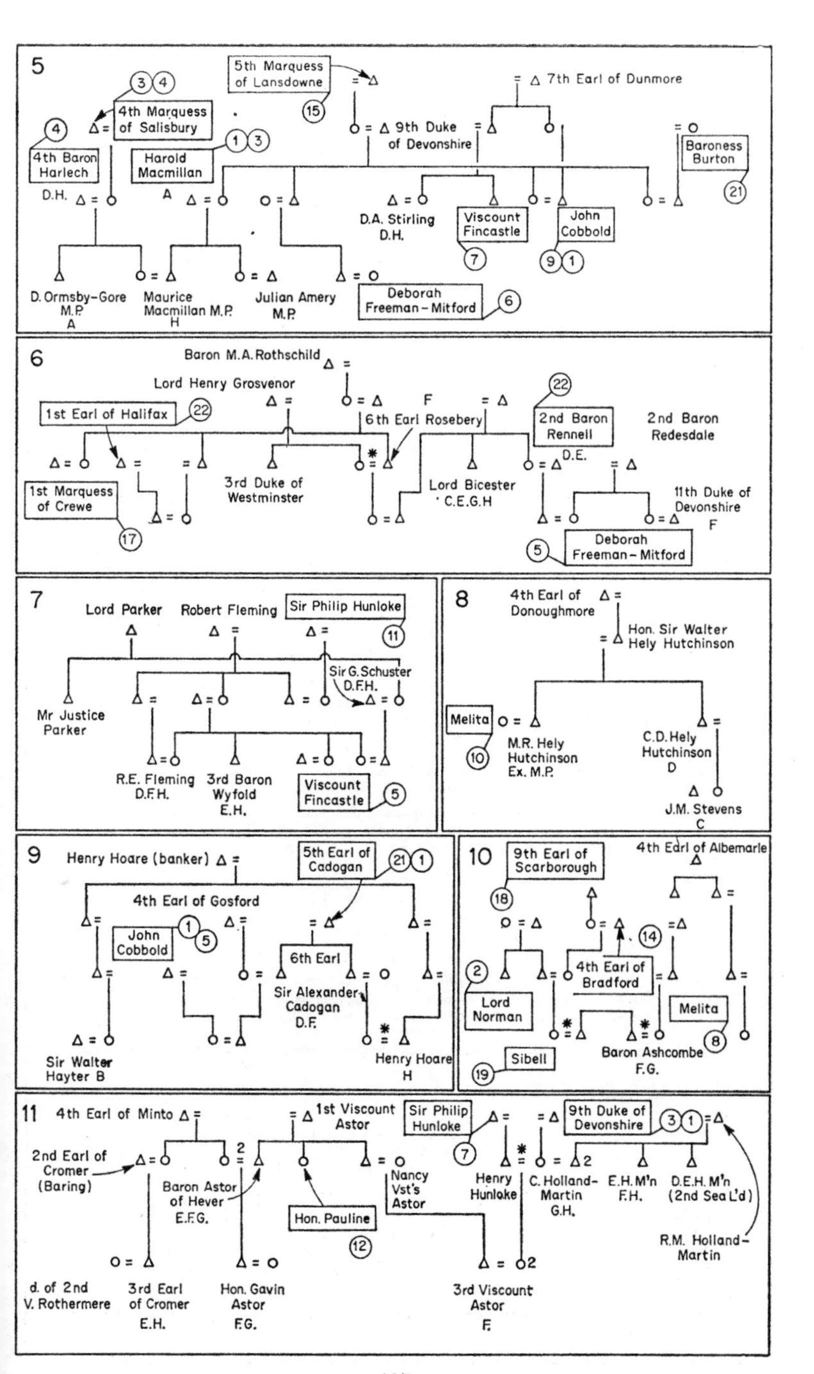
5
5th Marquess of Lansdowne
15
7th Earl of Dunmore
3
4
4th Marquess of Salisbury
4
4th Baron Harlech
1
3
Harold Macmillan
9th Duke of Devonshire
Baroness Burton
21
D.H.
A
D.A. Stirling
D.H.
Viscount Fincastle
John Cobbold
7
9
1
D. Ormsby-Gore M.P. A
Maurice Macmillan M.P. H
Julian Amery M.P.
Deborah Freeman-Mitford
6
6
Baron M.A. Rothschild
Lord Henry Grosvenor
22
1st Earl of Halifax
22
F
6th Earl Rosebery
2nd Baron Rennell
2nd Baron Redesdale
D.E.
1st Marquess of Crewe
17
3rd Duke of Westminster
Lord Bicester
C.E.G.H
11th Duke of Devonshire
F
5
Deborah Freeman-Mitford
7
Lord Parker
Robert Fleming
Sir Philip Hunloke
11
Sir G. Schuster
D.F.H.
Mr Justice Parker
R.E. Fleming
D.F.H.
3rd Baron Wyfold
E.H.
Viscount Fincastle
5
8
4th Earl of Donoughmore
Hon. Sir Walter Hely Hutchinson
Melita
10
M.R. Hely Hutchinson Ex. M.P.
C.D. Hely Hutchinson D
J.M. Stevens
C
9
Henry Hoare (banker)
5th Earl of Cadogan
21
1
4th Earl of Gosford
John Cobbold
1
5
6th Earl
Sir Alexander Cadogan D.F.
Sir Walter Hayter B
Henry Hoare H
10
9th Earl of Scarborough
4th Earl of Albemarle
18
14
2
4th Earl of Bradford
Lord Norman
Melita
8
Sibell
19
Baron Ashcombe F.G.
11
4th Earl of Minto
1st Viscount Astor
Sir Philip Hunloke
9th Duke of Devonshire
3
1
2nd Earl of Cromer (Baring)
Baron Astor of Hever E.F.G.
Hon. Pauline
12
Nancy Vst's Astor
7
Henry Hunloke
C. Holland-Martin G.H.
E.H. M'n F.H.
D.E.H. M'n (2nd Sea L'd)
R.M. Holland-Martin
d. of 2nd V. Rothermere
3rd Earl of Cromer E.H.
Hon. Gavin Astor F.G.
3rd Viscount Astor F

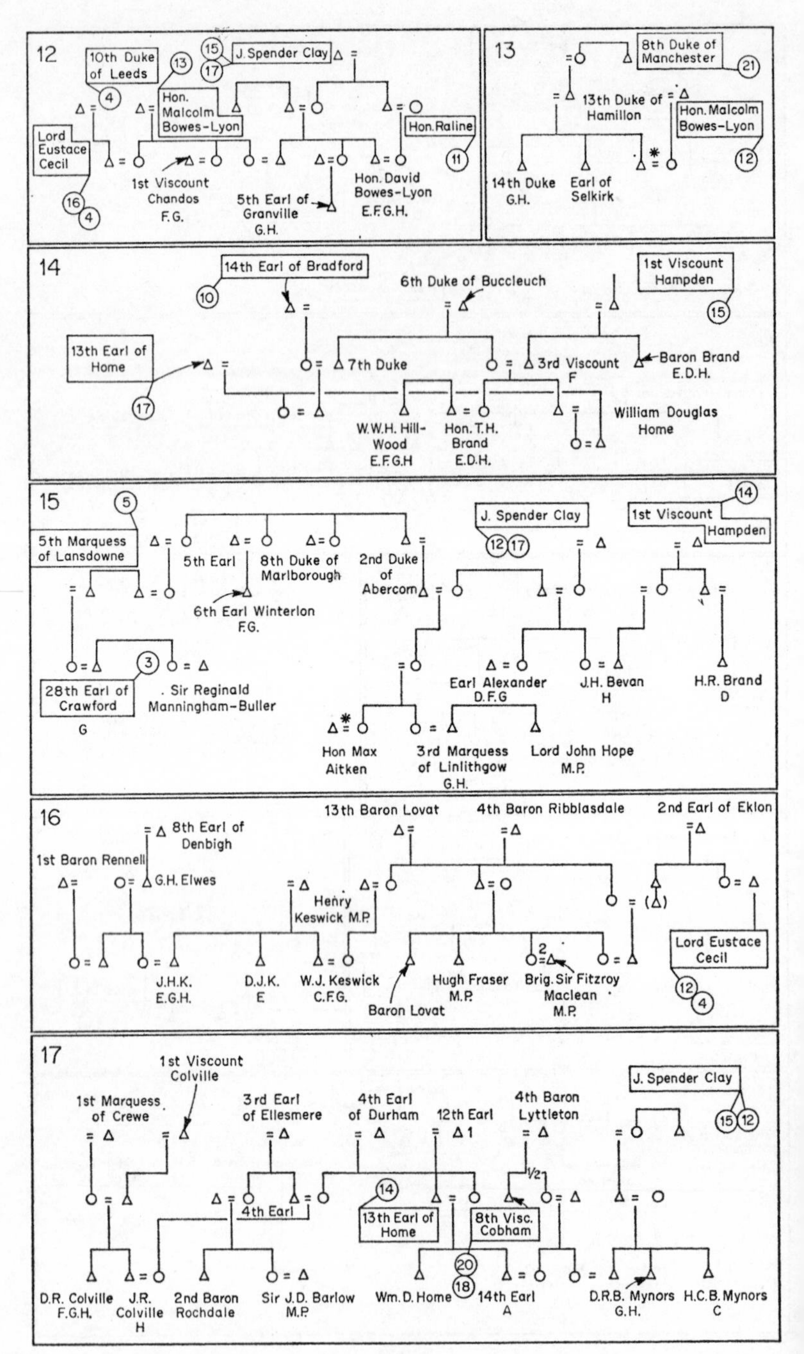
12
10th Duke of Leeds
Lord Eustace Cecil
Hon. Malcolm Bowes-Lyon
J. Spender Clay
Hon. Raline
1st Viscount Chandos F.G.
5th Earl of Granville G.H.
Hon. David Bowes-Lyon E.F.G.H.
13
8th Duke of Manchester
13th Duke of Hamilton
Hon. Malcolm Bowes-Lyon
14th Duke G.H.
Earl of Selkirk
14
14th Earl of Bradford
6th Duke of Buccleuch
1st Viscount Hampden
13th Earl of Home
7th Duke
3rd Viscount F
Baron Brand E.D.H.
W.W.H. Hill-Wood E.F.G.H
Hon. T.H. Brand E.D.H.
William Douglas Home
15
5th Marquess of Lansdowne
5th Earl
8th Duke of Marlborough
2nd Duke of Abercorn
J. Spender Clay
1st Viscount Hampden
6th Earl Winterton F.G.
28th Earl of Crawford G
Sir Reginald Manningham-Buller
Earl Alexander D.F.G
J.H. Bevan H
H.R. Brand D
Hon Max Aitken
3rd Marquess of Linlithgow G.H.
Lord John Hope M.P.
16
8th Earl of Denbigh
1st Baron Rennell
G.H. Elwes
13th Baron Lovat
4th Baron Ribblesdale
2nd Earl of Eklon
Henry Keswick M.P.
Lord Eustace Cecil
J.H.K. E.G.H.
D.J.K. E
W.J. Keswick C.F.G.
Baron Lovat
Hugh Fraser M.P.
Brig. Sir Fitzroy Maclean M.P.
17
1st Viscount Colville
1st Marquess of Crewe
3rd Earl of Ellesmere
4th Earl of Durham
12th Earl
4th Baron Lyttleton
J. Spender Clay
4th Earl
13th Earl of Home
8th Visc. Cobham
D.R. Colville F.G.H.
J.R. Colville H
2nd Baron Rochdale
Sir J.D. Barlow M.P.
Wm. D. Home
14th Earl A
D.R.B. Mynors G.H.
H.C.B. Mynors C

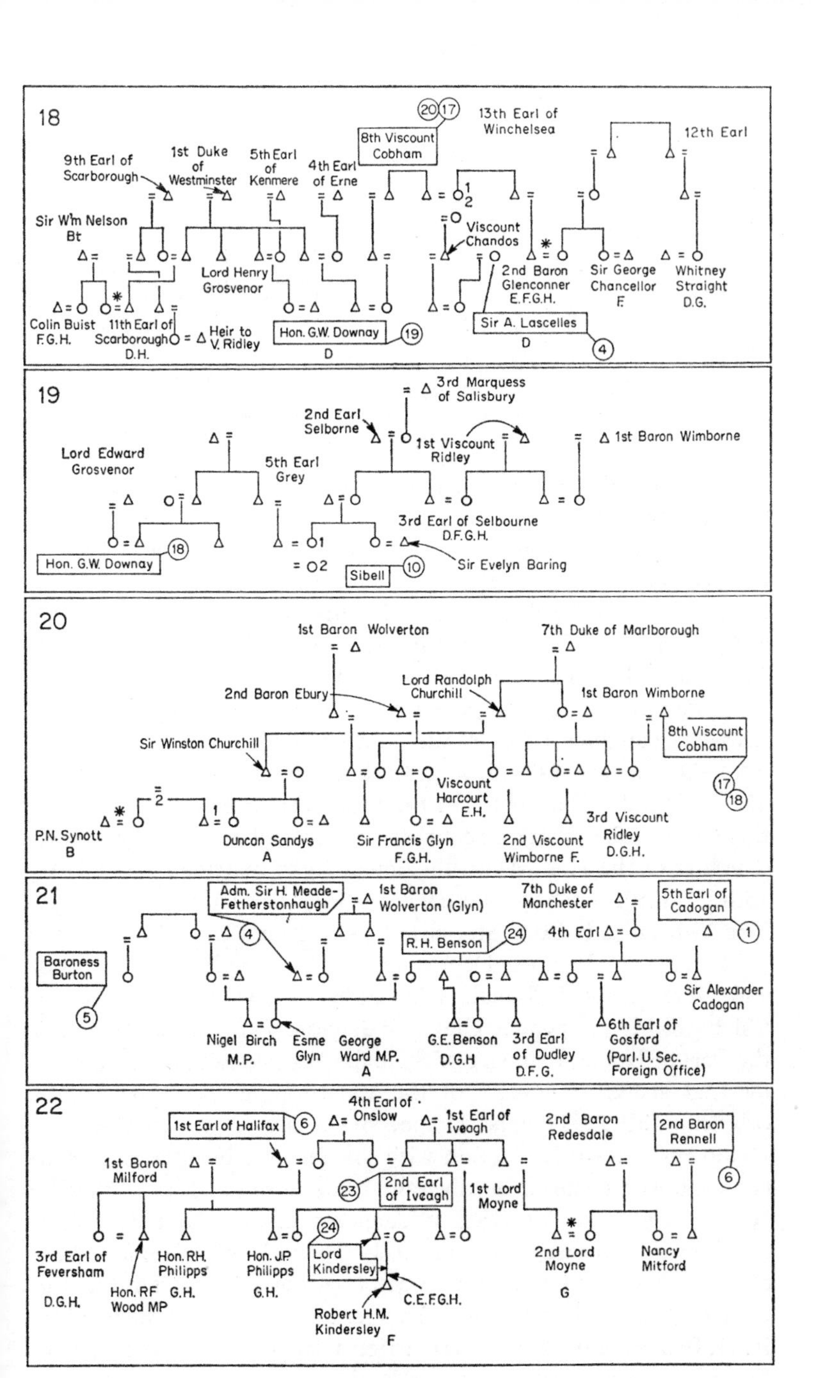
18
9th Earl of Scarborough
1st Duke of Westminster
5th Earl of Kenmere
4th Earl of Erne
8th Viscount Cobham
13th Earl of Winchelsea
12th Earl
Sir Wm Nelson Bt
Viscount Chandos
Lord Henry Grosvenor
2nd Baron Glenconner E.F.G.H.
Sir George Chancellor F.
Whitney Straight D.G.
Colin Buist F.G.H.
11th Earl of Scarborough D.H.
Heir to V. Ridley
Hon. G.W. Downay
D
Sir A. Lascelles
D
19
3rd Marquess of Salisbury
2nd Earl Selborne
1st Viscount Ridley
1st Baron Wimborne
Lord Edward Grosvenor
5th Earl Grey
3rd Earl of Selbourne D.F.G.H.
Hon. G.W. Downay
Sibell
Sir Evelyn Baring
20
1st Baron Wolverton
7th Duke of Marlborough
2nd Baron Ebury
Lord Randolph Churchill
1st Baron Wimborne
8th Viscount Cobham
Sir Winston Churchill
Viscount Harcourt E.H.
P.N. Synott B
Duncan Sandys A
Sir Francis Glyn F.G.H.
2nd Viscount Wimborne F.
3rd Viscount Ridley D.G.H.
21
Adm. Sir H. Meade-Fetherstonhaugh
1st Baron Wolverton (Glyn)
7th Duke of Manchester
5th Earl of Cadogan
4th Earl
R.H. Benson
Baroness Burton
Sir Alexander Cadogan
Nigel Birch M.P.
Esme Glyn
George Ward M.P. A
G.E. Benson D.G.H
3rd Earl of Dudley D.F.G.
6th Earl of Gosford (Parl. U. Sec. Foreign Office)
22
4th Earl of Onslow
1st Earl of Iveagh
1st Earl of Halifax
2nd Baron Redesdale
2nd Baron Rennell
1st Baron Milford
2nd Earl of Iveagh
1st Lord Moyne
3rd Earl of Feversham D.G.H.
Hon. RF Wood MP
Hon. RH. Philipps G.H.
Hon. J.P. Philipps G.H.
Lord Kindersley
Robert H.M. Kindersley F
C.E.F.G.H.
2nd Lord Moyne G
Nancy Mitford

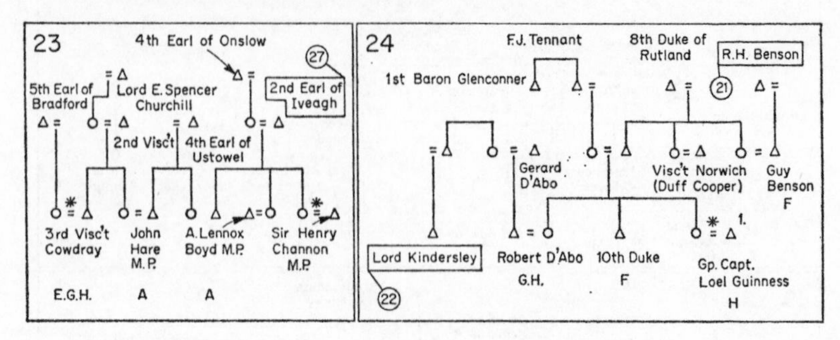

(now the 4th Viscount), managing director of Lazard's, was also a witness at the Tribunal.

The name of Viscount Hampden links diagrams 14 and 15, for the 1st Viscount's daughter was mother to Mr J. H. Bevan, brother-in-law of Earl Alexander of Tunis. Earl Alexander married a daughter of the 5th Earl of Lucan, whose wife was a daughter of Mr J. Spender-Clay. This brings us back to diagrams 11 and 12, by-passed in the previous paragraph. A son of Mr J. Spender Clay married a daughter of the 1st Viscount Astor. Diagram 11 shows the Astor-Devonshire link; diagram 12 shows that the granddaughter of Mr J. Spender Clay married the Hon. David Bowes-Lyon, and traces some other marriage connections of members of his family. A daughter of the Hon. Malcolm Bowes-Lyon married a son of the 13th Duke of Hamilton; another son is First Lord of the Admiralty. The 14th Duke is Lord Steward of the Queen's Household.

Mr H. C. B. Mynors, Deputy Governor of the Bank of England and witness at the Tribunal, is descended on his mother's side from a sister of Mr J. Spender Clay (*see* diagram 17). His brother, and the Earl of Home, Minister of State for Commonwealth Relations, married sisters, members of the Lyttleton family. The Earl's brother, William Douglas Home, son-in-law of the 4th Viscount Hampden, links this diagram with diagram 14. Further Lyttleton connections are shown on diagram 18. The son of Lord Chandos (Oliver Lyttleton) married a daughter of Sir Alan Lascelles (diagram 4), brother-in-law of the 1st Baron Lloyd. The first wife of Lord Chandos' father was a member of the Tennant family, also referred to in the last diagram. This repeats the name of the late Mr R. H. Benson. One of his sons married a daughter of the 2nd Earl of Dudley (diagram 21). The Earl's sister married the 4th Baron

Wolverton and a daughter of this marriage became the wife of Mr Nigel Birch, MP. He was Economic Secretary to the Treasury at the time of the decision to raise the Bank Rate and also a member of the Keswick shooting party mentioned in the evidence, a party which also included a member of the Hambro Bank family.[1] Diagram 21 also shows two other members of the Government, the Secretary of State for Air, brother of the 3rd Earl of Dudley, and the Earl of Gosford, Parliamentary Under-Secretary of State to the Foreign Office. Their two families are linked by a marriage in the previous generation.

The next diagram (22) introduces Lord Kindersley, Director of the Bank of England and a prominent Tribunal witness. His brother married a niece of the 2nd Earl of Iveagh, father-in-law of the Rt. Hon. Alan Lennox-Boyd, MP, Minister of State for Colonial Affairs. The Earl of Iveagh is father-in-law to a sister of another Conservative Minister, the Rt. Hon. John Hare, MP, whose wife is sister to Viscount Cowdray, who was mentioned in evidence at the Tribunal in connection with the Pearson Group of Companies.[2] These connections are shown on diagram 23. The final diagram refers to some further connections of Lord Kindersley.

Some of the diagrams, for example diagram 9, have not been referred to in the text. To have traced all the ramifications of kinship and affinity through all the diagrams would have been confusing, and would have obscured our main aim, that of tracing links between members of the six categories.

Seventy-three of the persons in the six categories appear in the kinship diagrams. We know that there could have been more had not the diagrams been abridged. Eight Ministers are included in the diagrams; and three Senior Civil Servants. For the other four categories there are more names than persons, since there are multiple directorships. Nine of the category C names appear, twenty-five of the category D names, twenty of the category E names, and thirty-two of the category F names. The only category to be markedly under-represented in the diagrams is category B (top Civil Servants) with only three included of a total of seventy-three in the category. This may arise partly from the method used in compiling the diagrams.

Some estimate of the extent of multiple directorships may be

[1] *Proceedings*, p. 98: Q. 3705 ff.

[2] *Proceedings*, p. 32: Q. 926; p. 33; Q. 946-9; p. 130: Q. 4886 ff.

gained if the number of names on the diagrams in categories C, D, E, and F is compared with the number of persons: eighty-six as compared with sixty-two. Finally, in comment on the diagrams, only about 18 per cent of all the names in the categories appear in the diagrams. On the hypothesis that all persons in the categories are linked by kinship or affinity (one to which we do not subscribe) it would take a great deal more research to include them in a series of diagrams.

V

So far in this article we have presented facts baldly without attempting to assess their meaning and significance. It would have been unwise to have done so in view of the bias of the sample and the incompleteness of the data. Our study must be regarded, then, mainly as a contribution to the 'ethnography' of finance, politics, and administration. But we cannot conclude without attempting briefly to relate what we have said to one aspect of social structure which is of particular interest to us.

We have referred to the tradition of intermarriage between banking families. Also by tradition, some merchant bankers become directors of the Bank of England. It is not surprising then that the kinship diagrams show connections between directors of merchant banks, and between merchant banks and directors of the Bank of England. Nor is it surprising that we find that positions in certain firms are occupied by adjacent generations of the same family. The positions of chairman of Lazard Bros. and director of the Bank of England, for example, are now occupied by Lord Kindersley and were once occupied by his father.

What might seem surprising is that kinship connections of this kind have persisted through many changes in the scale and functions in banking, in the organization of industry, and in the complexity of politics. Bagehot,[1] referring to the family basis of private banking at the end of last century, argued that it was inappropriate for modern large-scale organization. Weber has also argued that bureaucratic, 'civil-service-type' structure, in which recruitment and promotion are based on specific technical qualifications, and in which authority vests in the office and not in the person, is the most appropriate to modern conditions, while traditional structures are

[1] Bagehot, op. cit., p. 272 ff.

unsuitable from the point of view of effectiveness. But Weber also argues that, for effectiveness' sake, decision-making and execution ought to be separate. And he notes that: '. . . administrative structures based on different principles intersect with bureaucratic organization.'[1]

Some of the organizations to which we have referred seem to have the separation of decision-making and executive functions to which Weber refers. Possibly they incorporate both traditionalistic and bureaucratic structure. They have both directors and managers, generally different sets of persons, possibly of different social background and training. While there have been studies of the influence of kinship as a mode of succession amongst managers,[2] we are not aware of any study which has extended to boards of directors.

Weber's point about the intersection of different structural principles has not been followed up by empirical research in the area covered in this article. Gouldner's examination of some hypotheses derived from Weber in the light of facts about factory social structure could be taken as a model for such work.[3]

The intersection of different social principles has another, individual aspect, that of role conflict. Our evidence shows that many people occupy several social roles. For example, a person may have one role in a kinship system, be a member of one or more boards of directors, and a member of various clubs and associations.

The evidence at the Parker Tribunal referred in many places to this problem, but especially as it related to the dual roles of director of a merchant bank and of the Bank of England, which were occupied by Lord Kindersley and Mr W. J. Keswick. Commenting generally on this kind of problem, Mr Cobbold addressed the Parker Tribunal as follows:

> It seems to me that a similar position often arises both in business matters and, more generally, in other walks of life, where an honest man must often divorce one set of interests from another. . . . The position arises almost every day in banking, where a banker is not expected to use, for his bank's profit, secret information about a customer's affairs;

---

[1] H. H. Gerth and C. Wright Mills (trans. and ed.), *From Max Weber, Essays in Sociology* (Kegan Paul, London 1947).

[2] R. Clements, *Managers—a Study of their Careers in Industry* (Allen and Unwin, London 1958). Rosemary Stewart *et al.*, *Management Succession* (Acton Soc. Trust, London 1958).

[3] A. W. Gouldner, *Patterns of Industrial Bureaucracy* (Routledge and Kegan Paul, London 1955).

and:

> . . . the existence of the problem (even if it arises infrequently) must pose the question whether the present arrangement is on balance best suited to the national interest. I am most strongly of the opinion that it is.[1]

Mr Cobbold seemed aware that there were disadvantages in a situation where individuals were faced, as a consequence of discrepancy between structural principles, with conflicts of loyalty or allegiance. But he was personally convinced that these were outweighed by the advantages. This raises a general problem of comparative social structure. The field we have ourselves surveyed provides extensive data relevant to this problem. These data suggest that 'top decision-makers', as well as being linked by kinship, business interests and similar background, are also divided by competing, even conflicting interests. Indeed, kinship itself, in certain circumstances, may act as a divisive as well as a uniting force.

To carry out the research into the problems we have briefly outlined would require investigation of a wider field than we have surveyed, and the use of techniques other than those we have used. Interviews, direct observation of behaviour, complete quantitative analysis of such items as leisure-time activities, as well as the construction of complete kinship diagrams, would be necessary. This latter technique would close many gaps in knowledge of British social structure. Sociologists, including ourselves, have tended to concentrate on the study of working-class groups or small local communities where there is much knowledge of the operation of kinship in social life. For our 'top decision-makers' we have only biographical material, inspired comment, and little more. It is possible that sociologists have avoided the problem of kinship in 'higher circles' because of the formidable problems presented for empirical field research. We can see that there may be many problems of this kind but there is no reason why the published sources of data should not be fully used.

[1] *Proceedings*, p. 208.

15

THE BRITISH POLITICAL ÉLITE

W L GUTTSMAN

This kind of distribution of power position has been plotted for some of the major élite groups. Naturally not all affiliations have been enumerated. It seemed right to concentrate on membership and office holding of groups which rank comparatively high in the exercise of economic or political power or influence, while disregarding positions of mere social prestige, such as leadership in voluntary organizations, charities, professional bodies and the like. Apart from the élite categories enumerated or analysed in Tables 15.3–7,[1] trade union leadership, membership of the House of Commons,[2] peerages and leading positions in party organizations have been counted. Membership of some lesser Government Boards has also been noted. The data on which this analysis has been based are almost entirely taken from *Who's Who* and other biographical reference works, and the entries there may be occasionally incomplete. Cross-checking of membership of Royal Commissions and Committees, however, does not suggest that there are significant omissions in those entries which refer to the *cursus honorum* of an individual.

In listing the membership of committees or advisory bodies, only one entry is given in each category. But even without allowing for the membership of a host of committees and advisory bodies—up to ten have been found in quite a few cases—the results suggest that within the group of the 'elect' élite membership is unequally distributed. At the bottom end there are 200-odd (out of a total of over 500) for whom no activity in any other élite group is known. At the other end are the *pluralists of power*, men who over a number of years or occasionally even simultaneously, exert influence through a number of advising or decision-making bodies. Power attracts such men and power breeds more power and influence.

[1] Tables 4–7 inclusive do not appear in this extract.

[2] In the case of members of the Government membership of the House of Commons is not specifically mentioned.

First published in The British Political Elite *by W. L. Guttsman, MacGibbon and Kee, 1963.*

Table 15.3. The Social Background of some Contemporary Élite Groups

	1 Labour Govt., 1945	2 Labour Govt., 1951	3 Cons. Govt., 1951	4 Cons. Govt., 1960	5 Heads of Civil Service, 1958	6 Ambassadors and Ministers, 1953	7 Leaders of Industry and Business, 1950–5	8 Directors of large Insurance Cos., 1958	9 Directors of Bank of England and 'Big 5', 1958	10 Army, 1953	11 Judiciary, 1953	12 Bishops, 1953
Aristocrats	2	3	14	15	—	—	3	—	—	—	—	—
Working Class	38	30	1	1	—	—	1	—	—	—	—	—
Etonians	5	5	24	17	3	—	8	46	50	—	—	—
Harrow, Winchester, Rugby, Marlborough	2	5	16	10	11	—	8	34	33	—	—	—
All Public Schools	15	23	52	48	—	65	29	—	—	21	36	27
Sandhurst, Dartmouth, Woolwich	—	—	1	—	—	—	1	12	8		—	—
Grammar Schools	11	16	8	18	—	—	15	—	—	—	—	—
'State Secondary Schools'					—	—	—	—	—	4	8	7
Elementary School only	30[a]	22[a]	—	—	—	—	1	—	2	—	—	—
Oxford or Cambridge University	15	23	40	46	50	—	22	57	83	—	—	—
Other Universities	9	8	3	3	15	—	8	10	14	—	—	—
Total in Category	66[b]	66[b]	65	66	73[a]	75	65	149[c]	166[c]	34	58	43

A Minister of Health (Eton and Cambridge) becomes the head of a Cambridge College, a member of an Area Board of a Nationalized Industry, Vice-Chancellor of the University, heads a Departmental Committee, chairs one Royal Commission and later another (Sir H. U. Willink). A leading industrialist (Rugby and Cambridge) is not only a Director of the Bank of England, and a President of the Federation of British Industries. He also chairs an advisory Council and a Royal Commission, and no sooner has the work of the latter come to an end than he is invited to head another committee on the future of Broadcasting (Sir Harry Pilkington). The Chairman and Managing Director of one of the largest industrial concerns, ranking twentieth place among the 100 giants (King Edward VI Grammar School, Birmingham, no university), joins within a decade a number of highly important bodies: the Advisory Council of the D.S.I.R., the Atomic Energy Authority, and the Board of Governors of the B.B.C. He becomes a director of the Commonwealth Development Finance Corporation and finally heads a small inquiry into the future of a vast nationalized undertaking. Its report, involving far-reaching changes of organization and policy, is accepted by the Government (Sir Ivan Stedeford). A solicitor (Rugby,

---

Notes on Sources, etc., columns:

1–4, 7. Original analysis. 'Leaders of Industry and Business' are leading officers (Presidents, Chairmen, Vice-Presidents, Vice-Chairmen, Hon. Gen. Secretaries, Hon. Treasurers of the British Employers' Confederation, the Federation of British Industries and the Association of British Chamber of Commerce).

5, 8, 9. T. Lupton and C. Shirley Wilson: 'The City Men Who Decide', *Manchester School*, January 1959. No data for post-school education were available for 82 of the 388 men in the three categories.

6. Sir R. Williams: *Whose Public Schools* (Bow Group Pamphlet), p. 14.

10, 11, 12. James Harvey and Katherine Hood: *The British State* [Lawrence and Wishart, London 1958] (Army: Rank of Lieutenant General and above; Judiciary: Members of Supreme Court and the Lord Justices of Appeal).

[a] Data about schooling were not available in the case of 9 members of the 1945 Government and in 4 cases in 1951. Internal evidence does suggest, however, that the majority, if not all of them, received only elementary education.

[b] In the case of Labour ministers the figure of those with a working-class background is to some extent an estimate based on educational and occupational background. Information about father's background was in many cases not available.

[c] No data for post-school education were available for 82 of the 388 men in the three categories. Figures for those educated at grammar schools and at other public schools are not available separately.

Oxford) becomes Headmaster of Rugby and later Chairman of the B.B.C. (Sir Arthur Fforde). Another Governor of that body (Eton and Cambridge) is a Peer, nephew of a Prime Minister, a one-time Chairman of the Scottish Division of the National Coal Board (Earl Balfour). The Vice-Chancellor of an English university (Tonbridge School, Oxford—Modern Greats) becomes a Vice-Chairman of the B.B.C. and of the British Council, Chairman of an important Advisory Council. He is a member of a number of other important bodies in the educational field, sits on the General Nursing Council and on the Governing Board of the National Institute for Research in Nuclear Science (Sir Philip Morris).

The reasons for such peregrinations in this penumbra of politics are not quite clear. Is there a shortage of men capable of heading important government missions and willing to do so? Is previous good performance a guarantee for success in very disparate fields, or does public confidence in the work of a committee depend on the renown of the man who heads it? If so, the name is generally not one that has an ancient ring. The reputations come today from the field of industry or science, the universities and Whitehall. Pluralities of power are widely distributed; in interpreting the spread of membership among different élite groups which is summarized in Table 15.8 we must bear in mind that the picture is inevitably truncated. Not all élites have been included and the net of affiliations is incomplete. The men included are far from having completed their span of influence; if the same groups be examined after another decade the total of affiliations would be larger.

Table 15.8 gives an indication of the hierarchical structure of power-holding among the members of the various élite groups.

In the Conservative, *as well* as in the Labour Government, half of those who held office are so far without membership in other élite groups. But here the similarity ends. If we compare the pattern of affiliations revealed in the charts at the end of this chapter, quite a different set of configurations emerges. Nearly one-half of those members of the Conservative Administration who have affiliations with other élite groups are connected with the leadership of industry and finance, either as members of the board of industrial giants, or as directors of leading banks or insurance companies, or as spokesmen of principal economic pressure groups. Among the Labour leadership only a mere handful have joined the boards of either nationalized industries or large private enterprises. Of the

Table 15.8. Cross Membership of Élite Groups

Affiliations with other élite groups	Lab. Govt., 1945–51	Cons. Govt., 1951–5	Directorate of culture	Scientific directorate	Govt. committee men
None	56	45	25	26	57
One	36	22	17	25	61
Two	14	15	11	8	47
Three	6	4	8	10	21
Four	1	2	1	2	8
Five or more	—	—	3	3	6
Total	113	88	65	74	200
Total of memberships	86	76	84	100	284

two who have followed a ministerial career with high positions in industry—Lord Shawcross as a Director of Shell and Lord Wilmot as Director and Deputy Chairman of Boulton & Paul—one has since severed his connection with the Labour Party. Labour ministers, on the other hand, have been active on Government Committees and Royal Commissions to a much greater extent than their opposite numbers.

The membership of the other three élite groups does not only present a great degree of involvement in other élite positions, but the diagrams show the power and the weight of some of these affiliations. The 57 Chairmen of Government Committees do not only hold another 126 élite positions, but these include 13 peerages, 13 directorships in banks, insurance companies, large industrial undertakings and boards of nationalized industries. None of them had held extremely high positions in the Civil Service at home and abroad, and eleven belonged to the upper levels of the Judiciary.

AFFILIATIONS OF MEMBERS OF THE LABOUR GOVERNMENT 1945-51, WITH OTHER ÉLITE GROUPS

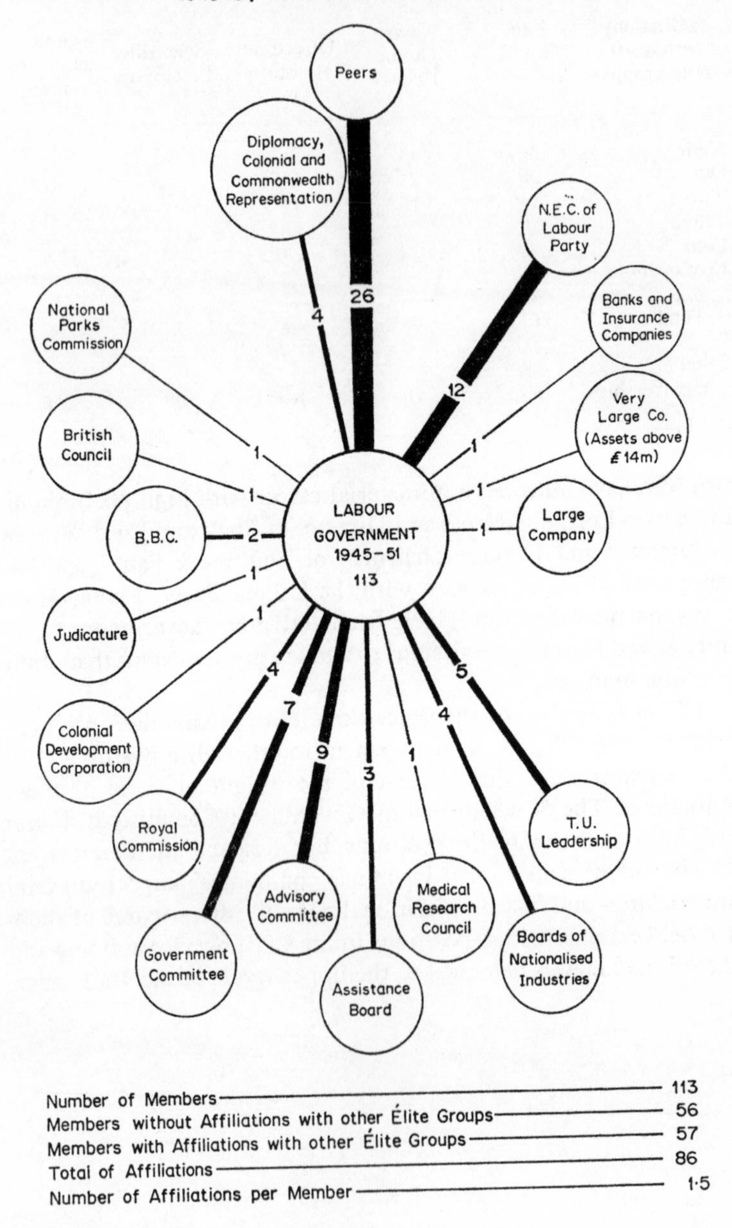

AFFILIATIONS OF MEMBERS OF THE CONSERVATIVE GOVERNMENT, 1951–55, WITH OTHER ÉLITE GROUPS

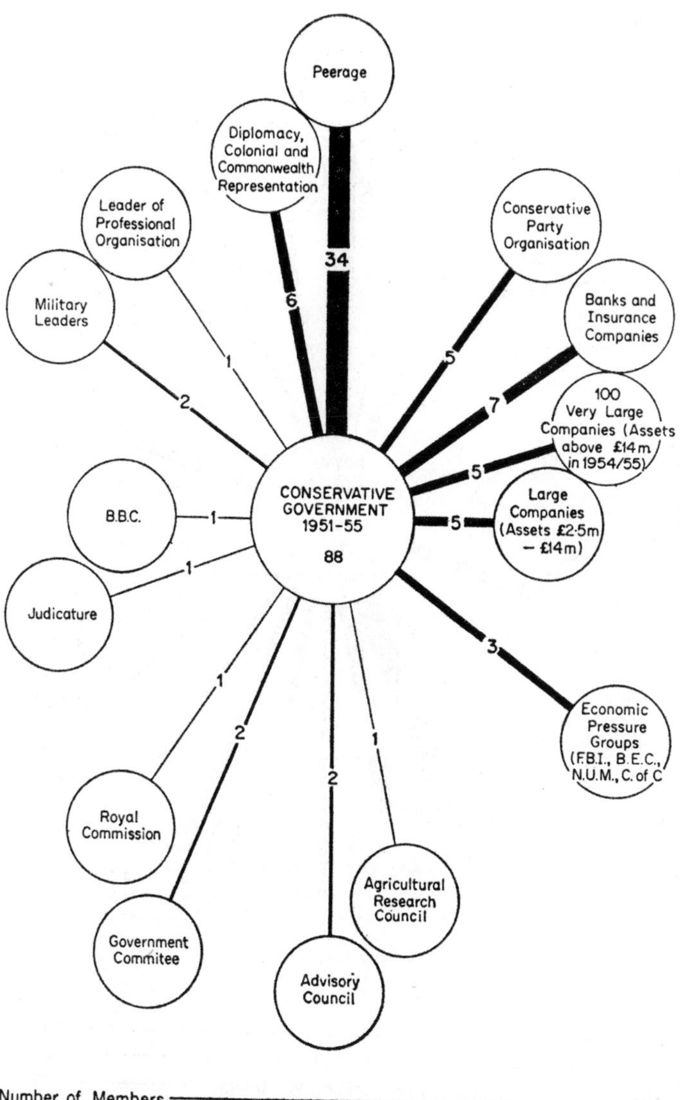

Number of Members	88
Members without Affiliations with other Élite Groups	45
Members with Affiliations with other Élite Groups	43
Total of Affiliations	76
Number of Affiliations per Member involved	1·8

AFFILIATIONS OF ROYAL COMMISSIONERS AND CHAIRMEN OF COMMITTEES WITH OTHER ÉLITE GROUPS

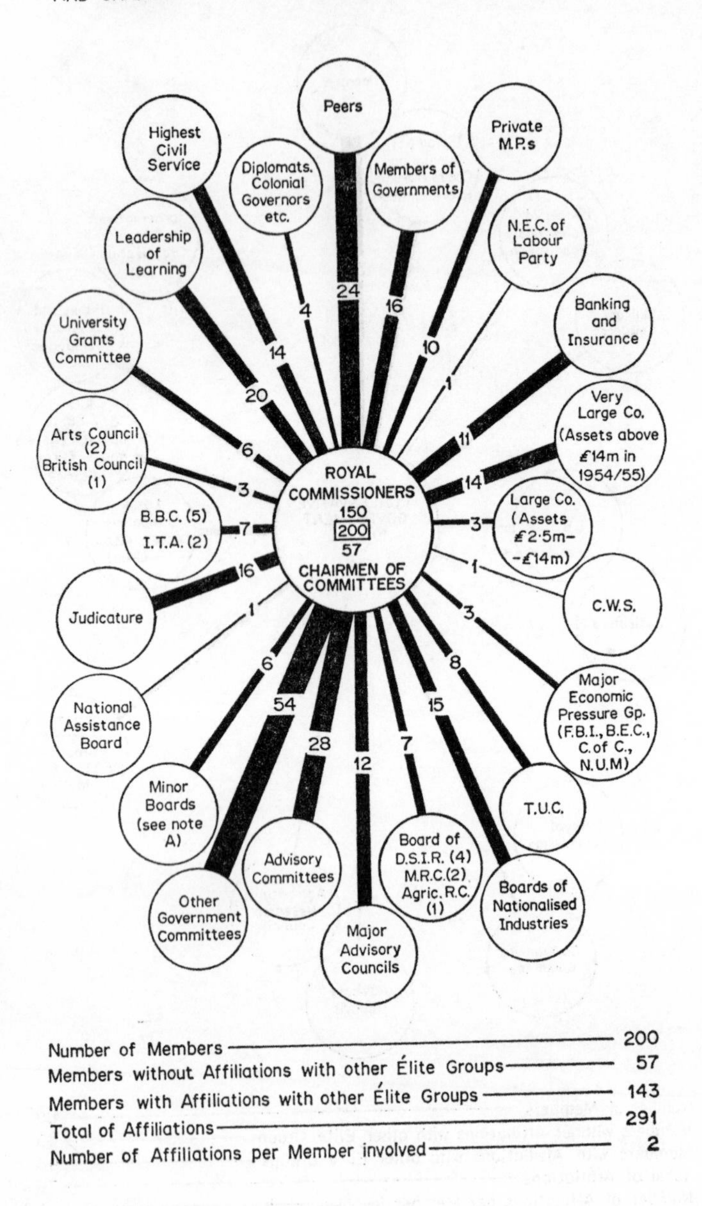

16

THE CONTRIBUTION OF THE PUBLIC SCHOOLS AND OXBRIDGE: 1 'BORN TO RULE'

H GLENNERSTER AND R PRYKE

The third and most important of all the reasons for taking action on the public schools is the crucial part they play in the power structure of our society.

We believe that it can be argued that positions of power and influence are still dominated to a remarkable degree by those from public schools; that there is no evidence of any great improvement in this situation in recent years; that, at the growing points of power, in the large industrial firms, the influence of the public schools has been growing; and that, finally, the most important link in this chain of power, between the public schools and Oxford and Cambridge, has not weakened at all.

Table 16.1 shows the extent to which the leading positions in society are filled by those from public schools. The worst offender was the late Tory Cabinet. Only three members, Marples, Barber and Heath, did not come from public schools. This might be dismissed as untypical and has anyway been remedied by the election. But the proportion of public-school men amongst city directors must be just as high. Nearly half of all city directors went to six public schools. In a whole range of important posts in the public service two out of three of the occupants came from public schools—senior civil servants, ambassadors, generals and judges. Almost exactly the same ratio holds good amongst business leaders. Next down the list come influential people of one kind and another—members of royal commissions, governors of the B.B.C., and so on. Nearly half of these have attended public schools. Finally, there are the top managers of companies employing over 10,000 employees. These are a much larger group than the others we have been considering, but one in three are public-school men, and this proportion is rising.

But only 2·5 per cent of the population can enjoy a public-school

First published in The Public Schools, *Fabian Society, 1964.*

Table 16.1. Percentage of Posts Filled by those with a Public-School Education

	%
Conservative Cabinet (1964)[a]	87
Judges (1956)[b]	76
Conservative M.P.s (1964)[c]	76
Ambassadors (1953)[d]	70
Lieutenants General and above (1953)[d]*	70
Governors of the Bank of England (1958)[e]†	67
Bishops (1953)[d]	66
Chief executives in 100 largest firms (1963)[f]	64
Air Marshals (1953)[d]	60
Civil servants above assistant secretary (1950)[g]	59
Directors of leading firms (1956)[h]	58
Chairmen of government committees of enquiry (1944–60)[i]	55
Members of royal commissions (1960)[i]	51
Civil servants above and including assistant secretary (1950)[g]	48
All city directors (1958)[e]†	47
B.B.C. governors (1949–59)[i]	44
Members of Arts and British councils (1950–59)[i]	41
Labour Cabinet (1964)[a]	35
Top managers of 65 largest firms (1953)[j]	33
Members of government research councils (1950–5)[i]	31
Labour M.P.s (1964)[c]	15

* Boarding schools only.
† Only six of the leading schools.

Sources:
[a] *Who's Who*, etc.
[b] *Economist* 21 and 28 July 1956.
[c] *The Times* 17 October 1964.
[d] James Harvey and Katherine Hood *The British State* [Lawrence and Wishart, London 1958] (boarding schools only).
[e] T. Lupton and S. Wilson *The Manchester School* [see chapter 14] (the six schools were Eton, Harrow, Winchester, Charterhouse, Rugby, Marlborough).
[f] *Business*, November 1963.
[g] R. Keith Kelsall *Recruitment of higher civil servants* [Routledge, London, 1955].
[h] G. H. Copeman in *British business leaders*. [Leaders of British Industry (Gee, London (1955).]
[i] W. L. Guttsman *The British Political Élite* [Heinemann, London 1963].
[j] Acton Society Trust *Management succession.*

education. It is from this tiny group that so many powerful positions in society are filled. In practice the group is smaller still, for the major schools take a disproportionate share of the top jobs filled by public-school men. The examples of the city directorates are a case in point.

It is often argued that as the state system of education improves, so the influence of the public schools will decline. If this were true, one would expect to find that the improvements in state education in this century had already had a substantial effect. This has not happened.

Members of the Cabinet

Taking all members of the Cabinet from 1868–1916, 68 per cent came from public schools. In the period 1916–55, the figure had only fallen to 52 per cent. However, this decline is mainly due to the rise of the Labour Party, and not the democratization of either party. Between 1886 and 1916 just over 80 per cent of Conservative Cabinet ministers had been to public school. Between 1916 and 1955 the average fell to 70 per cent. In 1959 it was 87 per cent. The proportion of public-school men in Labour Cabinets has also risen. In the 1924 and 1931 governments 17 per cent of the members came from public schools. In the new Labour Cabinet, 35 per cent come from public school.

Members of Parliament

A similar pattern is to be found among M.P.s. Between 1918 and 1939, 78 per cent of Conservative M.P.s went to public schools, according to J. P. S. Ross in *Electors and elected*. In 1959, according to Butler and Rose (1) the proportion was 72 per cent. But Ross only had information for 80 per cent of M.P.s. Since an M.P. whose education is difficult to find out about is less likely to have attended a public school, the proportions for public-school men in these years are a little too high. This is clear from the figures for 1951 where Ross's figures overlap with David Butler's, who had more complete information. Taking this factor into account, the trend is clear. The proportion of Conservative M.P.s from public schools has remained almost stationary since the first world war.

The proportion of Labour M.P.s from these schools is now double that between the wars, though still only a fifth of the Tory figure.

The Civil Service

At the beginning of the century the proportion of entrants by competitive examination coming from public schools was 80 per cent. This had fallen to about 70 per cent just before the war and is now just over 50 per cent.

Table 16.2. Type of School last attended by those entering the Home Civil Service by Open Examination, 1909–63

	1909–14	1909–39	1956–63
Independent	80·1	71·6	51·3
Direct grant	9·1	10·3	12·0
L.E.A.	5·9	15·3	37·0
Others	4·8	2·9	—

Sources: 1909–39, R. Keith Kelsall *Higher civil servants in Britain* [Routledge, London 1955]; 1956–63, civil service commissioners' annual reports.

A closer study of what has been happening is more depressing. In the first place, the young men who took these examinations before 1914 all began their education in the 1890s, and however much we may criticize our present state system of education it is incomparably better than that of the 1890s. The gap that existed between elementary board school and the education received by someone going to Winchester and New College in the 1890s has narrowed very substantially. It cannot be said that the drop in public-school representation has shown a comparable change. The proportion of public-school entrants has fallen by a third.

Also, in the postwar period the trend has been checked and even reversed. This is particularly significant, since it is from 1956 onwards that one would expect to see the first fruits of the 1944 Act, the 'opening up' of the grammar schools, and more generous university grants.

The civil service entry should be the least affected by old-school-tie traditions. The very slow improvement in the representation of those from ordinary state schools over the past 50 years gives little room for optimism that there will be radical changes in occupations where entry is less competitive.

Businessmen

In an article in the magazine *Business* in November 1963 Nigel Farrow produced figures showing the educational background of the chief business executives in the hundred largest companies as defined by the size of their assets. 'Chief executive' was defined as either chairman of the directors or else the managing director: 64 per cent of these men had been to schools who are members of the H.M.C. (that is, not only independent schools).

We took the same 100 companies in 1938 and repeated the analysis, using the *Stock Exchange Year Book*, 1938, *Who's Who*, etc.: 90 of the companies or their equivalent were in existence. The comparable figure was 57 per cent. Since in the 1938 list about a third of the people concerned could not be found in reference books, the figures are not entirely comparable. However, it is clear that at the very least there has been no reduction in the public-school contribution to the business world, and there may well have been an increase. The public-school element in the city is so large that there is hardly room for a reduction to have occurred.

Lower down the business hierarchy, the public-school element is less prominent, but it has increased rapidly.

Management succession analysed the background of all managers above foreman level in firms then employing over 10,000 people. This included 65 companies. Those managers who entered the firms in the first years of this century and were born before 1895 came overwhelmingly from elementary and local schools. Only 8 per cent came from public schools. Of those born between 1920 and 1924, who entered the firms in the late 1940s, 30 per cent came from public schools.

There is little other detailed information of this kind, but what there is suggests that there has been remarkably little change in the educational background of the élite. In 1926 Professor Tawney showed, in *Equality*, (2) that 66 per cent of judges had been to English public schools, and in 1956 the proportion was 65·5 per cent (*Economist*, July 1956). The proportion of public-school boys in the traditional seats of power has changed very little. Where change has occurred, as in the Civil Service, it has been very gradual. In the new centres of power in our society—the giant companies—public-school influence has grown.

A tightening grip

There is every prospect that an increasing number of the top jobs in our largest industrial firms will be filled by public-school men. Even if the public schools' grip on other power points weakens, their hold on industry is almost certain to grow stronger.

One reason why the public schools' grip on industry will tighten is the way in which managers are now selected. 'In management selection procedures since the war' state McGivering, Matthews and Scott, *Management in Britain* (3) (p. 70), 'great emphasis has often been placed on the possession of "social skill", administrative ability or "capacity for teamwork"—or on some other variant of what is newly considered to be the co-operative approach essential to effective leadership. These social qualities are vague . . . their incidence in the individual cannot be assessed accurately short of a fairly lengthy period of observation. It is not surprising, therefore, if with the best of intentions, decisions about them in selection procedures tend to be based on known qualifications which are *believed* to confer them, rather than on an assessment of the qualities themselves.'

The public schools are widely believed to produce boys with just these 'social skills'. A boy with this background, therefore, has an advantage over non-public-school competitors for managerial posts.

This advantage will apply especially when young men are being selected for training schemes designed to lead to top jobs. Schemes of this type have been adopted by many large firms since the war. In 1954–5, R. V. Clements studied the careers of managers at 28 firms of varying sizes in the Manchester area. He found that a considerable number, especially among those who had been appointed most recently, were ex-managerial trainees. Clements says that 'the majority attended public boarding schools; the rest, a sizeable minority, went to the better grammar schools. . . . For successful entry to one of these schemes, a public school training plus possibly experience and luck was at first sufficient. More modern and more stereotyped schemes usually require a university education following attendance at a public school.' (*Managers: a study of their careers in industry*, (3) p. 38.)

Numerous remarks by businessmen and public-school headmasters show that industry welcomes those with a public-school education. The headmaster of Ellesmere College said that 'in our conventions and in our interviews with heads of industry we are given to understand most clearly that they are anxious more than ever to have boys from public schools' (*Observer*, 21 June 1959).

As McGivering says (p. 66), 'there has been a marked heightening of interest both on the part of industry in the ex-public-school boy, and on the part of the public school in industry. The Director of the Public Schools Appointments Bureau recently acknowledged that the "generosity of over 340 firms and companies" has enabled the work of the bureau to expand considerably over the last six years.'

Never have industry and the public schools been in closer contact or more anxious to serve each other. This is shown not only by the work of the appointments bureau, but also by the financial assistance which industry has given to public schools. The Industrial Fund for the Advancement of Science and the contribution which industry makes to public-school appeals have already been described. The relationship between industry and the public schools is well illustrated by one of the appeal brochures we obtained. On the front cover of the Bromsgrove appeal, in bold type, are the words, 'An appeal on behalf of free enterprise in the training of midland youth for midland industry.'

The conclusion is clear: the public schools' grip on industry will tighten, partly because they are thought to possess the qualities for which those who run the new management selection and training schemes are looking, and partly because the contacts between industry and the public schools have become extremely close. As Peter Shore says (*Conviction*, p. 38),[1] 'it is this close connection between industry and the public schools that has prevented and will prevent any major break in the continuity of our ruling class. In Britain, at any rate, the emergence of a new industrial society is not producing a new ruling class but is providing instead a new managerial base for the established order.'

Oxbridge the key to power

The advantage which an education at Oxford or Cambridge gives is well illustrated by the results of the civil service examinations. Among those entering the administrative grade by open competition

[1] Shore, P. in N. Mackenzie (ed.) *Conviction* (MacGibbon, London, 1958).

the proportion from Oxbridge has, except in the years following the two world wars, stood at over 80 per cent since the beginning of the century. This is very remarkable, for with the rise of provincial universities the proportion of university students at Oxford and Cambridge has declined. Because Oxbridge holds a key to power, it is of the utmost importance who goes there, and how they get there.

According to the Robbins report (5) in 1961 well over half of the Oxford and Cambridge entrants were from independent schools, but less than a third were from grammar schools. At the other universities the position is very different. Nearly three-quarters of their entrants came from grammar schools, and only 15 per cent from independent schools. In 1961 the proportion of Oxbridge entrants from independent schools was slightly smaller than in 1955; 54 per cent in 1961 as against 57 per cent in 1955.

The high proportion of public-school men among those who enter Oxford and Cambridge suggests that a public-school education is a great advantage in obtaining entry. This has been confirmed by the recently published appendices to the Robbins report. They show that 80 per cent of applicants from independent schools who had one good A level pass were accepted by Oxford and Cambridge. The comparable figure for maintained-school applicants with one good A level was 35 per cent. With three or more good A levels 88 per cent of independent school boys were accepted and 65 per cent of maintained-school boy applicants. It can be seen that for a pupil from a private school the chance of acceptance varies little according to the number of A levels he passes. It does markedly with a boy from a maintained school.

It may be said that a third year in the sixth form is necessary for entrance to Oxbridge. True, a higher proportion of sixth-formers stay on for a third year at public schools than at grammar schools. But the public schools' advantage in gaining Oxbridge places is only partly explained by their large number of third-year sixth-formers. For although the public schools gain about half of the places at Oxford and Cambridge, they only contain about a quarter of all boys in third-year sixth forms; while the grammar schools, which account for well over half of those in third-year sixth forms, only obtain 30 per cent of Oxbridge places. The proportion of places won by the direct grant schools is similar to their proportion of third-year sixth-formers (*Ministry of education statistics*, 1963, part I; and ministry figures).

Although the public schools' great success in obtaining Oxbridge places is not due simply to the high proportion of boys who stay into the third-year sixth, it could be due to better teaching and higher academic standards. In many grammar schools the number of third-year sixth-formers is very small and, instead of [following] a specially designed course, they may have to repeat much of the second-year syllabus. And as the public schools probably have more teachers with first-rate qualifications this might be expected to raise the academic level. If this was the whole explanation of public-school boys' success at gaining entrance to Oxford and Cambridge, it might be expected that their performance at university would be better than other entrants; or at least as good. But as the table below shows, the position is much worse.

Table 16.3. Oxbridge Degree Results by Type of Secondary Education: Men, 1958

	good %	poor %
H.M.C. and direct grant:		
Boarders	32	49
Day boys	45	30
L.E.A. grammar	50	33

Source: J. G. H. Newfield, paper to British Association, 3 September 1963.

It can be seen that only about a third of the public-school boys obtained good degrees (first and upper second class) and that about half received poor degrees (third, pass, and fail degrees). Among former grammar boys the proportions were reversed: half obtained good degrees and only a third were poor. Of course, it may be true that public-school boys do so well when they seek admission and so badly when they take their degrees because they have been 'forced'. If this explanation is valid, and it probably contains some truth, it does not provide an excuse for those in charge of admissions, who should be able to distinguish between those who have the capacity to do well at university and those who have not.

Even more important, this explanation cannot be used to defend the public-school system. If it is true that public-school boys have an advantage because they have been forced, then those who are able to afford a public school education are, in effect, pushing their children to the front of the queue and purchasing admission to Oxford and Cambridge.

Knowing their place

The latest argument used to explain the high proportion of Oxbridge places obtained by public-school boys is that relatively fewer boys from maintained schools apply. The Robbins committee adopted this position, and the Oxford administration office has recently produced figures which show that in 1964 the proportion of applicants offered places is slightly higher for grammar than for public-school boys (*Guardian*, 13 March 1964). But why do so few grammar-school boys bother to apply? According to the Robbins committee (para. 220), the main explanation is that 'they feel convinced that their chances are small. This in turn is probably connected with the relative lack of contact between the colleges of Oxford and Cambridge and maintained schools.'

How often have we been told before that 'there is really no problem; it is all a matter of proper communications'. If grammar-school boys had an equal chance at Oxford and Cambridge surely the word would have been passed round by grammar-school masters. And if the colleges were really worried about the high proportion of places taken by public-school boys, they would have made contact with the grammar schools long ago. Colleges with a low proportion of grammar-school men have only to announce that they plan during the next few years to increase the proportion from say 20 to 50 per cent. The number of applicants will shoot up.

Some colleges at Oxford and Cambridge admit so few grammar boys that it is hardly surprising if only a comparatively small number bother to apply. They know when they are not wanted. The variation between colleges in the proportion of public-school men is so large that it is hard to avoid the conclusion that some colleges are more favourable to public-school men than others. The extent to which the proportion varies at Oxford colleges is shown in Table 16.4.

Table 16.4. Undergraduates from Independent Schools at Oxford Colleges 1962

	%		%
Trinity	80·6	University College	50·6
Christ Church	70·0	St John's	50·4
Oriel	66·4	Keble	48·6
New College	66·1	Exeter	45·3
Worcester	64·7	Jesus	41·9
Hertford	62·6	St Edmund's Hall	40·8
Lincoln	61·2	Wadham	39·6
Corpus Christi	58·5	Pembroke	37·6
Balliol	56·9	Queen's	37·2
Magdalen	54·5	St Catherine's	30·4
Merton	52·9	St Peter's	29·3
Brasenose	52·4		

Source: Oxford Magazine, April 1961.

It can be seen that at Trinity and Christ Church about three-quarters of the students are from independent schools, but that at St Peter's and Queen's the proportion is only about a third. Nor is it true that the colleges with a high proportion of public-school men have skimmed the best. When ranked according to the proportion of graduates who obtained firsts and seconds, Trinity and Christ Church were respectively 18th and 17th.

Not long ago Steven Watson, a tutor at Christ Church, gave the following description of the way in which undergraduates were selected at his college (*Oxford Magazine*, December 1960):

> Some colleges feel that other things being equal, they should prefer to accept the son of an old member rather than someone with no connections. . . . At Christ Church about two thirds will gain admission on the various scholarship examinations by faculties. The remaining third will be taken on by quite another system. They will sit a common entrance examination with fewer papers. On these they will be required to show a decent level of intellectual competence. In this selection the interview will play an important part. So too will the confidential reports made by the schools upon them. . . . Experience has taught dons the value of candid opinions from public school masters whom they know. They distrust hyperbole from those they do not know. . . . The need to civilise those who are born to great responsibilities, the desire to be tender to the claims of loyal old members will, for a long time to come, continue to work to the benefit of the public schools rather than the obscurer grammar schools.

According to Wilson (pp. 62–3)[1], it is on the public schools that

> the middle and upper classes rely to retain their privileges and values. . . . It is a point of some importance that the real motives of the middle classes for sending their children to public schools are to some extent different from the conscious or expressed motives. Thus a typical middle class defendant of the system would talk about discipline, leadership, 'good' (middle class) teachers, morality, mixing with one's fellows, and so on. Somewhere in his mind, however—perhaps at the back of it, but nowadays more probably fairly far in front—are the social and economic advantages: the university, the highly paid job, the useful contacts, the approved manners.

The middle and upper classes are right—when they send their children to public school they are not simply paying for a good education, they are starting their children on the road to power and influence. The principal commodity which those who send their children to public schools are buying is not education but privilege.

Class always tells

This has been disputed on two grounds. First, it has been suggested that public-school men gain such a high proportion of top posts because of their merit. Second, it is argued that their advantage derives from their class background and family connections, rather than their education.

In an attempt to show that the success of those with a public-school education is due to merit, Dancy uses a most ingenious argument. He says (pp. 116–7)[2] that

> appointments to the civil service, which are made *solely* on merit, go to public school men in a proportion which is indeed greater than sixth form numbers would warrant, but it is not less than the proportion in which other top appointments go to public school men. If public school men have the ability to command two thirds of the top civil service appointments, why should we suspect favouritism when we find them occupying a similar proportion of the best jobs in other professions?

This argument has a number of serious weaknesses. First, it ignores the possibility that the civil service attracts those public-school men who have the best degrees and the highest intelligence. As Rupert Wilkinson has pointed out (in the *British Journal of Sociology*, December 1962), the underlying purpose behind the development of the public-school system was the training of capable public servants.

[1] Wilson, J. *Public Schools and Private Practice* (Allen and Unwin, London 1962).

[2] Dancy, J. C. *The Public Schools and the Future* (Faber and Faber, London 1963).

Second, there is evidence, some of which was given earlier and some of which Dancy quotes (pp. 95–6) that when firms select potential managers they have a predisposition to favour public-school men but place comparatively little emphasis on intelligence.

Third, if merit were the only factor at work, it might be expected that those in positions of power and influence would, like civil servants, be drawn fairly evenly from the different public schools. But, as we have seen, a very high proportion were educated at a few top schools. And how are we to explain that very few men from schools like Manchester Grammar, which are highly selective, and give a very good education, are to be found in top positions? Those who believe that public-school men rise because of their merit will find it hard to show that the only reason why old Etonians fill such a high proportion of top places is because of their outstanding talent. Was it, for instance, entirely without significance that eight of the nine men whom Macmillan used to sound out the Tory Party during its leadership crisis were, like Sir Alec Douglas-Home, educated at Eton?

The argument 'that the advantage which public school men enjoy in obtaining top positions is due to their class background and family connections and not to their education' seems plausible at first sight, because almost all public-school boys come from fairly wealthy families. But it is difficult to believe that a public-school education counts for nothing. Parents who pay high fees to send their children to these schools obviously believe that it is important, or they would not waste their money.

The variety and range of advantages enjoyed by public-school boys cannot be explained by family connections alone. Nor can they be satisfactorily attributed solely to class background, for increasingly in our society it is education rather than family wealth or parental occupation which is used as a guide to social status. Public schools are a transmission belt for class privilege. . . .

NOTES

(1) D. E. Butler and R. Rose, *British General Election of 1959* (Macmillan, London 1960).
(2) Allen and Unwin, London.
(3) Liverpool University Press 1960.
(4) Allen and Unwin 1958.
(5) *Report of the Committee on Higher Education*, Cmd 2154 (H.M.S.O., London 1963).

17

THE CONTRIBUTION OF THE PUBLIC SCHOOLS AND OXBRIDGE: 2

PUBLIC SCHOOLS COMMISSION

First published in The Public Schools Commission: First Report, vol. II, *H.M.S.O.*

Table 17.1. Social Class of Fathers [Appendix 6]

Social class	Boarding pupils					Day pupils				
	Public boys	Public girls	Public mixed	Total public schools	R.E. sample[1]	Public boys	Public girls	Public mixed	Total public schools	R.E. sample
	%	%	%	%	%	%	%	%	%	%
I and II										
Professional and Managerial	84	84	89	84	82	81	89	86	85	82
III										
(*a*) Non-manual	4	2	7	4	5	10	5	9	8	7
(*b*) Manual	2	1	2	1	1	5	1	5	3	4
IV										
Semi and unskilled	1	—	1	—	—	1	1	—	1	2
Armed forces	10	13	1	11	12	2	4	—	3	5
Total	100	100	100	100	100	100	100	100	100	100
Father's occupation stated	8,038	3,870	177	12,085	409	2,898	2,783	21	5,702	541
No. of leavers	8,299	4,363	186	12,848	503	2,993	2,987	23	6,003	677

Note: The information supplied by the schools on the occupation of fathers was, in many cases, ambiguous and classification was necessarily arbitrary. In view of this, these figures should be treated with caution.

Source: Kalton G. *The Public Schools* (Longmans, London 1966). 3.11. p. 35. (H.M.C. figures are taken from the H.M.C. School Entrants' Survey.) Commission Questionnaire.

[1] R. E. Sample: Schools selected to form a sample of other recognized efficient secondary schools. (See *Report* vol. 2, Appendix 6 for details).

Table 17.2. Proportion of Leavers whose Mother or Father is an Old Pupil [*Appendix 6*]

	Public boys		Public girls		Public mixed		Total public schools		R.E. Sample	
	Boarding pupils	Day pupils	Boarding pupils	Day pupils	Boarding pupils	Day pupils	Boarding pupils	Day pupils	Boarding pupils	Day pupils
	%	%	%	%	%	%	%	%	%	%
Proportion of pupils whose mother/father was an old pupil	17	7	10	3	11	4	14	5	3	2
Details given	7,676	2,405	4,332	2,946	186	23	12,219	5,374	482	673
No. of pupils	7,741	2,815	4,363	2,987	186	23	12,290	5,825	503	677

Note: Information on the 325 pupils at H.M.C. boys' schools (168 boarding and 157 day) who transferred to other schools is not available.

Sources: Kalton—additional information.
Commission Questionnaire.

Table 17.3 University awarding first degrees [Appendix 6]

University	Public boys	Public girls	Public mixed	Total public schools	R.E. sample
	%	%	%	%	%
Oxford and Cambridge	78	20	44	61	17
Other English and Welsh	18	64	47	32	57
Other	4	16	8	7	25
Total	100	100	100	100	100
University stated	3,841	1,646	59	5,546	230
No. of teachers	4,392	2,870	90	7,352	458

Source: Kalton 4.4. p. 47. Commission Questionnaire.

Table 17.4. The Proportions of Independent and Direct-grant School Pupils at Various Stages of Education Compared with the Proportions from those Schools in a Selection of Professions and Positions [*Appendix 8, Section 4*]

	Numbers		Percentages[d]				
	Total	Total whose school is known	Six of the major public schools[b]	All public schools	Other independent recognized efficient schools	Total all independent recognized efficient schools	Direct grant[d] schools
14-year-olds at school in England and Wales (1967)	642,977	all	0·15	2·6	2·19	4·8	2·4
17-year-olds at school in England and Wales (1967)	113,689	all	0·6	9·3	4·4	13·7	8·9
School-leavers (England and Wales) going to all Universities 1965–6	36,471	all	1·07	15·6	3·3	18·9	13·4
School-leavers (England and Wales) going to Oxford and Cambridge 1965–6	4,655	all	4·7	35·1	7·0	42·1	18·7
Vice Chancellors, Heads of Colleges, Professors of all English and Welsh Universities (1967)[f]	1,646	925	5·8	32·5	0·9	33·4	12·7
Heads of Colleges, Professors of Oxford and Cambridge (1967)	256	217	11·5	49·3	2·7	52·0	10·6
Labour Cabinet (1967)	21	19	15·8	42·0	—	42·0	—
Conservative Cabinet (1963)	23	22	63·6	90·9	—	90·9	—
M.P.s Labour (1966)	363	363	2.4	19·5	0·5	20·0	4·9
M.P.s Conservative (1966)	253	253	35·0	76·6	2·0	78·6	2·0
Admirals, Generals and Air Chief Marshals (1967)	22	20	25·0	55·0	—	55·0	15·0
Physicians and Surgeons at London teaching hospitals and on General Medical Council (1967)	244	232	9·4	68·0	1·2	69·2	12·5

Fellows of the Royal Society elected between 1962 and 1966[g]	138	122	6·5	24·6	—	24·6	13·0
Governor and Directors of the Bank of England (1967)	18	17	29·4	76·5	—	76·5	5·8

Notes:

[a] It should be remembered that the people concerned would in many cases have attended school some considerable time ago. For example, someone in his late fifties would have been at school in the 1920s.

[b] Charterhouse, Eton, Harrow, Marlborough, Rugby and Winchester.

[c] The sources are given below.

[d] The percentages are taken of the total whose school is known.

[e] The results are presented in the form of histograms in Diagram 7 of Volume I.

[f] In this and the following professions or positions former pupils of Scottish schools are included. Pupils at Scottish schools have not, however, been included in the totals of those at present receiving education because the categories of school in Scotland do not come within the same definitions as those in England and Wales. Inclusion of Scottish figures would not in any case significantly alter the table.

[g] Excluding 3 non-scientific members of the Royal Society elected in this period.

Sources:

1. Proportion of pupils at recognized efficient schools: 1967 figures, provided by the Department of Education and Science.
2. Pupils from recognized efficient schools going on to Oxford and Cambridge and other universities: 1965–6 figures provided by the Department of Education and Science from a 10 per cent sample of school leavers.
3. Vice Chancellors, Heads of Colleges and Professors of Oxford and Cambridge colleges and other universities: information taken from the Universities' Year Book 1967.
4. Cabinet as at September 1967: information from Dod's Parliamentary Companion.
5. Members of Parliament: information from Dod's Parliamentary Companion.
6. Admirals: Navy List 1967. Generals: Army List 1967. Air Chief Marshals: Air Force List 1967.
7. Members of the General Medical Council: Hospitals Year Book 1967. Surgeons and Physicians at London teaching hospitals: Universities Year Book 1967.
8. Directors of firms: 1967 Kompass Directors' Directory.
9. Church of England Bishops: Church of England Year Book 1967.
10. Judges and Q.C.s: 1967 Whitaker.
11. Fellows of the Royal Society (1962–6): information from 1967 Year Book.
12. Governor and Directors of the Bank of England: 1967 Whitaker.
13. Information about the schools attended in respect of 3, and 6 to 12 above taken from *Who's Who* 1967.

Table 17.5. Civil and Diplomatic Service Recruitment [Appendix 8, Section 5]. Administrative Class: details of Competitors and Successes 1963–7 by Schools

Method II

Type of school	Competitors (Note *b*)					Successes (Note *c*)				
	1963	1964	1965	1966	1967	1963	1964	1965	1966	1967
A. Public schools	207	161	162	156	210	26	27	51	34	49
B. Other independent schools	23	51	51	56	19	7	3	5	8	2
C. Direct grant schools	48	59	67	80	132	7	17	12	19	31
D. Maintained schools	166	134	151	227	335	15	17	24	31	44
E. Foreign and other schools	13	5	2	17	11	1	1	1	2	2
Total	457	410	433	536	707	56	65	93	94	128

Method I

Type of school	Competitors (Note *b*)					Successes (Note *d*)				
	1963	1964	1965	1966	1967	1963	1964	1965	1966	1967
A. Public schools	46	46	55	33	31	9	16	18	5	5
B. Other independent schools	15	14	13	5	3	1	1	4	1	—
C. Direct grant schools	19	14	32	20	12	5	3	7	6	3
D. Maintained schools	71	45	53	35	33	12	5	3	6	9
E. Foreign and other schools	4	2	3	4	3	—	—	—	—	1
Total	153	121	156	97	82	27	25	32	18	18

Notes:

[a] Method I is the traditional method of entry to the Administrative Class and involves a short qualifying examination, a 40-minute interview before the Final Interview Board, and optional academic papers set and marked at Final Honours level. Method II involves a short qualifying examination in General Subjects, group tests and interviews lasting two days and an interview before the Final Board. Candidates competing by Method II must have, or obtain in the year in which they compete, a degree with at least Second Class Honours: there is no stipulation as to class of degree for Method I candidates.

[b] 'Competitors' exclude voluntary withdrawals but include all other candidates who competed in at least one stage of the selection process. 'Dual' Method I/II candidatures counted twice.

[c] 'Successes' cover all candidatures for the Administrative Class; they include 10, 13, 14, 12 and 20 candidates in 1963, 1964, 1965, 1966 and 1967 respectively who were also successful for and preferred the Foreign/Diplomatic Service. The total of successes for 1967 (Method II) includes one candidate from the 1966 competition.

[d] As Note *c*: the numbers for the Foreign/Diplomatic Service were 5, 2, 4, 2 and nil in 1963, 1964, 1965, 1966 and 1967 respectively.

Foreign/Diplomatic Service Competitors and Successes 1963–7 by Schools

Method II

Type of school	Competitors (Note *a*)					Successes (Note *b*)				
	1963	1964	1965	1966	1967	1963	1964	1965	1966	1967
A. Public schools	146	119	135	136	162	15	15	19	16	16
B. Other independent schools	18	29	33	32	9	—	2	2	1	—
C. Direct grant schools	17	22	26	33	44	1	3	1	3	7
D. Maintained schools	66	61	89	106	137	4	4	2	7	7
E. Foreign and other schools	4	3	3	6	10	—	1	1	1	—
Total	251	234	286	313	362	20	25	25	28	30

Method I

Type of school	Competitors (Note *a*)					Successes				
	1963	1964	1965	1966	1967	1963	1964	1965	1966	1967
A. Public schools	27	20	33	19	22	4	1	2	—	—
B. Other independent schools	9	4	4	1	1	1	—	—	—	—
C. Direct grant schools	7	2	13	13	6	—	—	—	2	—
D. Maintained schools	27	22	21	14	13	—	1	2	—	—
E. Foreign and other schools	3	1	—	2	2	—	—	—	—	—
Total	73	49	71	49	44	5	2	4	2	—

Notes:

[a] 'Competitors' exclude voluntary withdrawals but include all other candidates who competed in at least one stage of the selection process. 'Dual' Method I/II candidatures counted twice.

[b] 'Successes' cover all candidatures for the Diplomatic Service; they include 3, 8, 2 and 2 candidates in 1963, 1964, 1966 and 1967 respectively who were also successful for and preferred the Administrative Class.

Administrative Class Competitors and Successes 1963–7 by Schools and Universities

Method II

Type of school	Oxford and Cambridge candidates			Other candidates		
	Competitors	Successes	Success ratio	Competitors	Successes	Success ratio
A. Public schools	670	162	1:4·1	226	25	1:9·0
B. Other independent schools	76	13	1:5·8	124	12	1:10·3
C. Direct grant schools	231	65	1:3·6	155	21	1:7·4
D. Maintained schools	340	73	1:4·7	673	58	1:11·6
E. Foreign and other schools	9	—	—	39	7	1:5·6
Total	1,326	313	1:4·2	1,217	123	1:9·9

Method I

Type of school	Oxford and Cambridge candidates			Other candidates		
	Competitors	Successes	Success ratio	Competitors	Successes	Success ratio
A. Public schools	136	46	1:3·0	67	7	1:9·6
B. Other independent schools	14	4	1:3·5	28	3	1:9·3
C. Direct grant schools	58	20	1:2·9	40	4	1:10·0
D. Maintained schools	106	21	1:5·0	144	14	1:10·3
E. Foreign and other schools	2	1	1:2·0	14	—	—
Total	316	92	1:3·4	293	28	1:10·5

Foreign/Diplomatic Service Competitors and Successes 1963–7 by Schools and Universities

Method II

Type of school	Oxford and Cambridge candidates			Other candidates		
	Competitors	Successes	Success ratio	Competitors	Successes	Success ratio
A. Public schools	556	75	1:7·4	142	6	1:23·7
B. Other independent schools	47	3	1:15·7	68	2	1:34·0
C. Direct grant schools	97	11	1:8·8	51	4	1:12·8
D. Maintained schools	171	19	1:9·0	288	5	1:57·6
E. Foreign and other schools	9	1	1:9·0	17	2	1:8·5
Total	880	109	1:8·1	566	19	1:29·8

Method I

Type of school	Oxford and Cambridge candidates			Other candidates		
	Competitors	Successes	Success ratio	Competitors	Successes	Success ratio
A. Public schools	79	7	1:11·3	42	—	—
B. Other independent schools	6	—	—	12	1	1:12·0
C. Direct grant schools	24	2	1:12·0	18	—	—
D. Maintained schools	37	—	—	60	3	1:20·0
E. Foreign and other schools	2	—	—	6	—	—
Total	148	9	1:16·4	138	4	1:34·5

18

RECRUITMENT TO THE CIVIL SERVICE ADMINISTRATIVE CLASS

G K FRY

First published in Statesmen in Disguise *by G. K. Fry, Macmillan, 1969.*

Table 18.9. Administrative Recruitment: Father's Occupation, 1948–63

Group	Method I				Method II			
	Competitors		Successes		Competitors		Successes	
	1948–56	1957–63	1948–56	1957–63	1948–56	1957–63	1948–56	1957–63
I	434	338	103	60	918	1,042	99	152
II	754	355	131	72	1,169	1,011	74	104
III	479	181	76	25	590	487	29	30
IV	34	40	5	7	40	63	1	6
V	13	4	4	—	16	9	3	2
Unknown	6	23	—	5	13	37	2	—
Total	1,720	941	319	169	2,746	2,649	208	294

Source: Sixth Report from the Estimates Committee (1964–5) p. 31.

Note: The occupational groups are those defined by the Registrar-General:
- I Administrators, managers, senior professional and scientific occupations.
- II Intermediate professional, managerial and technical occupations.
- III Highly skilled workers, foremen, supervisors, clerks.
- IV Skilled and semi-skilled.
- V Unskilled.

Table 18.10. Analysis of Method II, 1960–6

Year	No. of applications		No. qualified in written exam		No. qualified at C.S.S.B.		No. qualified at F.S.B.	
	Oxbridge	Non-Oxbridge	Oxbridge	Non-Oxbridge	Oxbridge	Non-Oxbridge	Oxbridge	Non-Oxbridge
1960	269	132 (5)	130	16 (1)	108	14 (1)	39	3 (1)
1961	315	196 (10)	153	47	109	24	50	10
1962	315	214 (18)	139	57 (3)	91	29 (2)	42	11 (1)
1963	284	224 (19)	156	68 (4)	103	28 (2)	48	8
1964	269	250 (22)	146	66 (1)	120	39	53	12
1965	303	272 (8)	176	95 (1)	131	57 (1)	67	26 (1)
1966	281	444 (16)	169	175 (4)	127	108 (2)	59	35

Source: Information supplied by the Civil Service Commissioners.
Note: The figures in brackets denote candidates who did not attend university and have been included in the main figure.

19

THE PUBLIC SCHOOLS AND THE ARMY

C B OTLEY

First published in New Society, *17 November 1966.*

Table 19.1. The Contribution of the Public Schools to Sandhurst 1890–1960

	Entrants from ten major public schools	Total all entrants from public schools	Total all entrants
	%	%	No.
1890	46	80	290
1900	52	92	353
1910	51	92	347
1920	32	81	637
1930	40	83	444
1939	30	85	587
1950	19	60	327
1960	16	51	250
Averages	36	80	3,235

Table 19.2. The Contribution of the Public Schools to Woolwich 1855–8 – 1939

	Entrants from ten major public schools	Total all entrants from public schools	Total all entrants
	%	%	No.
1855–8	10	22	146
1869	38	73	76
1890	41	72	120
1900	47	85	281
1910	57	89	139
1920	45	85	129
1930	52	89	124
1939	35	91	195
Averages	41	77	1,210

Table 19.3. The Contribution of Public Schools to the British Army Élite, 1870–1959[a]

	Contribution of ten major public schools	Contribution of all public schools	Total members of élite
	%	%	No.
1870	21	29	80
1897	25	37	63
1913	47	59	58
1926	48	77	48
1939	60	82	45
1959	42	83	36
Averages	38	56	330

[a] Lieutenant-generals, generals and field-marshals

PART TWO

THE ANALYSIS OF POWER

INTRODUCTION

This section is designed to illustrate the important conceptual problems involved in the analysis of power in Britain. Since all the extracts have been discussed in the *Introduction*, it is only necessary here to place them in context. The selections from Peter Worsley and David Lockwood are papers given at the 1964 conference of the British Sociological Association reprinted in a monograph edited by Paul Halmos on the development of industrial societies. Worsley attempts to provide a sociological extension of power beyond the confines traditionally set by political science. In this he shows why it is that in the most 'proletarianized' of societies the institutions of the property-owning classes have remained so pervasively in existence. The factors that he mentions—including especially the nature of legitimation—include more than directly governmental or strictly political considerations. Lockwood amplifies certain points in this discussion both by pointing out the ways in which the discussion of the distribution of power is infinitely more difficult than a similar discussion of the distribution of population, and in indicating the tricky problems implied by the notion of élite—or ruling-class—manipulation. Bottomore's extract is a discussion of the élite and ruling-class concepts, maintaining that some sort of selective synthesis between the two is possible. This raises a theme encountered in the Introduction and found in the selections from Poulantzas and Miliband. Dahl's review of power-élite theorists has been included because although it is now somewhat old it is a useful classic statement of the problems faced by the sociologist in maintaining that in a given society there is a certain concentration of power. Nicol Poulantzas' article (a review of Ralph Miliband's *The State in Capitalist Society*[1]) argues against the empiricist, a-theoretical, and subjectivist nature of Miliband's book. Thus, to take just one point, that Miliband shows that there is a degree of direct participation of capitalists within the state apparatus is not important for Poulantzas, because in terms of his theoretical problematic the relationship between the State and the capitalist class is a simple objective relationship. The congruence of interest does not

[1] R. Miliband: *The State in Capitalist Society* (Weidenfeld and Nicholson, London 1969), see pp. 136 above.

follow because one group participates *within* the other; it is a product of the character of the system itself. Miliband replies to most of Poulantzas' points. In the argument quoted here he points out how Poulantzas gets into a structural determinism in which the State is seen as merely determined by these objective relations. We have ended with this pair of articles because they are representative of methodological disagreements between two analysts of broadly similar political views and suggest some fruitful areas for future consideration.

20

THE DISTRIBUTION OF POWER IN INDUSTRIAL SOCIETY

PETER WORSLEY

In so far as people's behaviour takes account of the existence of others, and is affected by expectations about others, we call it 'social'. Some of this behaviour is *specifically purposive;* it aims to produce effects. But not all of it is, and not all behaviour of interest to the social scientist is 'social', in Weber's sense of the term. Weber himself, indeed, emphasized that 'sociology is by no means confined to the study of "*social action*"; this is only . . . its *central* subject matter. . . .' (1) *Causally* determined action, as well as 'meaningfully' determined action, is part of the sociologist's subject-matter. So, although 'meaningfully' behaviour may be 'non-social', causally it can never be without social *consequences*.

Restricting ourselves, however, to 'social' action, we can be said to act politically whenever we exercise constraint on others to behave as we want them to. The allocation of resources to further these ends is an economic allocation. The overall assertion of values entailed is an operation of political economy.

These conceptual departure-points imply a very wide conception of politics, what we may call Politics I (2). By this definition, the exercise of constraint in any relationship is political. All kinds of pressure, from mass warfare and organized torture to implicit values informing inter-personal conversation, make up the political dimension. Looked at this way, there is no such thing as a special kind of behaviour called 'political'; there is only a political dimension to behaviour. Yet the vulgar (and often, academic) use of the term 'politics'—what we shall call 'Politics II' (3)—restricts the term to the specialized machinery of government, together with the administrative apparatus of state and party organization. To follow the implications of this usage through, strictly, would involve us in denying to simple undifferentiated societies the privilege of having a political system at all (4). Moreover, we also recognize that extra-governmental organizations within advanced societies

First published in Sociological Review Monographs, *8, 1964.*

dispose of power, and have their own constellations of power: we speak of 'university politics'. By this, we do not mean, merely and obviously, that organizations like universities or trade unions, either continuously or intermittently, bring pressure to bear upon government, and are thereby behaving 'politically'—and only on such occasions. Nor do we mean that party politics emerges from and intrudes into sub-cultures. We mean, rather, that these sub-cultural groups are, latently and constantly, organized power-groupings. They have an internal system through which this power is deployed; externally, their mere existence is a fact which governments, even the most authoritarian, have to take account of. Normally, too, such power-groupings make sure governments *do* take account of their interests; they are not merely passive.

Politics II is a dying conceptual apparatus, the prerogative predominantly of a few formal constitutional theorists and legal theorists. More imaginative (i.e. sociological) political thinkers have always operated with a wider conception of politics: whether constitutional theorists, practising (not necessarily 'practical', a term which carries too many value-loaded assumptions) politicians, or ordinary people. The operation has, again, been a social as well as a logical one: the definition of the relationship between King and nobility, lord and vassal, the citizen and the state; the assertion of *new* 'rights'—of *habeas corpus*, freedom of conscience, votes for women—or, equally, the restriction of rights—religious intolerance, or 'the politics of inequality'. All these activities have involved the constant redefinition and restructuring of the specialized machinery of government in the light of changing social values and pressures. Politics, in fact, is something that happens in *society*, not only in governments. Governments themselves are only parts of societies. In recent years, the experience of mass politics has induced in political scientists a more sociological approach to politics, notably in their increasing interest in extra-governmental power-centres, and in the way that these interact with government. The vogue for 'pressure-group' studies has been one healthy product.

Nevertheless, governments *are* very special parts of this overall field of power. Experientially, this is obvious enough to anyone who has ever, say, paid taxes (like Mr Edmund Wilson (5)) been conscripted into the army, or landed in gaol. Analytically, however, the problem remains: does the peculiar importance of government derive from the fact that it is *specialized* to dispose of power?

The answer must be 'no'—other organizations are also specialized to dispose of power, whether trade unions, armies, public relations firms, or churches. It is the kind and range of power that is in question. Nor is it enough to say that governments exercise *legitimate* power; so do other organizations and sub-cultures. Interest-groups have a right to express themselves; indeed, we conceive of this as a vital part of the democratic process. In the heyday of laissez-faire, governments were content to delegate very many powers that today they jealously arrogate to themselves alone. The state was a weak 'nightwatchman', holding the ring, intervening only when chaos threatened. But both that state and today's much stronger state shared one fundamental attribute—they were the repositories of *ultimate* legitimacy. True, the ultimacy might be remote: a theoretical pre-eminence of the feudal monarch as *primus inter pares*. It might be too tenuous to put to the test, when to use power to dispose of force (as in 1832) would be to risk an end to the legitimacy on which the system depended.

'Ultimate legitimacy' defines the constant element, but the *de facto* powers of the state have changed so enormously—over the last century in Western Europe, for example—that it becomes metaphysical to talk of 'the functions of the state' as if these were absolutes. This is a level of generality too high to be of much utility, unhelpful in distinguishing analytically between, say, the contemporary South African polity, that of Lord Palmerston's Britain, Stalin's U.S.S.R., Ben Bella's Algeria, Hitler's Germany, or Johnson's U.S.A. For the state changes as 'civil society' changes. This makes for very different kinds of state. Élites are displaced; classes emerge and disintegrate. The study of these historically-specific types of state takes us a long way from metaphysics into the real analysis of power.

Nor is there a finite fund of power, any more than there is a fixed 'wages fund'. New sources and resources of power come into being; others disappear. The area of operation of the state therefore varies; so does the area arrogated by other organizations and sub-cultures. The definition of the legitimacy of the state largely consists in delimiting what is properly the sphere of the state and of no other agency—where, when, and how the state may operate. And who defines this legitimacy? Those who control the instruments of power—from machine-guns to television-networks—may define legitimacy entirely themselves. What we do, they may say, is right.

More normally, they try to present a more sophisticated and 'disinterested' rationale of rule, and endeavour to persuade the governed of its appropriateness.

In the latter situation, legitimacy is internalized, more or less, by the governed. How crucial this subjective acceptance can be was last brought out most vividly in this country in 1919—well-described by a noted Labour militant in his account of Lloyd George's interview with the leaders of the Triple Alliance:

> . . . 'Gentlemen,' Lloyd George remarked, 'you have fashioned, in the Triple Alliance of the unions represented by you, a most powerful instrument. I feel bound to tell you that in our opinion we are at your mercy. The army is disaffected and cannot be relied upon. Trouble has occurred already in a number of camps. We have just emerged from a great war and the people are eager for the reward of their sacrifices, and we are in no position to satisfy them. In these circumstances, if you carry out your threat and strike, then you will defeat us.'
>
> 'But if you do', went on Lloyd George, 'have you weighed the consequences? The strike will be in defiance of the Government of the country and by its very success will precipitate a constitutional crisis of the first importance. For if a force arises in the State which is stronger than the State itself, then it must be ready to take on the functions of the State, or withdraw and accept the authority of the State. Gentlemen', asked the Prime Minister quietly, 'have you considered, and if you have, are you ready?' 'From that moment on', said Robert Smillie, 'we were beaten and we knew we were.'
>
> After this the General Strike of 1926 was really an anti-climax. The essential argument had been deployed in 1919 (6).

The internalization of the legitimacy of Government was thus far more decisive than that Government's mere possession of rifles (7). Values are thus important to revolutionaries as well as governments, i.e. to any political movement except those (e.g. fascism) which glorify 'power in itself' (8) (and this is an ideology, too). Power is used *for something;* its use has effects.

Power does not exist 'in itself': it flows between people. And everybody has some of it, some area of choice, of ability to affect things his way. It may only be the power to be negative, to 'vote with one's feet'; in the extreme, only to choose death—but that is a choice, and, as the study of martyrology alone shows us, one which is by no means without social consequences. But some people have overwhelming and decisive power. Power is not randomly distributed, but institutionalized.

II

The identification of the rulers, therefore, must involve an examination of the distribution of power generally within civil society. In British society, there are only two institutional orders, however, within which very great power is concentrated: the political order and the economic order. This is not true for all societies. In some, for example, those in control of the means of violence are specially important. In the U.S.A., organized religion is a far more potent force than in this country (9), especially at the community level. The identification of the power élite, the delineation of the distribution of power, are matters for empirical investigation. But a simplistic kind of political behaviourism does not carry us very far. It is commonly assumed, for example, that the role of the military in the U.S.A. is very much more considerable than in the U.K. This may well be (10), but the truth or falsity of the proposition cannot be ascertained merely by reference to the public aggressiveness of the U.S. military, because the U.S. political system, unlike the British, entails a high degree of public competition for and scrutiny of estimates.

Sheer publicity, therefore, tells us little about the *importance* of the military. Indeed, as a general proposition, the more effective the lobby, the less public its activities. Those with the ear of government do not need to organize mass lobbies of the House of Commons (11). For the U.S.A., Selznick has shown how the really powerful and effective interest-group constitutes a kind of 'constituency' which intermeshes with its governmental counterpart and becomes difficult to distinguish from it (12). When sectional interest-group and government are so closely identified, there is little likelihood of clamorous public wrangling. There is no need for the interest-group to 'intervene': it is *there* already, or quite happy with things as they are. Quietness, then, is by no means an index of a pressure group's impotence or unconcern: it more usually indicates a high degree of consensus. In Britain, such consensus has been developed over centuries, as far as the military are concerned.

There is a deep-seated tradition of subservience of the military to the civil power, which derives from a suspicion of standing armies that goes back as far as Cromwell. Since then, the Army has always been carefully identified with 'society'. Its ethos was shaped during the era when its high officers were overwhelmingly drawn from the ranks of the landed aristocracy. But for a long time the Army has not been as attractive an avenue for the ambitious as industry or the City. As a result, recruitment of officers is becoming slightly more democratized, although the high officers' ranks still reflect the social pattern of thirty years ago, and retain a strong representation of landed, minor gentry, families. Self-recruitment from 'military families' there has always been, but whereas formerly the senior ranks attracted the wealthy and well-connected, during recent decades those from the less wealthy and well-connected military families have also been able to make their way up the ladder (13).

Only in wartime has the military successfully and seriously obtruded itself into the formation of public policy—or even tried to—but at such times, military policy *is* the central issue in public policy. Viscount Montgomery's public pronouncements are striking in their atypicality—and are self-consciously 'deviant' and outrageous into the bargain. This is the licensed and publicized military, which eminence makes possible, more akin to the cathartic role of the court jester or the Hyde Park Corner speaker than, say, to the ideology of the French military caste—which *has* been a most serious independent political force in recent years (14).

The British military, then, has never become a caste—it is too closely woven into the culture of the ruling classes. It is no longer, however, one of the major magnetic power-centres attracting the enterprising and the ambitious, probably because, increasingly, it no longer makes the key military decisions. These are made abroad, and the military machine which once coped with the Indian sub-continent, to mention no other area, finds itself stretched in dealing with Cyprus and other backwaters of the world.

Many of these features are reproduced in another formerly central institution of British society, the Church of England, which has been recently described as 'by far and away the most important social institution in the land', and 'by far and away the largest organizer of youth in the country' (15). Yet, in quantitative terms alone, it now exercises direct and regular influence over less than three million adult members, plus a further 1,161,000 Sunday school children aged between 3 and 14. By contrast, the *Daily Mirror* had a readership of nearly thirteen million people in 1954—one-third of the population aged 16 and over (16) and 'Granadaland' alone embraces some eight million adults.

The Army, the Church, and the Law are not what they were. But ordination still does not mean alienation: four Oxbridge colleges produced nearly one-quarter of the Church of England bishops between 1860 and 1960 (17), and the public schools and older universities still dominate recruitment. The class connections of the lower clergy, however, have become less specifically tied to the upper classes (and 22 per cent of contemporary ordinands attended secondary modern and similar schools) (18). Like the Army, as the Church has become less attractive to the upper classes, it increasingly finds its new recruits from formerly excluded social strata, and its senior leaders from within specifically *churchly* families. If the Church is no longer 'the Conservative Party at prayer', it is also still a long way from being 'that nation on Sunday'. Paradoxically, its democratization, which might well be a future source of religious strength, reflects its diminished social position. It no longer attracts those in search of decisive power; prelates have less to be proud about: education has long slipped from their grasp; morals are increasingly becoming the bailiwick of the B.M.A. (19), and ideology of the mass media.

As serious centres of power, then, we are concerned predominantly with the political and economic orders. It is significant that Dahrendorf, who emphasizes, pluralistically, that all institutions carry their quantum of power, in fact only singles out economic and political power for special analysis (20). For Britain, the close association between the two élites at the apex of these institutional orders—the governing élite and the coalesced property-owning landed aristocracy and industrial bourgeoisie—has recently been very closely documented by Guttsman (21), together with the entry of 'new men' unto the ranks of the governing élite (largely via the mechanisms for upwards mobility presented by the Labour movement (22) and an extended educational system).

The uninterrupted, albeit modified, dominance of the property-owning classes, in a society which has long been the most highly 'proletarianized' in the world, is surely one of the most striking phenomena of modern times (23). To paraphrase Sombart, we might well ask: 'Warum gibt es keine Rewolution in Vereinigten Königreich?'

The answer does not lie in the possession of machine-guns by the ruling class. In this century, only in 1926 has armed force ever been in sight. The challenge of the masses—who created a whole series of instruments of self-expression and self-assertion, from the co-operatives and the trade unions to the Labour Party—has never been a revolutionary one. To find a situation where the deployment of naked force was a necessary technique of ruling we have to go back to the mobilization of troops to confront the Chartists in 1848 at Kennington Common, or the earlier mobilization in 1812 against the Luddites when the Duke of Wellington put into the field more troops than he had commanded in the Peninsular War (24).

The exploration of this continuity and stability involves examination of the modification of both the ruling class and the ruled. The former were able to accede to the demands of the masses, for they vote flexibly and gradually; in the economic sphere, concessions to the 'welfare' demands of the newly-vocal enfranchised masses were also made skilfully and gradually. In the process, the theory and practice of *laisser faire* had to be thrown overboard. Gradually, the State assumed more and more responsibility for more and more areas of social life. In an age when the nationalized sector of the economy is responsible for half the investment spending, a third of the employment income, and a quarter of the national product, Herbert Spencer's resistance to state interference, whether in the shape of the Post Office, the public mint, poor relief, 'social' legislation, colonization, organized sanitation, or state education, seems remote indeed.

The extensions of the franchise in 1832, 1867 and 1884, were the crucial steps, politically. Yet the beginnings of reform produced no sharp polarization of forces. In the crucial period 1832–68, 'the classes were represented in almost the same proportions in each of the two parliamentary groupings'—'left-centre' (Liberal) and 'right-centre' (Conservative). After 1867, the new middle classes gradually crept onto the governmental scene (normally holding offices of lower prestige and 'administrative' content). Not until 1923 did a non-aristocrat hold the office of Foreign Secretary (25), and not until 1929 was a British government elected on full adult suffrage.

The entry of the middle classes into the centres of political power was thus a long-drawn-out process (26); the emerging proletariat, in its turn, only very gradually distinguished itself from the party of the middle classes.

Much more was involved in the difficult enterprise of modernization than political changes alone. On their own these might well have led to the rule of the masses so feared by sections of the élite. The modernization of British society was a much more many-sided process, the rationalization and stabilization of a whole 'political culture'. This enculturation was not accomplished by some undifferentiated 'ruling class': more specifically, many of the crucial reorganizations were the achievement of the Liberal Party, and bore the stamp of liberalism, even though that party, theoretically the repository of anti-bigness, anti-statism, and the cult of the individual, nevertheless had quite determinedly reorganized *itself* as a centralized, hierarchical machine, modelled on Chamberlain's Birmingham caucus system, and as a political party with a mass, *extra*-Parliamentary base (27). Self-rationalization was the climax to a long series of rationalizations of the wider society in the third quarter of the nineteenth century, a watershed between the society symbolized by Palmerston and modern mass democracy: reform of the Civil Service (the Northcote-Trevelyan reforms), of the Army (Cardwell's reforms, 1868–71), and of education, both for the élite (the development of public schools on the Rugby pattern) and for the masses (the development of primary education, 1870–80). For the newly literate, a special literature industry was founded (28). Via education, a proportion of the working class could find its way into the middle classes. Convinced by their personal experience of the reality of upwards social mobility, they constituted, and constitute, an important reservoir of believers in the notion of *la carrière ouverte aux talents* (29): their consciousness is structured by their own experience of mobility in the 'middle levels of power', to use Mills' phrase, and generalized into a theory applicable to the society as a whole.

The persistence of patterns of deference and traditionalistic loyalty among other large segments of the lower strata cannot be documented here, nor has it yet been adequately documented anywhere. 'Deference', however, only explains part of the mass vote which the Conservative Party has been able to mobilize since modern politics began in the 1870s. The sense of identity and solidarity with traditional rulers of society is a much more complex phenomenon than the term 'deference' implies. It was a much more *active* and modernizing assertion than that, classically defined by Disraeli:

> The Tory Party, unless it is a national party, is nothing. It is not a confederacy of nobles, it is not a democratic multitude; it is a party formed from

all the numerous classes in the realm—classes alike and equal before the law, but whose different conditions and different aims give vigour and variety to our national life (30).

Separately, at first—in associations of Conservative working men —the newly enfranchised were brought into association with their rulers. With the final rapid partition of the whole globe between the Western Powers in the last quarter of the century, a new mystique—of imperialism—was generated. The efficacy of such a mystique as a means of attaching the working class to the inherited order was again brilliantly perceived by Disraeli: 'I look to the cultivation of public opinion, and *especially to the working classes* for the maintenance of the British Empire' (31).

This solidarity, then, was far more complex than any crude label like 'feudal', 'deference-pattern', or even 'traditionalism' would imply. The imperialist note, indeed, was strikingly *un*traditional, and was resisted for a long time in both Conservative and Liberal circles, as well as Labour (32). As Guttsman has pointed out, the feudal heritage was, in fact, a *distant* one (and had been profoundly challenged and modified via Civil War and industrialization): 'English romantic thought accepted the basic tenets of the Enlightenment: freedom of thought, equality before the law, but it reacted against the libertarian and egalitarian views of the French revolution' (33). The latter tradition was taken up and developed by the working class; it could not easily form a part of the self-legitimation of the ruling class.

Simple, 'objective' classification of occupations, then, or of the distribution of power, does not take us very far in explaining the success of British conservatism in attracting one-third of the trade union vote even to this day. Counting heads is essential in order to establish some primary facts about who people are, but even in order to know what to count at this level, we operate with (often implicit) theoretical assumptions. To get any further, to explore deeper levels of behaviour, we have to move beyond this kind of classificatory activity into the field of 'political culture'. Of course, crude classification and correlation is analytically easier (if technically, perhaps, complicated enough) than more sophisticated exploration; it is also less controversial (34). The difficulties entailed in exploration arise intrinsically from the fact that human consciousness is involved, for we are dealing with *attitudes*, shaped by many variables. But the really fertile fields for sociological investigation lie precisely in the exploration of the interplay between the subjective and the objective (35). Class does not, metaphysically, mean anything 'in itself'. It is always acted upon, interpreted, mediated, by somebody, and it is the social agencies which inject *meaning* into class, and transmit these meanings to people, that must increasingly concern us. They concern us increasingly, both because this is the needed development in intellectual and analytical terms, and because, empirically, the mechanisms by which consciousness is manipulated are of growing importance in modern society.

In speaking of the study of 'political culture', I have in mind the way in which the gross quantitative facts of class differentiation, so amply demonstrated by Robbins (36), for example, actually translate into cultural activity. The ethos of the public school we know a good deal about; the ethos of the educationally less-privileged is barely documented. Obviously, having adequate material conditions in the home is half the battle. But battles are often won by marginal inputs of resources, and the other half of this particular battle is much less obvious. It lies in the shaping of motivation and aspirations: in the consequences of the experience of middle-level mobility for the psyche of the mobile; and, for others, in the complex adaptation to failure, stasis or descent, in the varying forms delineated by Merton: conformity, innovation, ritualism, retreatism, and the forms which often lie between these ideal types (37).

'Who owns what?' thus remains a crucial question, but what 'they' *do* with 'it' has been inadequately explored. Similarly, what is crucially missing in most power studies is any account of actual decision-making at the top (intrinsically difficult to obtain access to, of course, except usually long after the event) (38). And few sociologists have yet explored the consequences of dis-privilege with the subtlety of Hoggart's work. One systematic instance can be given, however: Bernstein's analysis of the behavioural and psychic consequences for the individual of internalized modes of speech which are both socially derived (class-linked) and also have consequences for the social distribution of roles in so far as they *reproduce* class divisions (39).

Sociology, in fact, needs to become more subtle. It must enter the difficult field of the exploration of consciousness (40). The study of the distribution of power, in particular, is not likely to make much serious headway unless it concentrates much more centrally on the analysis of the formation and maintenance of legitimation (41). In the long chain of connections between values and political behaviour, attention has so far been primarily—and naturally enough—focused upon the specific end-product: in our society, principally the vote; and comparatively little upon the process of political socialization. 'Pressure-group' studies are the bridge into this crucial area, where Politics I gives rise to Politics II. Political scientists, in their studies of the specialized field of Politics II, have in fact been pointing to processes which have their parallels in the overall cultural field of Politics I. The discernment by MacKenzie, for example, of the 'iron law of oligarchy' in the two major political parties, has been paralleled by the demonstration of similar élite tendencies in the largest British trade union (42). Kornhauser (43) and Mills (44), and Lipset, Trow and Coleman in their study of the International Typographical Union (45), have pushed further into the zone between specialized politics and culture in general. Finally, a different range of studies demonstrated how attitudes towards authority, individualism, minorities, outsiders, etc., manifest themselves not only within the context of institutionalized politics, but also in other power-relations, and even at the level of interpersonal relations, e.g. studies of the authoritarian personality (46), of specifically working-class authoritarianism (47), or such ideal typologies as Eysenck's scheme of 'tender-' and 'tough-mindedness' (48). Biography and history impinge upon each other; for this reason, complacency about the consequences of non-democracy within private organizations for the wider society is a dangerous state of mind (49). Similarly, tendencies towards 'massification' in the institutional sphere—the erosion away of the autonomy of secondary associations, portrayed by Kornhauser and Mills—are paralleled by 'mass' phenomena in wider cultural spheres, for example, in the arts (50). It is from a diffuse awareness of this circumstance that recent radicalism has concerned itself with such matters as the cultural content of films and the aesthetic quality of public architecture and design as well as with a purely 'structural' critique of the power order (51). 'Culture' and 'political culture' are not discrete areas.

'Massification' and 'bureaucratization' increasingly thrust themselves forward as apposite analytical frameworks within which the analysis of the distribution of power in industrial society can be analysed. They have been conceived of, sometimes, as *alternative* frameworks to the more familiar frameworks of analysis in which property has been seen as the crucial determinant of social differentiation, and thereby of the unequal distribution of power and of opposed political interest-groupings. In the light of the abundant evidence concerning the intimate links between wealth and élite position (52), there seems little need to assume that we have, in fact, arrived at a situation where the managers, the meritocrats, or the technocrats, are in control. Yet there are important centres of power where the possession of private wealth is not a virtual prerequisite, directly or indirectly, for high office. Historically, the organizations of the Labour movement have been the most important such centres. Even though Winchester and Oxbridge have been abundantly represented upon the Labour Front Bench for some years; even if teachers had displaced miners by 1945 as the strongest occupational group amongst Labour M.P.s (53); and even if Labour M.P.s *as a whole* have absorbed the values of their Parliamentary milieu, the high road to Labour power is still ensured by trade-union support rather than by the possession of private wealth (54).

Michels' field of investigation for his classic study of the process of oligarchy-formation was therefore excellently chosen, in terms of research strategy, since by looking at a 'Social-Democratic' (i.e. Marxist) party, he could effectively eliminate the variable of private property in examining the location of power and the genesis of 'vested interests'. The agency of revolutionary change had itself become bureaucratized. Adapting to the wider society, it became 'a state within a state', no longer intent on revolutionary transformation *of* society but living in self-contained independence within it (55).

His findings (anticipated by Weber) were thus prophetically relevant to the study of whole societies where power no longer depends upon the possession of capital, but upon 'ownership' of the machinery of politics. Analysis which postulated the emergence of a 'new class' in Eastern Europe thus extended the range of social organizations to which Michels' analysis of bureaucracy and oligarchy could be applied, from a focus upon non-capitalist organizations *within* the wider (capitalist) society, to whole non-capitalist societies (56).

A new set of problems—problems of political power, analytically separable from the phenomenon of the power of private wealth—had emerged on to the scene. Political theory itself innovated as socialized economies replaced private proprietorship. Even within the capitalist world, society becomes ever more social. The corporate giants are decisive (57), and the concomitant implications of corporateness for the millions involved in the corporations have been spelt out, albeit impressionistically and polemically in the main, in theories of 'the lonely crowd', of 'organization men', and of men who 'fear freedom' (58).

Though they are only partial and inadequate explanatory models for societies where private wealth is still crucial, as in Britain, theories of 'mass society', bureaucracy and oligarchy seem peculiarly relevant for the non-capitalist world, and for the novel forms of polity emerging in the new, non-industrialized countries. Only here have large-scale revolutionary movements retained their revolutionary dynamic, unlike movements among the proletarians of the developed world, sustained as the former are by the pressure of hungry peasants. But hunger alone explains little. 'Not without reason . . .', Durkheim once remarked, 'have so many religions dwelt on the advantages and moral value of poverty. It is actually the best school for teaching self-restraint' (59).

Hunger 'explains' fatalism no more adequately than it 'explains' revolution. As Lockwood has observed, 'The generation of conflict . . . is never a simple matter of a conflict of material interest, but also involves the normative definition of the situation' (60). To explain revolution, we have to look, again, at the agents and agencies of political socialization. The transformation of lethargic and traditionalistic peasants into *the* revolutionary force of the twentieth century has been largely accomplished by political élites which have successfully manipulated the new media of communication to unify and activate their audiences. Without this machinery, isolation and fatalism could not be easily broken down. And once in power, the ideology of legitimacy is effectively manufactured, consolidated, and instilled by virtue of control over the mass media, not machine-guns alone. In these societies, the power élite is very often not a wealth élite (at least in the first place). The country's wealth belongs to foreigners: the élite itself is indeed a 'new' kind of class, of 'new men' (usually Westernized and from the ranks of the minor Public Service).

It is because of growing sensitivity to the new power represented by the development of the modern machinery of government and of instruments of opinion-manufacture of greatly enhanced efficiency, in *all* societies, developed and under-developed, that concern about responsibility, control and accountability to the public have increasingly manifested themselves, from minor eruptions over Crichel Down in this country, to the Royal Commissions on the Press and on Broadcasting, the Bank Rate Tribunal, or the new-found enthusiasm for devolution, humanization, and participation, whether in the form of the Swedish Ombudsman or Yugoslav workers' control—or, in many new countries, in concern about the problem of reconciling a democratic ideology with an (inevitably) single-party state system.

In open societies, then, Politics II illuminates very little except when studied in the context of Politics I, for power is never concentrated exclusively in governments or parties. Politics I is, in fact, an abstraction from a total culture. Modern political science, therefore, must continue to interfuse, as it has been doing, with sociology, if the study of politics is to be fully meaningful.

NOTES

(1) *The Theory of Social and Economic Organization* (Free Press, Glencoe, Ill. 1947), pp. 114–15 (emphasis added). See also pp. 91–4.

(2) Cf. Gabriel A. Almond's Introduction to *The Politics of the Developing Areas* (Princeton University Press, 1960), pp. 7 ff.

(3) Arthur F. Bentley, in his *The Process of Government* (Principia Press, Evanston, Ill. 1935), makes a similar distinction (rather tautologically between 'government' as the performance of 'specified governing functions' (p. 261), and government as 'the process of . . . adjustment of . . . interest groups in a system . . . without any differentiated activity or organ . . .' (pp. 258–9). He also introduced a third category which seems analytically redundant, but has been important historically in that it encouraged people to look at pressure groups.

(4) The point was also noted by Bentley (p. 260); cf. Margaret Mead on the Arapesh: 'There are no political units', she writes, but follows this remark by stating: 'Clusters of villages are grouped into localities . . .', etc. *Sex and Temperament in Three Primitive Societies* (Routledge and Kegan Paul, London 1948), pp. 15–16.

(5) *The Cold War and the Income Tax: a Protest* (Farrar, Straus, N.Y. 1963).

(6) Aneurin Bevan, *In Place of Fear* (Heinemann, London 1952), pp. 20–1.

(7) The power of legitimacy may be further illustrated, from another crisis-situation in a democracy, this time from a Canadian professional bureaucracy, not a labour movement in revolt. When the populist-socialist Co-operative Commonwealth Federation came to power in Saskatchewan in 1944, the administration, despite its general hostility to the incoming Government, refrained, with minor exceptions, from actualizing their lack of sympathy (see S. M. Lipset, *Agrarian Socialism:* the Co-operative Commonwealth Federation in Saskatchewan, Oxford University Press, Toronto 1950, pp. 262 ff). Such occasions of sharp conflict of value-systems have

been rare in both Great Britain and Canada. They are therefore the more peculiarly significant and illuminating: they are critical, not 'atypical', instances.

(8) See Herbert Marcuse, *Reason and Revolution:* Hegel and the Rise of Social Theory (Routledge and Kegan Paul, London 1954), pp. 402–19.

(9) See Will Herberg, *Protestant, Catholic, Jew:* an essay in American religious sociology (Doubleday, New York 1955).

(10) See C. Wright Mills, 'The Military Ascendancy', in *The Power Élite* (Oxford University Press, New York 1956), pp. 198–224; and Fred J. Cook, *The Warfare State* (Jonathan Cape, London 1963).

(11) J. D. Stewart, *British Pressure Groups:* their rôle in relation to the House of Commons (Clarendon, Oxford 1958).

(12) P. Selznick, *TVA and the Grass-roots:* a study in the sociology of formal organization (University of California Press, 1953).

(13) Based on data in C. B. Otley's *The Social Background of Senior Generals in the British Army* (Ph.D. thesis in course of completion, University of Hull).

(14) Unlike the British military. For them, the liquidation of Empire did not proceed at their direct expense; the French Army, however, felt itself betrayed by civilians at home (like the German Army in 1918), and was subjected to the indignity of defeat by non-European peasant (and often Communist) guerillas.

(15) Leslie Paul, *The Deployment and Remuneration of the Clergy* (Church Information Office, London 1964), p. 26.

(16) *The National Readership Survey* (Institute of Incorporated Practitioners in Advertising, London 1954), p. 36.

(17) David H. J. Morgan, *The Social and Educational Backgrounds of English Diocesan Bishops in the Church of England, 1860–1960,* M.A. thesis, University of Hull, 1964.

(18) Paul, op. cit., p. 111.

(19) Public comment on the annual publication of the BMA publication *Getting Married* is fast becoming an index of the state of opinion on sex and marriage issues. The recent report on *Venereal Disease and Young People* (British Medical Association, London 1964), though heavily criticized as a monument of unscientific investigation, is nevertheless in keeping with the tendency to treat these problems as secular (socio-medical), rather than spiritual ones.

(20) Ralf Dahrendorf, *Class and Class Conflict in Industrial Society* (Routledge and Kegan Paul, London 1959).

(21) W. L. Guttsman, *The British Political Élite* (Heinemann, London 1963).

(22) See Zygmunt Bauman, *Klasa-Ruch-Elita:* studium socjologiozne dziej´w Angielskiego ruchu robotniczego (Panstwowe Wydawnictwo Naukowe, Warsaw 1960), the English summary of which at pp. 352–6 tantalizingly invites a full translation.

(23) For a stimulating recent discussion, see Perry Anderson, 'Origins of the Present Crisis', *New Left Review,* 23, January–February 1964, pp. 26–53.

(24) E. P. Thompson, *The Making of the British Working-class* (Gollancz, London 1963), p. 564.

(25) Guttsman, op. cit., p. 78.

(26) 'When the middle classes got votes, and seats in Parliament with them, in 1832, there was for a long time surprisingly little change in the social composition of the House of Commons. The new wealthy did not for the most part want to become legislators, or to spend their time away from business affairs. They only wanted to have a Parliament that would pass the laws

they required; and they remained content, for the most part, to let the gentry sit in the House of Commons, provided this condition was met. They had plenty to do locally . . .' G. D. H. Cole, *Studies in Class Structure* (Routledge and Kegan Paul, London 1961), p. 65.

(27) '. . . the parties, hitherto confined to Parliament, made their way into the constituencies and gradually covered the whole country with the network of their organization', Ostrogorski, cited in R. T. MacKenzie, *British Political Parties* (Mercury Books [Heinemann], London 1964), p. 8.

(28) Raymond Williams, *The Long Revolution* (Chatto and Windus, London 1961).

(29) See Denis Marsden and Brian Jackson, *Education and the Working Class:* some general themes raised by a study of 88 working-class children in a northern industrial city (Routledge and Kegan Paul, London 1962).

(30) Quoted in MacKenzie, op. cit., p. 147.

(31) Loc. cit., p. 147 (emphasis added).

(32) Bernard Semmel, *Imperialism and Social Reform:* English social-imperial thought 1845–1914 (Allen and Unwin, London 1960); and Ronald Robinson and John Gallagher, *Africa and the Victorians* (Macmillan, London 1961).

(33) Guttsman, op. cit., p. 66.

(34) On the distinction between *correlation* and *explanation* in political theory, see W. G. Runciman, *Social Science and Political Theory* (Cambridge University Press, London 1963), pp. 123–34.

(35) In the terms of research strategy, R. T. MacKenzie's current research into the phenomenon of working-class conservatism offers to grasp the most luxuriant nettle in the field.

(36) *Report of the Committee on Higher Education*, Cmnd 2154 (H.M.S.O., London 1963), Chapters 6 and 7, and Appendix 1, Parts II and III.

(37) e.g. the *ressentiment* expressed by the 'pessimists' recently described by D. F. Swift, 'Who Passes the 11 Plus?', *New Society*, No. 75, 5 March 1964, pp. 6–9.

(38) A recent study of British businessmen remarks that 'the first problem of properly-equipped and qualified academic investigators will be to persuade the subject to submit to study. . . . It is one thing to put junior managers on the couch; another to interrogate men who make £20,000 a year and tend to be contemptuous of academic investigators. A further difficulty is that those business men who will show a reasonable degree of co-operation will not necessarily be representative either of the business community as a whole, or of their industry, region, or size and type of firm,' Roy Lewis and Rosemary Stewart, *The Boss:* the life and times of the British business man (Dent, London 1963), Appendix, p. 273.

(39) B. Bernstein, 'Some Sociological Determinants of Perception', *British Journal of Sociology*, Vol. IX, no. 2, June 1958, pp. 159–74, and 'Language and Social Class', *British Journal of Sociology*, Vol. XI, no. 3, September 1960, pp. 271–6.

(40) A rare example of one study that does pose this problem, as the sub-title emphasizes, is David Lockwood's *The Blackcoated Worker:* a study in Class Consciousness (Allen and Unwin, London 1958).

(41) Not that the sociological study of the organization of the machinery of force has proceeded very far, either. S. Andreski's *Military Organization and Society* (Routledge and Kegan Paul, London 1954); C. B. Otley's above-mentioned study of senior British generals [note 13]; P. Abrams' 'Democracy, Technology, and the Retired British Officer', in Samuel P.

Huntington (ed.), *Changing Patterns of Military Politics* (Free Press, Glencoe 1962); and M. Janowitz's *The Professional Soldier:* a social and political portrait (Free Press, Glencoe 1960), are notable exceptions by sociologists, to which should be added S. Finer's stimulating *The Man on Horseback:* the rôle of the military in politics (Pall Mall, London 1962).

(42) Joseph Goldstein, *The Government of British Trade Unions:* a study of apathy and the democratic process in the Transport and General Workers' Union (Allen and Unwin, London 1952).

(43) William Kornhauser, *The Politics of Mass Society* (Routledge and Kegan Paul, London 1959).

(44) C. Wright Mills, 'The Mass Society', *The Power Élite* [note 10], Chapter 13.

(45) S. M. Lipset, M. A. Trow and J. S. Coleman, *Union Democracy:* the internal politics of the International Typographical Union (Free Press, Glencoe 1956).

(46) T. W. Adorno and others, *The Authoritarian Personality* (Harper, New York 1950).

(47) S. M. Lipset, *Political Man* (Mercury Books [Heinemann], London 1963), Chapter IV.

(48) H. J. Eysenck, *Sense and Nonsense in Psychology* (Penguin Books, Harmondsworth 1957), pp. 288 ff.

(49) It appears to be exhibited by Lipset in *Political Man*, when, by dichotomizing internal and external systems, he suggests that 'many organizations [which] may never fulfil the conditions for a stable internal democracy [may] still contribute in important ways to the democratic process in the total society' (p. 396).

(50) See 'The Purposes of Broadcasting', Chapter III, *Report of the Committee on Broadcasting*, Cmnd 1753 (H.M.S.O., London 1960).

(51) For a recent provocative discussion of the relationship between attitudes to sex and wider culture—including political values, see Alex Comfort, *Sex and Society* (Duckworth, London 1963).

(52) e.g. in addition to works cited above, R. K. Kelsall's *Higher Civil Servants in Britain:* from 1870 to the present day (Routledge and Kegan Paul, London 1955); D. V. Glass (ed.) *Social Mobility in Great Britain* (Routledge and Kegan Paul, London 1954); T. Lupton and C. Shirley Wilson, 'The City Men who Decide', *Manchester School*, January 1959, etc., etc.

(53) Guttsman, op. cit. [note 25], pp. 242–3. Not that 'middle-classness' necessarily involves a diminution of socialist conviction; the Left-wing minority within the Labour Party has included a high proportion of middle-class M.P.s (op. cit., pp. 267–75), and a Left-wing intellectual like Michael Foot is returned by a mining constituency.

(54) The trade unions have 12 direct representatives among the 28 members of the National Executive Committee of the Labour Party, and can, in effect, control 18 places: '[The NEC] has never attempted to move in any direction which a majority of the affiliated trade unions were not prepared to follow' (MacKenzie, op. cit., pp. 517–18).

(55) See the recent study by P. Nettl, 'The German Social-Democratic Party as a Political Model, 1890–1914', *Past and Present*, London (forthcoming); also Howard Becker, *German Youth: Bond or Free* (Kegan Paul, Trench, Trubner, London 1946), for similar tendencies among youth movements.

(56) Milovan Djilas, in *The New Class:* an analysis of the communist system (Thames and Hudson, London 1957), put the argument most sharply and least scientifically.

(57) The analogy of feudalism has attracted many observers, e.g. Ralph

Samuel, 'Bastard Capitalism', in *Out of Apathy*, ed. E. P. Thompson (Stevens, London 1960), pp. 24–5. See also Lewis and Stewart, op. cit. [note 38], p. 55 (quoting *The Economist*), and p. 49 (quoting Lord Keynes).

(58) And less impressionistically in R. M. Titmuss, *Essays on the Welfare State* (Unwin University Books, London 1963), esp. Chapter 3, 'Pensions Systems and Population Change', and Chapter 11, 'The Irresponsible Society'. See also the essays by Brian Abel-Smith and Peter Townsend in *Conviction* (MacGibbon and Kee, London 1958).

(59) Emile Durkheim, *Suicide:* a study in sociology (Routledge and Kegan Paul, London 1952), p. 254.

(60) 'Some Remarks on "The Social System"', *British Journal of Sociology*, Vol. VII, no. 2, June 1956, p. 140.

21

THE DISTRIBUTION OF POWER IN INDUSTRIAL SOCIETY - A COMMENT

D LOCKWOOD

Dr Worsley has been given a difficult task. We have asked him to talk about the 'distribution' of power in modern societies knowing full well that this is an entirely different matter from talking about the distribution of, say, population, income, or even educational opportunity. It is difficult enough, as Professor Titmuss has recently shown, to determine with any exactitude the distribution of something so apparently specific as income and wealth. How much more difficult then to assess the relativities of something as diffuse as power; especially if, following Professor Bierstedt's definition, you regard power as latent force; the ability to employ force, not its actual employment, the ability to apply sanctions, not their actual application. But to make matters worse, power must not only refer to the capacity to realize one's ends in a conflict situation against the will of others; it must also include the capacity to prevent opposition arising in the first place. We often hear that the study of power should concentrate on the making and taking of important decisions. But in one sense power is most powerful if the actor can, by manipulation, prevent issues coming to the point of decision at all. Finally, of course, to determine the extent of power, we must know how successful its employment is; in other words, we must know what the goals and objectives of those who employ it actually are.

The difficulties inhering in the objective assessment of the distribution of power are, moreover, as Dr Worsley has already noted, especially troublesome when we are dealing with contemporary society, because a knowledge of how important decisions come to be made, of how and to what extent conscious attempts at manipulation occur, and of the actual goals being pursued by those wielding power, are all relatively more inaccessible than for the historical past; or, at any rate, the recent historical past. There are exceptions, such as the glimpses into the chaotic workings of high

First published in Sociological Review Monographs, *8, 1964.*

finance that were disclosed by the Bank Rate Tribunal; but they are exceptions which prove how little we really know and how badly we imagine. Even such important studies as Rogow and Shore's account of the nationalization of steel (1), or Clegg and Adams' investigation of the shipbuilding and engineering dispute of 1957 (2), do not fully explicate what was perhaps the decisive element in these more dramatic confrontations of power: namely, the actual range of interests which were activated by the immediate issues at stake, the degree to which they involved interests of a wider, class-based kind.

It is obvious, then, that discussions about the structure of power in the society as a whole (as opposed to the distribution of power within corporate bodies such as trade unions and political parties, about which we are proportionately less ignorant) are bound to involve judgements which become progressively more arbitrary the closer we get to the heart of the problem. By this I mean—and here I share Dr Worsley's point of view—the further we get away from such considerations as the numerical strength, degree of organization and other resources of the groups concerned, or the social characteristics, homogeneity, and affiliations of the various élites, and the closer we get to the problem of how, through time, power is actually employed to alter or to maintain a given institutional allocation of rewards, facilities and personnel. As we move away from the anatomy of power to its physiology, the scope for the intrusion of more or less arbitrary judgements about how the system 'really works' becomes correspondingly greater. For example, this recourse to 'judgement' is, I think, just as clearly evident in Professor Parsons' essay on 'The Distribution of Power in American Society' as it is in the basically demographic study of the 'power élite' by Professor Mills which Parsons is reviewing (3).

Dr Worsley's own judgement about the distribution of power in British society is contained in the proposition that 'the uninterrupted, albeit modified dominance of the property-owning classes in a society which has long been the most highly "proletarianized" in the modern world' must be regarded as 'one of the most striking phenomena of modern times'. From the context in which this sentence occurs, I understand that it contains a suggestion as to how power is to be measured. It is one which is basically similar to that put forward by Professor Marshall: namely, that 'if a class is strong enough to secure or to preserve those institutions that favour its activities, it may be said to be "governing" to that extent' (4). What Dr Worsley appears to be saying, then, is that the relatively small minority who own a great deal of the private wealth of the country are still the dominant power group in the society because they have been able to maintain more or less intact the institution of private economic power (and the gross inequalities of wealth) during a period which has seen the rise of a labour movement which has had nationalization and a greater equality in the distribution of wealth as its major political objectives. He would presumably share the conclusion of Mr Bottomore, who, in referring to the evidence of the redistribution of private wealth, writes that 'the upper class in Britain has been able to resist with considerable success the attacks upon its economic interests, and that in this sense of having power to defend its interests it has maintained itself during the present century as a ruling class' and that what seems to have taken place is 'not so much a reduction in the power of the upper class as a decline in the radicalism of the working class' (5). The present degree of inequality in the ownership of wealth is, of course, all the more surprising when set against the background of several obvious institutional developments which formally, at any rate, impose certain constraints upon the power of wealth as such: a universal franchise, collective bargaining, social services, even outright nationalization. For someone like Mr Crosland these and similar changes represent such a profound alteration of our society that he would regard the term 'capitalism' as applied to it as a complete misnomer. I myself would tend to agree with Dr Worsley that 'who owns what remains a crucial question; but what "they" do with it has been inadequately explored'. His point that there is no 'finite fund of power, any more than there is a fixed "wages fund"', while undoubtedly true, does not make life any easier for the analyst of power. It is, however, a salutary reminder that it is not enough, if we wish to study power realistically, to trace, as Professor Friedman has done (6), the *legal* changes that have limited the way in which the power of private capital *used to be used*. The relationships between economic and political power are exceedingly complex. For example, if Clegg and Adams are right in asserting that under conditions of full employment employers cannot succeed in imposing a 'wages freeze' (even with the support of the government), and if by now it is widely accepted that the maintenance of full employment is a precondition of gaining and retaining political power, then the voting power of the post-Keynesian wage-earner is a political resource that indirectly affects his bargaining power in the labour market. On the other hand, if we follow the line of argument suggested by Professor Wilson in his book on the politics of commercial television (7), the wealth expended on new forms of advertising, which are directed at this self-same wage-earner, may be having a much greater impact upon his sub-political aspirations, and hence be influencing his conception of the 'good society' much more profoundly, than all the wealth which the business community devotes in one way or another to overt political propaganda (8). Whatever the relationships between economic resources and political power or between political resources and economic power actually are in these two particular instances, it is with the net effect of complex and changing relationships of this *type* that the analysis of power must deal before we can decide how far something like the distribution of private wealth is really a safe index of the 'dominance' of the property-owning classes.

For it seems to me that it is to prejudge an historical development compounded of many such, and inadequately studied, complexities of power, if it is assumed that the viability of capitalist economic institutions is an index of, and, thereby, in great measure, if not wholly, attributable to, the *power* of the property-owning classes. I think it is easier to make this point by referring to Dr Worsley's mention of Sombart. 'To paraphrase Sombart', he writes, 'we might well ask: "Warum gibt es Keine Revolution in Vereinigten Königreich?" '. Since this statement follows directly after Dr Worsley's affirmation of 'the uninterrupted, albeit modified dominance of the property-owning classes', he presumably intends us to see a relationship between the two. But which? It is one thing to say that the property-owning classes are still dominant because there wasn't a socialist revolution; but it is quite another thing to say that there wasn't a socialist revolution because of the dominance of the property-owning classes. Dr Worsley appears to take the second view. He argues at several points that the best form of power rests not on coercion but on a successful appeal to its legitimacy; and that, in particular, the dominant groups in this country have been very successful in avoiding the open use of force. But does he wish to go further than this and argue that this successful appeal to legitimacy (and the avoidance of revolution) was in large measure a product of the successful manipulation of the lower classes, either by 'tactical concessions' or through what the Webbs used to call 'the capitalist domination of the mental environment'? He says that the 'study of power is not likely to make much serious headway unless it concentrates much more on the analysis of the formation and maintenance of legitimation' and suggests that 'those who control the instruments of power—from machine-guns to television-networks—may define legitimacy entirely themselves'. But how far would he go in arguing that the 'uninterrupted, albeit modified dominance of the property-owning classes' is a history of domination by means of engineered consensus? It seems to me that this is a crucial question, since, if the legitimacy of the institution of private property is not in large part a product of managed consensus, or manipulation, then the theory that the persistence of this institution (and its consequences for the distribution of wealth) is a measure of the *power* of the propertied classes, falls to the ground.

This is an important problem, though one which is extremely difficult to solve (9). In talking about manipulation, of course, one does not have to postulate a united ruling class, motivated by undiluted self-interest, busily at work, full-time, devising with great foresight and cunning devious ways and means of keeping the masses in order. On the other hand, the wealthy and the powerful will, from time to time, be faced with exigencies or presented with opportunities which quite naturally they, severally or collectively, will seek to control to their own advantage and in accordance with the conceptions of rightfulness of which they are the exponents. The degree to which manipulation enters into the strategy of dominant groups, the means by which it is possible, and the success with which it meets, will, of course, vary considerably from one social structure to another. Modern societies, given their conceptions of 'progress', their continuing processes of institutionalized change, and their need for a high level of commitment on the part of the masses, are especially likely to create the frame of mind and the instrumentalities by which this form of power comes into play. Although the full comparative study of industrialization from this point of view has still to be written, the various elements involved in what Professor Marshall calls 'citizenship' were clearly to a very considerable extent parts of a consistent (though not perhaps 'planned' and almost certainly imperfectly realized) strategy of what Professor Bendix has called the 'civic integration' of the working classes (10).

What is extremely hard to say is what effects these 'institutionalized' changes had on the development of working-class movements by contrast with what one may call the 'spontaneous' changes brought about by industrialization itself (as well as the 'unintended consequences' of institutionalized change). To whatever degree 'sponsored mobility' through educational reform was intended as a social 'safety valve', the proliferation of non-manual jobs relative to manual jobs, which has made mobility a reality, was a produce of economic growth. Whatever strategy of social control was involved in the extension of political rights, the progressive industrial redistribution of the labour force, away from communities of a type most favourable to the development of solidary working-class feeling, was a concomitant change of a 'spontaneous' kind which presumably worked in the same direction. Again, the 'natural' bureaucratization of working-class organizations, of which Michels made so much (11), was itself an 'unintended consequence' of the extension of civic rights and the development of a national economy; but it helped to routinize the expression of protest in ways that could not have been clearly foreseen by those who advocated these rights.

Basically, of course, in order to be able to judge how far attempts at manipulation, in so far as the intention can be proven, were successful, it would be necessary to indulge in Max Weber's form of mental experimentation and ask how the working-class movement would have developed in the absence of such measures. Realistically, the closest approach would be to compare countries whose rates of 'spontaneous' industrial development were not dissimilar, but whose rates of 'civic integration' proceeded at different rates. But even then, the difficulties are not entirely removed. Lipset, for example, has argued that the earlier and more easily a working class received the right to vote and organize on an effective basis, the less radical the labour movement. But, of course, one might argue that the less radical the labour movement, the more likely it would be to receive these rights in the first place.

NOTES

(1) A. A. Rogow and Peter Shore, *The Labour Government and British Industry* (Blackwell, Oxford 1955).
(2) H. A. Clegg and Rex Adams, *The Employers' Challenge* (Blackwell, Oxford 1957).

(3) T. Parsons, *Structure and Process in Modern Societies* (Free Press, Glencoe 1960), Chapter 6.

(4) T. H. Marshall, *Citizenship and Social Class* (Cambridge University Press, Cambridge 1950), p. 123.

(5) T. B. Bottomore, *Élites and Society* (Sir Isaac Pitman and Sons Ltd., London 1964), p. 35.

(6) W. Friedman, *Law and Social Change in Contemporary Britain* (Stevens, London 1951), Chapter 2.

(7) H. H. Wilson, *Pressure Group* (Secker and Warburg, London 1961).

(8) A form of influence, which, incidentally, does not appear to appeal to the 'patrician' elements of the élite, who, themselves somewhat disoriented in their search for an up-to-date version of the 'deferential' voter, view this attempt to cultivate the loyalties of the 'affluent' worker by the 'huckster' elements in their ranks with moral distaste and some political alarm.

(9) Of course, in many respectable academic circles, just to raise the issue of manipulation is sufficient to be threatened by that analytical bogeyman 'the conspiracy theory of society', which is often sufficient to send the more timid brethren scurrying to the safer, opposite, but no less ludicrous position of 'modernized social contract theory'; so that it is now more 'sensible' to start from the assumption that consensus is completely independent of power than that consensus is imposed by power.

(10) In one case, at least, planned with high deliberation with a view to the subversion of a radical (or supposedly radical) socialist movement; though, as even the slightest knowledge of the course of Bismarck's social policy will indicate, planned amid considerable moral dissension within the ruling group itself. See W. Vogel, *Bismarcks Arbeiterversicherung* (Braunschweig 1951).

(11) Recent work seems to indicate that the de-radicalization of social democracy in Germany, which Michels attributed to the process of internal bureaucratization of trade-union and party organization, in fact reflected the, by then, well-advanced 'integration' of the German working class into the wider society.

22

RULING ÉLITE OR RULING CLASS?

T B BOTTOMORE

The concepts of 'ruling class' and 'governing élite' are used in descriptions and explanations of political happenings, and their value must be judged by the extent to which they make possible reasonable answers to important questions about political systems. Do the rulers of society constitute a social group? Is it a cohesive or divided, an open or closed group? How are its members selected? What is the basis of their power? Is this power unrestricted or is it limited by that of other groups in society? Are there significant and regular differences between societies in these respects, and if so, how are they to be explained?

The two concepts are alike in emphasizing the division between rulers and ruled as one of the most important facts of social structure (1). But they state the division in different ways: the concept of a 'governing élite' contrasts the organized, ruling minority with the unorganized majority, or masses, while the concept of a 'ruling class' contrasts the dominant class with subject classes, which may themselves be organized, or be creating organizations. From these different conceptions arise differences in the way of conceiving the relations between rulers and ruled. In the Marxist theory, which employs the concept of a ruling class, the conflict between classes becomes the principal force producing changes of social structure; but in the élite theories—in spite of the fact that Pareto praised highly Marx's conception of class struggle which he described as 'profoundly true' (2)—the relations between the organized minority and the unorganized majority are necessarily represented as more passive, and the resulting problem of how to explain the rise and fall of ruling élites, if it is confronted at all, has to be dealt with either by postulating a recurrent decadence in the élite (Pareto) or by introducing the idea of the rise of new 'social forces' among the masses (Mosca) which brings the theory close to Marxism.

A further difference between the two concepts lies in the extent to which they make possible explanations of the cohesion of the

First published in Élites and Society *by T. B. Bottomore, Sir Isaac Pitman and Sons Ltd., 1964.*

ruling minority. The 'governing élite', defined as those who occupy the positions of command in a society, is merely assumed to be a cohesive group, unless other considerations, such as their membership of the wealthy class, or their aristocratic family origins are introduced (as they are consistently by Mosca, and occasionally by Pareto). But the 'ruling class', defined as the class which owns the major instruments of economic production in a society, is shown to be a cohesive social group; first, because its members have definite economic interests in common, and, more importantly, because it is engaged permanently in a conflict with other classes in society, through which its self-awareness and solidarity are continually enhanced. Furthermore, this concept states in a precise form what is the basis of the minority's ruling position, namely its economic dominance, while the concept of the governing élite' says little about the bases of the power which the élite possesses, except in so far as it incorporates elements from the Marxist theory of classes. In Mills' study of the 'power élite', there is an attempt to explain the power position of the three principal élites taken separately—that of the business executives by the growth in size and complexity of business corporations; that of the military chiefs by the growing scale and expense of the weapons of war, determined by technology and the state of international conflict; and that of the national political leaders, in a somewhat less satisfactory way, by the decline of the legislature, of local politics and of voluntary organizations—but the unity of the power élite as a single group, and the basis of *its* power, are not explained. Why is there *one* power élite and not *three*?

The superiority of the concept of 'ruling class' lies in its greater fertility and suggestiveness and in its value in the construction of theories. But I have pointed out earlier some of its defects, and it is now necessary to consider whether these can be overcome. The most important step in this direction would be to give up the Marxist view of the concept as a description of a real phenomenon which is to be observed in all societies in the same general form, and to regard it instead as an 'ideal type', in the sense which Max Weber gave to this term (3). If we treat the concept in this way we can proceed to ask how closely the relationships in a particular society approach the ideal type of a ruling class and subject classes; and so employ the concept, properly, as a tool of thought and investigation. It is then possible to see clearly that the idea of a 'ruling class' originated in the study of a particular historical situation—the end of feudalism and the beginnings of modern capitalism (4)—and to consider how far, and in what respects, other situations diverge from this ideal type, as a result of the absence or weakness of class formation, the influence of factors other than the ownership of property in the creation of classes, and the conflict between different forms of power.

There are two sorts of situation in which we can see especially plainly a divergence from the ideal type of a ruling class. One is that in which, although there is an 'upper class'—that is to say, a clearly demarcated social group which has in its possession a large part of the property of society and receives a disproportionately large share of the national income, and which has created on the basis of these economic advantages a distinctive culture and way of life—this class does not enjoy undisputed or unrestricted political power, in the sense that it is able to maintain easily its property rights or to transmit them unimpaired from generation to generation. This kind of situation has been discerned by many observers particularly in the modern democracies, in which, as I noted earlier, there is a potential opposition between the ownership of wealth and productive resources by a small upper class, and the possession of political power, through the franchise, by the mass of the population. As de Tocqueville once wrote: 'Il est contradictoire que le peuple soit à la fois misérable et souverain.'

In order to determine whether in such a case there is a 'ruling class' it is necessary first to examine the degree in which the upper class has been successful in perpetuating its ownership of property. We shall have to note, on one side, that in the democratic countries during the present century a considerable number of restrictions have been placed upon the use of private property, and that there has probably been some reduction in the inequalities of wealth and income, as a result of progressive taxation, and of the growth of publicly owned property and publicly administered social services. On the other side we must note that the decline in the proportion of private wealth owned by the upper class has been modest and very slow, and that the redistribution of income through taxation has not proceeded very far. The situation in Britain was very carefully examined by John Strachey (5), who concluded that

> up to 1939 there had been little or no redistribution of the national income in favour of the mass of the population, either through trade union pressure or

> budgetary changes . . . the wage earners' standard of life had risen just about in step with the rise in the total national income, their share remaining about constant . . . the broad pattern of distribution which emerges . . . is that at the end of the period under discussion [1939] as at the beginning [1911] some 10 per cent of the population got nearly one-half of the national income and the other 90 per cent got the other half of the national income (6).

In the following period, up to 1951, there was some redistribution of income which resulted in transferring some 10 per cent of the total national income from property owners to wage-earners, but this trend was probably reversed again after 1951 (7). Strachey concludes:

> All this is evidence that capitalism has in fact an innate tendency to extreme and ever-growing inequality. For how otherwise could all these cumulatively equalitarian measures which the popular forces have succeeded in enacting over the past hundred years have done little more than hold the position constant? Is it not clear that, if the workings of the system had not been continuously modified, it would have produced just that ever sharper polarization which Marx diagnosed as its essential tendency? (8)

It is evidence, to put the matter in another way, that the upper class in Britain has been able to resist with considerable success the attacks upon its economic interests, and that in this sense of having the power to defend its interests it has maintained itself during the present century as a ruling class. The situation in the other democratic countries, with the exception of the Scandinavian countries, does not differ greatly from that in Britain; in all of them, right-wing governments have been in power during most of the present century and the redistribution of wealth and income has occurred slowly, if at all. One must be sceptical, therefore, of the view that the extension of voting rights to the mass of the population can establish at once—or has in fact established in the short period of time in which modern democracies have existed—popular rule, and eliminate the power of a ruling class. What seems to have taken place in the democratic countries up to the present time is not so much a reduction in the power of the upper class as a decline in the radicalism of the working class.

The second type of situation in which there is a divergence from the 'ruling class—subject classes' model is that in which the ruling group is not a class in Marx's sense. One instance is provided by those societies in which a stratum of intellectuals or bureaucrats may be said to wield supreme power—in China under the rule of the *literati*, or in India under the rule of the Brahmins. Another instance is to be found in the present-day Communist countries where power is concentrated in the leaders of a political party. In these cases, however, we need to examine carefully how far the ruling stratum is clearly distinguishable from a ruling class. In India, the Brahmins, during the ages when they were most powerful, were also substantial landowners, and they were closely allied with the landowning warrior castes in the imperial and feudal periods of India's history. On occasion, they themselves founded ruling or noble houses, and there seems to have been, at times, an amount of movement of individuals and families between the Brahmin and Kshatriya (warrior) castes, which the doctrines of caste exclusiveness expounded in the classical texts do not indicate.

Again, in China, the *literati* were recruited, in the feudal period, from the principal landowning families, and at other times they came in the main from wealthy families (9); so that they were always closely linked with an upper class. There is, moreover, another important economic aspect of the rule of these groups of intellectuals and administrators to which Karl Wittfogel has drawn attention (10). One of the principal instruments of production in China and India (and in a number of other ancient societies) (11) was the system of irrigation, and the *literati* and the Brahmins, without owning this property upon which agricultural production depended, still exercised a more or less complete control over its use. Consequently they possessed, in addition to their ownership of land, a vital economic power which, according to Wittfogel, was the principal support of their political dominance.

But notwithstanding these qualifications the distinction between social strata of this kind and ruling classes which base their power directly upon the legal ownership of property remains. The possession of the means of administration may be, as Max Weber argued, an alternative to the possession of means of economic production, as a basis of political power (12). This distinction is perhaps more obvious in the case of the present-day Communist countries, in which there is no private ownership of the means of production, and in which the officials of the ruling party and the state control the economy. Wittfogel has attempted, in a very ingenious way, to assimilate this type of political power to the general category of 'oriental despotism' (13), but I think the differences are too great—the existence of private ownership of land and other resources, and the intimate bonds between the officials and the property-owning classes in one case, and the specific characteristics of rule by a political party in the other (14)—for this attempt to be successful. The political system of the Communist countries seems to me to approach the pure type of a 'power élite', that is, a group which, having come to power with the support or acquiescence of particular classes in the population, maintains itself in power chiefly by virtue of being an organized minority confronting the unorganized majority; whereas in the case of ancient China or India we have to deal with a system which combines the features of a ruling class and a power élite.

There is another element in the position of a ruling class, which has already been mentioned and which needs to be examined more fully in its bearing upon those situations in which the existence of such a class is doubtful. Since the power of a ruling class arises from its ownership of property, and since this property can easily be transmitted from generation to generation, the class has an enduring character. It is constituted by a group of families which remain as its component elements over long periods of time through the transmission of the family property. Its composition is not entirely immutable, for new families may enter it and old families may decline, but the greater part of its members continue from generation to generation. Only when there are rapid changes in the whole system of production and property ownership does the composition of the ruling class change significantly; and in that case we can say that one ruling class has been replaced by another. If, however, we were to find, in a particular society or type of society, that the movement of individuals and families between the different social levels was so continuous and so extensive that no group of families was able to maintain itself for any length of time in a situation of economic and political pre-eminence, then we should have to say that in such a society there was no ruling class. It is, in fact, this 'circulation of élites' (in the terminology of the élite theorists) or 'social mobility' (in the language of more recent sociological studies) that has been fixed upon by a number of writers as a second important characteristic of modern industrial societies—the first being universal suffrage—which must qualify severely, if it does not altogether exclude, the assertion that there is a ruling class in these societies. By this means we may arrive at the view, which was formulated by Karl Mannheim among others (15), that the development of industrial societies can properly be depicted as a movement from a class system to a system of élites, from a social hierarchy based upon the inheritance of property to one based upon merit and achievement.

This confrontation between the concepts of 'ruling class' and 'political élite' shows, I think, that, while on one level they may be totally opposed, as elements in wide-ranging theories which interpret political life, and especially the future possibilities of political organization, in very different ways, on another level they may be seen as complementary concepts, which refer to different types of political system or to different aspects of the same political system. With their help we can attempt to distinguish between societies in which there is a ruling class, and at the same time élites which represent particular aspects of its interests; societies in which there is no ruling class, but a political élite which founds its power upon the control of the administration, or upon military force, rather than upon property ownership and inheritance; and societies in which there exists a multiplicity of élites among which no cohesive and enduring group of powerful individuals or families seems to be discoverable at all. In order to establish such a classification we need to examine more closely . . . the circulation of élites, the relations between élites and classes, and the ways in which new élites and new classes are formed.

NOTES

(1) 'From the point of view of scientific research the real superiority of the concept of the ruling, or political, class ["political élite" in our terminology T.B.B.] lies in the fact that the varying structure of ruling classes has a preponderant importance in determining the political type, and also the level of civilization, of the different peoples'. G. Mosca, *Ruling Class* [McGraw Hill, London 1960].
(2) Pareto, *Les systèmes*, II, p. 405.
(3) An ideal-type concept 'brings together certain relationships and events of historical life into a complex which is conceived as an internally consistent system . . . this construction itself is like a *utopia* which has been arrived at by the analytical accentuation of certain elements of reality . . . it *is* no hypothesis but it offers guidance in the construction of hypotheses. It is not a *description* of reality but it aims to give unambiguous means of expression to such a description. . . . An ideal type is formed by the one-sided

accentuation of one or more points of view and by the synthesis of a great many diffuse, discrete, more or less present and occasionally absent *concrete individual* phenomena, which are arranged according to those one-sidedly emphasized viewpoints into a unified *analytical* construct'. Max Weber, *The Methodology of the Social Sciences* [Collier-Macmillan, London 1950], p. 90.

(4) As Croce observed of the whole theory of historical materialism: 'The materialistic view of history arose out of the need to account for a definite social phenomenon, not from an abstract inquiry into the factors of historical life'. B. Croce, *Historical Materialism and the Economics of Karl Marx* [Frank Cass, London 1966], p. 17.

(5) John Strachey, *Contemporary Capitalism* [Gollancz, London 1956], Chapter VIII, 'The Real Development'. Strachey draws upon a number of other studies, including Douglas Jay, *The Socialist Case;* and Dudley Seers, *The Levelling of Incomes since 1938* and *Has the Distribution of Income Become More Unequal?*

(6) op. cit., pp. 137–8.

(7) Ibid., p. 146. More recently, Richard M. Titmuss, in his *Income Distribution and Social Change* [Unwin University Books, London 1962], has undertaken the most thorough study yet made in Britain of the sources of information about the distribution of income. The chief purpose of his study is to inquire into the adequacy of the data which have been used by students of national income and which are derived mainly from reports and studies by the Board of Inland Revenue; and he shows in detail how inadequate they are to determine with any precision the distribution of income at a given time or its changes over time. Nevertheless, the additional factors which in his view need to be taken into account, especially in estimating the wealth and income which accrues to the upper class—life assurances, superannuation, tax-free lump sums on retirement, education covenants, discretionary trusts, expense accounts and capital gains—work in the main to increase inequality, and a study of their magnitude suggests that any movement towards greater equality of income or wealth, since 1938, has been, to say the least, of modest dimensions. Titmuss himself concludes that '. . . we should be much more hesitant in suggesting that any equalizing forces at work in Britain since 1938 can be promoted to the status of a "natural law" and projected into the future. As we have shown, there are often forces, deeply rooted in the social structure and fed by many complex institutional factors inherent in large-scale economies, operating in reverse directions. Some of the more critical of these factors, closely linked with the distribution of power, and containing within themselves the seeds of long-lasting effects—as, for instance, in the case of settlements and trusts—function as concealed multipliers of inequality. They are not measured at present by the statistics of income and only marginally by the statistics of wealth. Even so, there is more than a hint from a number of studies that income inequality has been increasing since 1949 whilst the ownership of wealth, which is far more highly concentrated in the United Kingdom than in the United States, has probably become still more unequal and, in terms of family ownership, possibly strikingly more unequal, in recent years' (p. 198).

(8) Strachey, op. cit., pp. 150–1.

(9) See [T. B. Bottomore, *Élites and Society* (Sir Isaac Pitman and Sons Ltd., London 1964)] p. 65.

(10) Karl Wittfogel, *Oriental Despotism* [Yale University Press, 1963].

(11) See Julian H. Steward *et al.*, *Irrigation Civilizations: a Comparative Study*.
(12) The characteristics of bureaucratic societies have been examined at length in a recent study: S. N. Eisenstadt, *The Political Systems of Empires* [Collier-Macmillan, London 1969].
(13) Wittfogel, op. cit.
(14) This is discussed further in a later chapter [of *Élites and Society*] see pp. 77–80.
(15) See especially, *Man and Society* [Routledge, London 1940], Part II, Chapter II.

23

A CRITIQUE OF THE RULING ÉLITE MODEL

ROBERT A DAHL

A great many people seem to believe that 'they' run things: the old families, the bankers, the City Hall machine, or the party boss behind the scene. This kind of view evidently has a powerful and many-sided appeal. It is simple, compelling, dramatic, 'realistic'. It gives one standing as an inside-dopester. For individuals with a strong strain of frustrated idealism, it has just the right touch of hard-boiled cynicism. Finally, the hypothesis has one very great advantage over many alternative explanations: it can be cast in a form that makes it virtually impossible to disprove.

Consider the last point for a moment. There is a type of quasi-metaphysical theory made up of what might be called an infinite regress of explanations. The ruling-élite model *can* be interpreted in this way. If the overt leaders of a community do not appear to constitute a ruling élite, then the theory can be saved by arguing that behind the overt leaders there is a set of covert leaders who do. If subsequent evidence shows that this covert group does not make a ruling élite, then the theory can be saved by arguing that behind the first covert group there is another, and so on.

Now whatever else it may be, a theory that cannot even in principle be controverted by empirical evidence is not a scientific theory. The least that we can demand of any ruling-élite theory that purports to be more than a metaphysical or polemical doctrine is, first, that the burden of proof be on the proponents of the theory and not on its critics; and, second, that there be clear criteria according to which the theory could be disproved.

With these points in mind, I shall proceed in two stages. First, I shall try to clarify the meaning of the concept 'ruling élite' by describing a very simple form of what I conceive to be a ruling-élite system. Second, I shall indicate what would be required in principle as a simple but satisfactory test of any hypothesis asserting that

First published in the American Political Science Review, vol. *52, No. 2, June 1958.*

a particular political system is, in fact, a ruling-élite system. Finally, I shall deal with some objections.

I. A simple ruling-élite system

If a ruling élite hypothesis says anything, surely it asserts that within some specific political system there exists a group of people who to some degree exercise power or influence over other actors in the system. I shall make the following assumptions about power:[1]

1. In order to compare the relative influence of two actors (these may be individuals, groups, classes, parties, or what not), it is necessary to state the scope of the responses upon which the actors have an effect. The statement 'A has more power than B' is so ambiguous as to verge on the meaningless, since it does not specify the scope.

2. One cannot compare the relative influence of two actors who always perform identical actions with respect to the group influenced. What this means as a practical matter is that ordinarily one can test for differences in influence only where there are cases of differences in initial preferences. At one extreme, the difference may mean that one group prefers alternative A and another group prefers B, A and B being mutually exclusive. At the other extreme, it may mean that one group prefers alternative A to other alternatives, and another group is indifferent. If a political system displayed complete consensus at all times, we should find it impossible to construct a satisfactory direct test of the hypothesis that it was a ruling-élite system, although indirect and rather unsatisfactory tests might be devised.

Consequently, to know whether or not we have a ruling élite, we must have a political system in which there is a difference in preferences, from time to time, among the individual human beings in the system. Suppose, now, that among these individuals there is a set whose preferences regularly prevail in all cases of disagreement, or at least in all cases of disagreement over key political issues (a term I propose to leave undefined here). Let me call such a set of individuals a 'controlling group'. In a full-fledged democracy operating strictly according to majority rule, the majority would constitute a controlling group, even though the individual members

[1] See Robert A. Dahl, 'The Concept of Power', *Behavioral Science*, vol. 2 (July 1957), pp. 201–15.

of the majority might change from one issue to the next. But since our model is to represent a ruling-élite system, we require that the set be *less than a majority in size*.

However, in any representative system with single-member voting districts where more than two candidates receive votes, a candidate *could* win with less than a majority of votes; and it is possible, therefore, to imagine a truly sovereign legislature elected under the strictest 'democratic' rules that was none the less governed by a legislative majority representing the first preferences of a minority of voters. Yet I do not think we would want to call such a political system a ruling-élite system. Because of this kind of difficulty, I propose that we exclude from our definition of a ruling élite any controlling group that is a product of rules that are actually followed (that is, 'real' rules) under which a majority of individuals could dominate if they took certain actions permissible under the 'real' rules. In short, to constitute a ruling élite a controlling group must not be *a pure artifact of democratic rules*.

A ruling élite, then, is a controlling group less than a majority in size that is not a pure artifact of democratic rules. It is a minority of individuals whose preferences regularly prevail in cases of differences in preference on key political issues. If we are to avoid an infinite regress of explanations, the composition of the ruling élite must be more or less definitely specified.

II. Some bad tests

The hypothesis we are dealing with would run along these lines: 'Such and such a political system (the U.S., the U.S.S.R., New Haven, or the like) is a ruling-élite system in which the ruling élite has the following membership.' Membership would then be specified by name, position, socio-economic class, socio-economic roles or what not.

Let me now turn to the problem of testing a hypothesis of this sort, and begin by indicating a few tests that are sometimes mistakenly taken as adequate.

The first improper test confuses a ruling élite with a group that has a high *potential for control*. Let me explain. Suppose a set of individuals in a political system has the following property: there is a very high probability that if they agree on a key political alternative, and if they all act in some specified way, then that alternative will be chosen. We may say of such a group that it has a *high potential for control*. In a large and complex society like ours, there may be many such groups. For example, the bureaucratic triumvirate of Professor Mills would appear to have a high potential for control.[1] In the City of New Haven, with which I have some acquaintance, I do not doubt that the leading business figures together with the leaders of both political parties have a high potential for control. But a potential for control is not, except in a peculiarly Hobbesian world, equivalent to actual control. If the military leaders of this country and their subordinates agreed that it was desirable, they could most assuredly establish a military dictatorship of the most overt sort; nor would they need the aid of leaders of business corporations or the executive branch of our government. But they have not set up such a dictatorship. For what is lacking are the premises I mentioned earlier, namely agreement on a key political alternative and some set of specific implementing actions. That is to say, a group may have a high potential for control and a *low potential for unity*. The actual *political effectiveness* of a group is a function of its potential for control *and* its potential for unity. Thus a group with a relatively low potential for control but a high potential for unity may be more politically effective than a group with a high potential for control but a low potential for unity.

The second improper test confuses a ruling élite with a group of individuals who have more influence than any others in the system. I take it for granted that in every human organization some individuals have more influence over key decisions than do others. Political equality may well be among the most Utopian of all human goals. But it is fallacious to assume that the absence of political equality proves the existence of a ruling élite.

The third improper test, which is closely related to the preceding one, is to generalize from a single scope of influence. Neither logically nor empirically does it follow that a group with a high degree of influence over one scope will necessarily have a high degree of influence over another scope within the same system. This is a matter to be determined empirically. Any investigation that does not take into account the possibility that different élite groups have different scopes is suspect. By means of sloppy questions one

[1] C. Wright Mills, *The Power Élite* (Oxford University Press, New York 1956), *passim*.

could easily seem to discover that there exists a unified ruling élite in New Haven; for there is no doubt that small groups of people make many key decisions. It appears to be the case, however, that the small group that runs urban redevelopment is not the same as the small group that runs public education, and neither is quite the same as the two small groups that run the two parties. Moreover the small group that runs urban redevelopment with a high degree of unity would almost certainly disintegrate if its activities were extended to either education or the two political parties.

III. A proposed test

If tests like these are not valid, what can we properly require?

Let us take the simplest possible situation. Assume that there have been some number—I will not say how many—of cases where there has been disagreement within the political system on key political choices. Assume further that the hypothetical ruling élite prefers one alternative and other actors in the system prefer other alternatives. Then unless it is true that in all or very nearly all of these cases the alternative preferred by the ruling élite is actually adopted, the hypothesis (that the system is dominated by the specified ruling élite) is clearly false.

I do not want to pretend either that the research necessary to such a test is at all easy to carry out or that community life lends itself conveniently to strict interpretation according to the requirements of the test. *But I do not see how anyone can suppose that he has established the dominance of a specific group in a community or a nation without basing his analysis on the careful examination of a series of concrete decisions*. And these decisions must either constitute the universe or a fair sample from the universe of key political decisions taken in the political system.

Now it is a remarkable and indeed astounding fact that neither Professor Mills nor Professor Hunter has seriously attempted to examine an array of specific cases to test his major hypothesis.[1] Yet I suppose these two works more than any others in the social science of the last few years have sought to interpret complex political systems essentially as instances of a ruling élite.

[1] Mills, op. cit., Floyd Hunter, *Community Power Structure* (University of North Carolina Press, Chapel Hill, 1953).

To sum up: the hypothesis of the existence of a ruling élite can be strictly tested only if

1. The hypothetical ruling élite is a well-defined group.
2. There is a fair sample of cases involving key political decisions in which the preferences of the hypothetical ruling élite run counter to those of any other likely group that might be suggested.
3. In such cases, the preferences of the élite regularly prevail.

IV. Difficulties and objections

Several objections might be raised against the test I propose.

First, one might argue that the test is *too weak*. The argument would run as follows: If a ruling élite *doesn't* exist in a community, then the test is satisfactory; that is, if every hypothetical ruling élite is compared with alternative control groups, and in fact no ruling élite exists, then the test will indeed show that there is no minority whose preferences regularly prevail on key political alternatives. But—it might be said—suppose a ruling élite *does* exist. The test will not *necessarily* demonstrate its existence, since we may not have selected the right group as our hypothetical ruling élite. Now this objection is valid; but it suggests the point I made at the outset about the possibility of an infinite regress of explanations. Unless we use the test on every possible combination of individuals in the community, we cannot be certain that there is not some combination that constitutes a ruling élite. But since there is no more *a priori* reason to assume that a ruling élite does exist than to assume that one does not exist, the burden of proof does not rest upon the critic of the hypothesis, but upon its proponent. And a proponent must specify what group he has in mind as his ruling élite. Once the group is specified, then the test I have suggested is, at least in principle, valid.

Second, one could object that the test is *too strong*. For suppose that the members of the 'ruled' group are indifferent as to the outcome of various political alternatives. Surely (one could argue) if there is another group that regularly gets its way in the face of this indifference, it is in fact the ruling group in the society. Now my reasons for wishing to discriminate this case from the other involve more than a mere question of the propriety of using the term 'ruling élite', which is only a term of convenience. There is, I think, a difference of some theoretical significance between a system in which a small group dominates over another that is opposed to it, and one in which a group dominates over an indifferent mass. In the second case, the alternatives at stake can hardly be regarded as 'key political issues' if we assume the point of view of the indifferent mass; whereas in the first case it is reasonable to say that the alternatives involve a key political issue from the standpoint of both groups. Earlier I refrained from defining the concept 'key political issues'. If we were to do so at this point, it would seem reasonable to require as a necessary although possibly not a sufficient condition that the issue should involve actual disagreement in preferences among two or more groups. In short, the case of 'indifference vs. preference' would be ruled out.

However, I do not mean to dispose of the problem simply by definition. The point is to make sure that the two systems are distinguished. The test for the second, weaker system of élite rule would then be merely a modification of the test proposed for the first and more stringent case. It would again require an examination of a series of cases showing uniformly that when 'the word' was authoritatively passed down from the designated élite, the hitherto indifferent majority fell into ready compliance with an alternative that had nothing else to recommend it intrinsically.

Third, one might argue that the test will not discriminate between a true ruling élite and a ruling élite together with its satellites. This objection is in one sense true and in one sense false. It is true that on a series of key political questions, an apparently unified group might prevail who would, according to our test, thereby constitute a ruling élite. Yet an inner core might actually make the decisions for the whole group.

However, one of two possibilities must be true. Either the inner core and the front men always agree at all times in the decision process, or they do not. But if they always agree, then it follows from one of our two assumptions about influence that the distinction between an 'inner core' and 'front men' has no operational meaning; that is, there is no conceivable way to distinguish between them. And if they do not always agree, then the test simply requires a comparison at those points in time when they disagree. Here again, the advantages of concrete cases are palpable, for these enable one to discover who initiates or vetoes and who merely complies.

Fourth, it might be said that the test is either too demanding or else too arbitrary. If it requires that the hypothetical élite prevails in *every single case*, then it demands too much. But if it does not require this much, then at what point can a ruling élite be said to exist? When it prevails in seven cases out of ten? Eight out of ten? Nine out of ten? Or what? There are two answers to this objection. On the one hand, it would be quite reasonable to argue, I think, that since we are considering only key political choices and not trivial decisions, if the élite does not prevail in *every* case in which it disagrees with a contrary group, it cannot properly be called a ruling élite. But since I have not supplied an independent definition of the term 'key political choices', I must admit that this answer is not wholly satisfactory. On the other hand, I would be inclined to suggest that in this instance as in many others we ought not to assume that political reality will be as discrete and discontinuous as the concepts we find convenient to employ. We can say that a system approximates to a true ruling élite system, to a greater or lesser degree, without insisting that it exemplify the extreme and limiting case.

Fifth, it might be objected that the test I have proposed would not work in the most obvious of all cases of ruling élites, namely in the totalitarian dictatorships. For the control of the élite over the expression of opinion is so great that overtly there is no disagreement; hence no cases on which to base a judgement arise. This objection is a fair one. But we are not concerned here with totalitarian systems. We are concerned with the application of the techniques of modern investigation to American communities, where, except in very rare cases, terror is not so pervasive that the investigator is barred from discovering the preferences of citizens. Even in Little Rock, for example, newspaper men seemed to have had little difficulty in finding diverse opinions; and a northern political scientist of my acquaintance has managed to complete a large number of productive interviews with White and Negro Southerners on the touchy subject of integration.

Finally one could argue that even in a society like ours a ruling élite might be so influential over ideas, attitudes and opinions that a kind of false consensus will exist—not the phony consensus of a terroristic totalitarian dictatorship but the manipulated and superficially self-imposed adherence to the norms and goals of the élite by broad sections of a community. A good deal of Professor Mills's argument can be interpreted in this way, although it is not clear to me whether this is what he means to rest his case on.

Even more than the others this objection points to the need to be circumspect in interpreting the evidence. Yet here, too, it seems to me that the hypothesis cannot be satisfactorily confirmed without something equivalent to the test I have proposed. For once again either the consensus is perpetual and unbreakable, in which case there is no conceivable way of determining who is ruler and who is ruled; or it is not. But if it is not, then there is some point in the process of forming opinions at which the one group will be seen to initiate and veto, while the rest merely respond. And we can only discover these points *by an examination of a series of concrete cases where key decisions are made*: decisions on taxation and expenditures, subsidies, welfare programmes, military policy, and so on.

It would be interesting to know, for example, whether the initiation and veto of alternatives having to do with our missile programme would confirm Professor Mills's hypothesis, or indeed any reasonable hypothesis about the existence of a ruling élite. To the superficial observer it would scarcely appear that the military itself is a homogeneous group, to say nothing of their supposed coalition with corporate and political executives. If the military alone or the coalition together is a ruling élite, it is either incredibly incompetent in administering its own fundamental affairs or else it is unconcerned with the success of its policies to a degree that I find astounding.

However I do not mean to examine the evidence here. For the whole point of this paper is that the evidence for a ruling élite, either in the United States or in any specific community, has not yet been properly examined so far as I know. And the evidence has not been properly examined, I have tried to argue, because the examination has not employed satisfactory criteria to determine what constitutes a fair test of the basic hypothesis.

24

THE PROBLEM OF THE CAPITALIST STATE

NICOL POULANTZAS

Ralph Miliband's recently published work, *The State in Capitalist Society*,[1] is in many respects of capital importance. The book is extremely substantial, and cannot decently be summarized in a few pages: I cannot recommend its reading too highly. I will limit myself here to a few critical comments, in the belief that only criticism can advance Marxist theory. For the specificity of this theory compared with other theoretical problematics lies in the extent to which Marxist theory provides itself, in the very act of its foundation, with the means of its own internal criticism. I should state at the outset that my critique will not be 'innocent': having myself written on the question of the State in my book *Pouvoir Politique et Classes Sociales*,[2] these comments will derive from epistemological positions presented there which differ from those of Miliband.

First of all, some words on the fundamental merits of Miliband's book. The theory of the State and of political power has, with rare exceptions such as Gramsci, been neglected by Marxist thought. This neglect has a number of different causes, related to different phases of the working-class movement. In Marx himself this neglect, more apparent than real, is above all due to the fact that his principal theoretical object was the capitalist mode of production, within which the economy not only holds the role of determinant in the last instance, but also the dominant role—while for example in the feudal mode of production, Marx indicates that if the economy still has the role of determinant in the last instance, it is ideology in its religious form that holds the dominant role. Marx thus concentrated on the economic level of the capitalist mode of production, and did not deal specifically with the other levels such as the State: he dealt only with these levels through their *effects* on the economy (for example, in the passages of *Capital*

[1] Weidenfeld and Nicholson, London 1969, 292 pp.

[2] Maspero, Paris 1968.

First published in New Left Review, *No. 58, 1969.*

on factory legislation). In Lenin, the reasons are different: involved in direct political practice, he dealt with the question of the State only in essentially polemical works, such as *State and Revolution*, which do not have the theoretical status of certain of his texts such as *The Development of Capitalism in Russia*.

How, by contrast, is the neglect of theoretical study of the State in the Second International, and in the Third International after Lenin, to be explained? Here I would advance, with all necessary precautions, the following thesis: the absence of a study of the State derived from the fact that the dominant conception of these Internationals was a deviation, *economism*, which is generally accompanied by an absence of revolutionary strategy and objectives —even when it takes a 'leftist' or Luxemburgist form. In effect, economism considers that other levels of social reality, including the State, are simple epiphenomena reducible to the economic 'base'. Thereby a specific study of the State becomes superfluous. Parallel with this, economism considers that every change in the social system happens first of all in the economy and that political action should have the economy as its principal objective. Once again, a specific study of the State is redundant. Thus economism leads either to reformism and trade-unionism, or to forms of 'leftism' such as syndicalism. For, as Lenin showed, the principal objective of revolutionary action is *State power* and the necessary precondition of any socialist revolution is the destruction of the bourgeois State apparatus.

Economism and the absence of revolutionary strategy are manifest in the Second International. They are less obvious in the Third International, yet in my view what fundamentally determined the theory and practice of 'Stalinist' policy, dominant in the Comintern probably from 1928, was nevertheless the same economism and absence of a revolutionary strategy. This is true both of the 'leftist' period of the Comintern until 1935, and of the revisionist-reformist period after 1935. This economism determined the absence of a theory of the State in the Third International and this *relation* (economism/absence of a theory of the State) is perhaps nowhere more evident than in its analyses of fascism—precisely where the Comintern had most need of such a theory of the State. Considerations of a concrete order both confirm and explain this. Since the *principal symptoms* of Stalinist politics were located in the relations between the State apparatus and the

Communist Party in the U.S.S.R., symptoms visible in the famous Stalin Constitution of 1936, it is very comprehensible that study of the State remained a forbidden topic *par excellence*.

It is in this context that Miliband's work helps to overcome a major lacuna. As is always the case when a scientific theory is lacking, bourgeois conceptions of the State and of political power have pre-emptied the terrain of political theory, almost unchallenged. Miliband's work is here truly *cathartic:* he methodically attacks these conceptions. Rigorously deploying a formidable mass of empirical material in his examination of the concrete social formations of the U.S.A., England, France, Germany or Japan, he not only radically demolishes bourgeois ideologies of the State, but provides us with a positive knowledge that these ideologies have never been able to produce.

However, the procedure chosen by Miliband—a *direct* reply to bourgeois ideologies by the immediate examination of concrete fact—is also to my mind the source of the faults of his book. Not that I am against the study of the 'concrete': on the contrary, having myself relatively neglected this aspect of the question in my own work (with its somewhat different aim and object), I am only the more conscious of the necessity for concrete analyses. I simply mean that a precondition of any scientific approach to the 'concrete' is to make explicit the epistemological principles of its own treatment of it. Now it is important to note that Miliband nowhere deals with the Marxist theory of the State as such, although it is constantly implicit in his work. He takes it as a sort of 'given' in order to reply to bourgeois ideologies by examining the facts in its light. Here I strongly believe that Miliband is wrong, for the absence of explicit presentation of principles in the order of exposition of a scientific discourse is not innocuous: above all in a domain like the theory of the State, where a Marxist theory, as we have seen, has yet to be constituted. In effect, one has the impression that this absence often leads Miliband to attack bourgeois ideologies of the State whilst placing himself on their own terrain. Instead of *displacing* the epistemological terrain and submitting these ideologies to the critique of Marxist science by demonstrating their inadequacy to the real (as Marx does, notably in the *Theories of Surplus-Value*), Miliband appears to omit this first step. Yet the analyses of modern epistemology show that it is never possible simply to oppose 'concrete facts' to concepts, but that these must be attacked by other parallel concepts situated in a different problematic. For it is only by means of these new concepts that the old notions can be confronted with 'concrete reality'.

Let us take a simple example. Attacking the prevailing notion of 'plural élites', whose ideological function is to deny the existence of a ruling class, Miliband's reply, which he supports by 'facts', is that this plurality of *élites* does not exclude the existence of a ruling *class*, for it is precisely these élites that constitute this class:[1] this is close to Bottomore's response to the question. Now, I maintain that in replying to the adversary in this way, one places oneself on his ground and thereby risks floundering in the swamp of his ideological imagination, thus missing a scientific explanation of the 'facts'. What Miliband avoids is the necessary preliminary of a critique of the ideological notion of élite in the light of the scientific concepts of Marxist theory. Had this critique been made, it would have been evident that the 'concrete reality' concealed by the notion of 'plural élites'—the ruling class, the fractions of this class, the hegemonic class, the governing class, the State apparatus—can only be grasped if the very notion of élite is rejected. For concepts and notions are never innocent, and by employing the notions of the adversary to reply to him, one legitimizes them and permits their persistence. Every notion or concept only has meaning within a whole theoretical problematic that founds it: extracted from this problematic and imported 'uncritically' into Marxism, they have absolutely uncontrollable effects. They always surface when least expected, and constantly risk clouding scientific analysis. In the extreme case, one can be unconsciously and surreptitiously contaminated by the very epistemological principles of the adversary, that is to say the problematic that founds the concepts which have not been theoretically criticized, believing them simply refuted by the facts. This is more serious: for it is then no longer a question merely of external notions 'imported' into Marxism, but of principles that risk vitiating the use made of Marxist concepts themselves.

Is this the case with Miliband? I do not believe that the consequences of his procedure have gone so far. It nevertheless remains true that, as I see it, Miliband sometimes allows himself to be unduly influenced by the methodological principles of the adversary. How is this manifested? Very briefly, I would say that it is visible

[1] Miliband, pp. 24 ff and 47.

in the difficulties that Miliband has in comprehending social classes and the State as *objective structures*, and their relations as an *objective system of regular connections*, a structure and a system whose agents, 'men', are in the words of Marx, 'bearers' of it—*träger*. Miliband constantly gives the impression that for him social classes or 'groups' are in some way reducible to *inter-personal relations*, that the State is reducible to inter-personal relations of the members of the diverse 'groups' that constitute the State apparatus, and finally that the relation between social classes and the State is itself reducible to inter-personal relations of 'individuals' composing social groups and 'individuals' composing the State apparatus.

I have indicated, in an earlier article in N.L.R., that this conception seems to me to derive from a *problematic of the subject* which has had constant repercussions in the history of Marxist thought.[1] According to this problematic, the agents of a social formation, 'men', are not considered as the 'bearers' of objective instances (as they are for Marx), but as the genetic principle of the levels of the social whole. This is a problematic of *social actors*, of individuals as the origin of *social action:* sociological research thus leads finally, not to the study of the objective co-ordinates that determine the distribution of agents into social classes and the contradictions between these classes, but to the search for *finalist* explanations founded on the *motivations of conduct* of the individual actors. This is notoriously one of the aspects of the problematic both of Weber and of contemporary functionalism. To transpose this problematic of the subject into Marxism is in the end to admit the epistemological principles of the adversary and to risk vitiating one's own analyses.

Let us now consider some of the concrete themes of Miliband's book in the light of this preamble.

1. The false problem of managerialism

The first problem which Miliband discusses, very correctly, is that of the *ruling class*, by way of reply to the current bourgeois ideologies of *managerialism*. According to these ideologies, the contemporary separation of private ownership and control has transferred economic power from entrepreneurs to managers. The latter

[1] 'Marxist Political Theory in Great Britain', N.L.R. 43.

have no interest as owners in the strict sense, and hence do not seek profit as their aim—in other words, profit is not a motivation of their conduct, but growth, or development. Since the ruling class is here defined by the quest for profit, and this quest no longer characterizes the directors of the economy, the ruling class itself no longer exists: we are now confronted with a 'plurality of élites', of which the managers are one. What is Miliband's response to this?[1] He takes these ideologies literally and turns their own arguments against them: in fact, managers do seek profit as the goal of their actions, for this is how the capitalist system works. Seeking private profit, they also make up part of the ruling class, for the contradiction of the capitalist system according to Marx, Miliband tells us, is 'the contradiction between its ever more social character and its enduringly private purpose'.[2] While not excluding the existence of some managerial goals relatively different from those of owners, Miliband considers managers as one among the distinct economic élites composing the ruling class.

I consider this a mistaken way of presenting the problem. To start with, the distinctive criterion for membership of the capitalist class for Marx *is in no way* a motivation of conduct, that is to say the search for profit as the 'aim of action'. For there may well exist capitalists who are not motivated by profit, just as there are non-capitalists (the petty-bourgeoisie in small-scale production, for instance) who by contrast have just such a motivation. Marx's criterion is the objective place in production and the ownership of the means of production. It should be remembered that even Max Weber had to admit that what defined the capitalist was not 'the lure of gain'. For Marx, profit is not a motivation of conduct—even one 'imposed' by the system—it is an objective category that designates a part of realized surplus value. In the same way, the fundamental contradiction of the capitalist system, according to Marx, is not at all a contradiction between its social character and its 'private purpose', but a contradiction between the socialization of productive forces and their *private appropriation*. Thus the characterization of the existing social system as capitalist in no way depends on the motivations of the conduct of managers. Furthermore: to characterize the class position of managers, one need not refer to the motivations of their conduct, but only to their place in production and their relationship to the ownership of the means of

[1] Miliband, ibid. [2] Miliband, p. 34.

production. Here both Bettleheim and myself have noted that it is necessary to distinguish, in the term 'property' used by Marx, formal legal property, which may not belong to the 'individual' capitalist, and *economic property or real appropriation*, which is the only genuine *economic power*.[1] This economic property, which is what matters as far as distribution into classes is concerned, still belongs well and truly to *capital*. The manager exercises only a functional delegation of it.

From this point of view, the managers as such do not constitute a distinct fraction of the capitalist class. Miliband, basing himself on the non-pertinent distinction of motivations of conduct, is led to consider the managers a distinct 'economic élite'. By doing so, he not only attributes to them an importance they do not possess, but he is prevented from seeing what is important. For in effect, what matters is not the differences and relations between 'economic élites' based on diverging aims, but something of which Miliband says virtually nothing, *the differences and relations between fractions of capital*. The problem is not that of a plurality of 'economic élites' but of fractions of the capitalist class. Can a Marxist pass over in silence the existent differences and relations, under imperialism, between comprador monopoly capital, national monopoly capital, non-monopoly capital, industrial capital, or financial capital?

2. The question of bureaucracy

The next problem that Miliband selects for discussion, again correctly, is that of the relation between the ruling class and the State. Here too Miliband's approach to the question is to provide a direct rebuttal of bourgeois ideologies. These ideologies affirm the *neutrality* of the State, representing the general interest, in relation to the divergent interests of 'civil society'. Some of them (Aron, for example) claim that the capitalist class has never truly *governed* in capitalist societies, in the sense that its members have rarely participated directly in the government; others claim that the members of the State apparatus, the 'civil servants', are neutral with respect to the interests of social groups. What is the general line of Miliband's response to these ideologies? Here too he is led to take up the

[1] Bettleheim [C.], *La Transition vers l'Economie Socialiste*, and Poulantzas, *Pouvoir Politique et Classes Sociales* [Maspero 1968], pp. 23 ff.

reverse position to these ideologies, to turn their argument against them. He does so in two ways. First of all he establishes that the members of the capitalist class have in fact often directly participated in the State apparatus and in the government.[1] Then, having established the relation between members of the State apparatus and the ruling class, he shows (a) that the *social origin* of members of the 'summit' of the State apparatus is that of the ruling class, and (b) that *personal ties* of influence, status and milieu are established between the members of the ruling class and those of the State apparatus.[2]

I have no intention of contesting the value of Miliband's analyses, which on the contrary appear to me to have a capital *demystifying* importance. Yet however exact in itself, the way chosen by Miliband does not seem to me to be the most significant one. Firstly, because the *direct* participation of members of the capitalist class in the State apparatus and in the government, even where it exists, is not the important side of the matter. The relation between the bourgeois class and the State is an *objective relation*. This means that if the *function* of the State in a determinate social formation and the *interests* of the dominant class in this formation *coincide*, it is by reason of the system itself: the direct participation of members of the ruling class in the State apparatus is not the *cause* but the *effect*, and moreover a chance and contingent one, of this objective coincidence.

In order to establish this coincidence, it would have been necessary to make explicit the role of the State as a specific instance, a regional structure, of the social whole. Miliband, however, seems to reduce the role of the State to the conduct and 'behaviour' of the members of the State apparatus.[3] If Miliband had first established that the State is precisely *the factor of cohesion of a social formation and the factor of reproduction of the conditions of production of a system* that itself determines the domination of one class over the others, he would have seen clearly that the participation, whether direct or indirect, of this class in government *in no way changes things*. Indeed in the case of the capitalist State, one can go further: it can be said that the capitalist State best serves the interests of the capitalist class only when the members of this class do not participate directly in the State apparatus, that is to say when the *ruling*

[1] Miliband, pp. 48–68.
[2] Ibid., pp. 69–145, especially 119–45.
[3] Ibid., pp. 68–118.

class is not the *politically governing class*. This is the exact meaning of Marx's analyses of nineteenth-century England and Bismarckian Germany, to say nothing of Bonapartism in France. It is also what Miliband himself seems to suggest in his analyses of social-democratic governments.[1]

We come now to the problem of the *members of the State apparatus*, that is to say the army, the police, the judiciary and the administrative bureaucracy. Miliband's main line of argument is to try to establish the relation between the conduct of the members of the State apparatus and the interests of the ruling class, by demonstrating either that the social origin of the 'top servants of the State' is that of the ruling class, or that the members of the State apparatus end up united to this class by personal ties.[2] This approach, without being false, remains descriptive. More importantly, I believe that it prevents us from studying the specific problem that the State apparatus presents; *the problem of 'bureaucracy'*. According to Marx, Engels and Lenin, the members of the State apparatus, which it is convenient to call the 'bureaucracy' in the general sense, constitute a specific *social category*—not a class. This means that, although the members of the State apparatus belong, by their class origin, to different classes, they function according to a specific internal unity. Their class origin—*class situation*—recedes into the background in relation to that which unifies them—their *class position:* that is to say, the fact that they belong precisely to the State apparatus and that they have as their *objective function* the actualization of the role of the State. This in its turn means that the bureaucracy, as a specific and relatively 'unified' social category, is the 'servant' of the ruling class, not by reason of its class origins, which are divergent or by reason of its personal relations with the ruling class, but by reason of the fact that its internal unity derives from its actualization of the objective role of the State. The totality of this role itself coincides with the interests of the ruling class.

Important consequences follow for the celebrated problem of the *relative autonomy* of the State with respect to the ruling class, and thus for the equally celebrated question of the relative autonomy of the bureaucracy as a specific social category, with respect to that class. A long Marxist tradition has considered that the State is only a simple tool or instrument manipulated at will by the ruling class. I do not mean to say that Miliband falls into this trap, which makes

[1] Ibid., pp. 96 ff.

[2] Ibid., pp. 119–45.

it impossible to account for the complex mechanisms of the State in its relation to class struggle. However, if one locates the relationship between the State and the ruling class in the social origin of the members of the State apparatus and their inter-personal relations with the members of this class, so that the bourgeoisie almost physically 'corners' the State apparatus, one cannot account for the relative autonomy of the State with respect to this class. When Marx designated Bonapartism as the 'religion of the bourgeoisie', in other words as characteristic of *all* forms of the capitalist State, he showed that this State can only truly serve the ruling class in so far as it is relatively autonomous from the diverse fractions of this class, precisely in order to be able to organize the hegemony of the whole of this class. It is not by chance that Miliband finally admits this autonomy only in the extreme case of Fascism.[1] The question posed is whether the situation today has changed in this respect: I do not think so, and will return to this.

3. The branches of the state apparatus

Miliband's approach thus to a certain extent prevents him from following through a rigorous analysis of the State apparatus itself and of the relations between different 'branches' or 'parts' of this apparatus. Miliband securely establishes that the State apparatus is not only constituted by the government, but also by special branches such as the army, the police, the judiciary, and the civil administration. Yet what is it that governs the *relations* between these branches, the respective importance and the relative predominance of these different branches among themselves, for example the relation between parliament and the executive, or the role of the army or of the administration in a particular form of State? Miliband's response seems to be the following:[2] the fact that one of these branches predominates over the others is in some way directly related to the 'exterior' factors noted above. That is to say, it is either the branch whose members are, by their class origin or connections, nearest to the ruling class, or the branch whose predominance over the others is due to its immediate 'economic' role. An example of the latter case would be the present growth of the role of the army, related to the current importance of military expenditures.[3]

[1] Ibid., p. 93. [2] Ibid., pp. 119 ff. [3] Ibid., pp. 130 ff.

Here too, I cannot completely agree with Miliband's interpretation. As I see it, the State apparatus forms an *objective system* of special 'branches' whose relation presents a *specific internal unity* and obeys, to a large extent, *its own logic*. Each particular form of capitalist State is thus characterized by a particular form of relations among its branches, and by the predominance of one or of certain of its branches over the others: liberal State, interventionist State, Bonapartism, military dictatorship or fascism. But each particular form of capitalist State must be referred back, *in its unity*, to important modifications of the relations of production and to important stages of class struggle: competitive capitalism, imperialism, state capitalism. Only *after* having established the relation of a form of State as a unity, *that is as a specific form of the system of State apparatus as a whole*, with the 'exterior', can the respective role and the mutual internal relation of the 'branches' of the State apparatus be established. A *significant* shift in the predominant branch in the State apparatus, or of the relation between these branches, cannot be *directly* established by the immediate exterior role of this branch, but is determined *by the modification of the whole system of the State apparatus and of its form of internal unity as such*: a modification which is itself due to changes in the relations of production and to developments in the class struggle.

Let us take as an example the present case of the *army* in the advanced capitalist countries. I do not think that the 'immediate' facts of the growth of military expenditure and increasing interpersonal ties between industrialists and the military are sufficient to speak of a *significant* shift of the role of the army in the present State apparatus: besides, in spite of everything, Miliband himself is very reserved in this matter. In order for such a shift to occur, there would have to be an important modification of the form of State as a whole—without this necessarily having to take the form of 'military dictatorship'—a modification which would not be due *simply* to the growing importance of military expenditure, but to profound modifications of the relations of production and the class struggle, of which the growth of military expenditures is finally only the *effect*. One could thus establish the relation of the army not simply with the dominant class, but with the totality of social classes—a complex relation that would explain its role by means of a shift in the State as a whole. I believe that there is no more striking evidence of this thesis, in another context, than present developments in Latin America.

4. The present form of the capitalist state

Can we then speak in the present stage of capitalism of a modification of the form of the State? I would answer here in the affirmative, although I do not believe that this modification is necessarily in the direction of a preponderant role of the army. Miliband also seems to give an affirmative reply to the question. How does he situate this present modification of the form of State?[1] If the relation between the State and the ruling class is principally constituted by the 'inter-personal' relations between the members of the State apparatus and those of the ruling class, the only approach that seems open is to argue that these relations are now becoming increasingly intense and rigid, that the two are practically interchangeable. In effect, this is just the approach which Miliband adopts. The argument seems to me, however, merely descriptive. Indeed, it converges with the orthodox communist thesis of *State monopoly capitalism*, according to which the present form of the State is specified by increasingly close inter-personal relations between the monopolies and the members of the State apparatus, by the 'fusion of State and monopolies into a single mechanism'.[2] I have shown elsewhere why and how this thesis, in appearance ultra-leftist, leads in fact to the most vapid revisionism and reformism.[3] In fact, the present modification of the form of State must mainly be sought and studied not in its simple effects, which are besides disputable, but in profound shifts of the articulation of economy and polity. This modification does not seem to me to alter the relative autonomy of the State which at present, as J. M. Vincent has recently noted in connection with Gaullism,[4] only assumes different forms. In brief, the designation of any existent State as the pure and simple agent of big capital seems to me, *taken literally*, to give rise to many misinterpretations—as much now as in the past.

[1] Ibid., especially pp. 123 ff.

[2] See the acts of the colloquy at Choisy-le-Roi on 'State Monopoly Capitalism' in *Economie et Politique*, Special Number.

[3] Poulantzas, op. cit., pp. 297 ff.

[4] *Les Temps Modernes*, August–September 1968.

5. The ideological apparatuses

Finally there is one last problem which seems to me very important, and which will provide me with the occasion to go further than I have done in my own work cited above. I wonder in effect if Miliband and myself have not stopped half-way on one critical question. This is the role of *ideology* in the functioning of the State apparatus, a question which has become especially topical since the events of May–June 1968 in France. The classic Marxist tradition of the theory of the State is principally concerned to show *the repressive role of the State*, in the strong sense of organized physical repression. There is only one notable exception, Gramsci, with his problematic of hegemony. Now Miliband very correctly insists in long and excellent analyses (*The process of legitimization*, I, II, pp. 179–264) on the role played by ideology in the functioning of the State and in the process of political domination: which I have tried to do from another point of view in my own work.

I think however that, for different reasons, we have both stopped half-way: which was not the case with Gramsci. That is to say, we have ended by considering that ideology only exists in ideas, customs or morals without seeing that ideology can be embodied, in the strong sense, in *institutions*: institutions which then, by the very process of institutionalization, belong to the system of the State whilst depending principally on the ideological level. Following the Marxist tradition, we gave the concept of the State a *restricted* meaning, considering the principally repressive institutions as forming part of the 'State', and rejecting institutions with a principally ideological role as 'outside of' the State, in a place that Miliband designates as the 'political system', distinguishing it from the State.[1]

Here is the thesis I would like to propose: the system of the State is composed of *several apparatuses or institutions* of which certain have a principally repressive role, in the strong sense, and others a principally ideological role. The former constitute the repressive apparatus of the State, that is to say the State apparatus in the classical Marxist sense of the term (government, army, police, tribunals and administration). The latter constitute the *ideological apparatuses of the State*, such as the Church, the political parties, the unions (with the exception of course, of the *revolutionary* party or trade-union organizations), the schools, the mass media

[1] Miliband, pp. 50 ff.

(newspapers, radio, television), and, from a certain point of view, the family. This is so whether they are *public* or *private*—the distinction having a purely juridicial, that is, largely ideological character, which changes nothing fundamental. This position is in a certain sense that of Gramsci himself, although one he did not sufficiently found and develop.

Why should one speak in the plural of the state ideological apparatuses, whilst speaking in the singular of the State repressive apparatus? Because the State repressive apparatus, the State in the classic Marxist sense of the term, possesses a very rigorous internal unity which directly governs the relation between the diverse branches of the apparatus. Whilst the State ideological apparatuses, by their principal function—ideological inculcation and transmission—possess a greater and more important autonomy: their inter-connections and relations with the State repressive apparatus appear, by relation to the mutual connections of the branches of the State repressive apparatus, vested with a greater independence.

Why should one speak of *State* ideological apparatuses; why should these apparatuses be considered as composing part of the State? I will mention four principal reasons:

1. If the State is defined as the instance that maintains the cohesion of a social formation and which reproduces the conditions of production of a social system by maintaining class domination, it is obvious that the institutions in question—the State ideological apparatuses—fill exactly the same function.

2. The condition of possibility of the existence and functioning of these institutions or ideological apparatuses, under a certain form, is the State repressive apparatus itself. If it is true that their role is principally ideological and that the State repressive apparatus does not in general intervene *directly* in their functioning, it remains no less true that this repressive apparatus is always present behind them, that it defends them and sanctions them, and finally, that their action is *determined* by the action of the State repressive apparatus itself. The student movement, in France and elsewhere, can testify to this for schools and universities today.

3. Although these ideological apparatuses possess a notable autonomy, among themselves and in relation to the State repressive apparatus, it remains no less true that they belong to the same system as this repressive apparatus. Every important modification of the form of the State has repercussions not only on the mutual

relations of the State repressive apparatus, but also on the mutual relations of the State ideological apparatuses and of the relations between these apparatuses and the State repressive apparatus. There is no need to take the extreme case of fascism to prove this thesis: one need only mention the modifications of the role and relations of the Church, the parties, the unions, the schools, the media, the family, both among themselves and with the State repressive apparatus, in the diverse 'normal' forms through which the capitalist State had evolved.

4. Finally, for one last reason: according to Marxist–Leninist theory, a socialist revolution does not signify only a shift in *State power*, but it must equally '*break*', that is to say radically change, the State apparatus. Now, if one includes ideological apparatuses in the concept of the State, it is evident why the classics of Marxism have—if often only in implicit fashion—considered it necessary to apply the thesis of the 'destruction' of the State not only to the State repressive apparatus, but *also to the State ideological apparatuses:* Church, parties, unions, school, media, family. Certainly, given the autonomy of the State ideological apparatuses, this does not mean that they must all be 'broken' in homologous fashion, that is, *in the same way* or at *the same time* as the State repressive apparatus, or that any one of them must be. It means that the 'destruction' of the ideological apparatuses has *its precondition* in the 'destruction' of the State repressive apparatus which maintains it. Hence the illusory error of a certain contemporary thesis, which considers it possible to pass here and now to the 'destruction' of the university in capitalist societies, for instance. But it also means that the advent of socialist society cannot be achieved by 'breaking' only the State repressive apparatus whilst maintaining the State ideological apparatuses intact, taking them in hand as they are and merely changing their function.

This question evidently brings us closer to the problem of the *dictatorship of the proletariat* and of the *cultural revolution:* but I have the feeling that it takes us farther from Miliband. I do not, however, want to enter here into the problem of the political conclusions of the Miliband's book, in which he shows himself very—too—discreet: the question remains open. I will end by recalling what I said at the beginning: if the tone of this article is critical, this is above all proof of the interest that the absorbing analyses of Miliband's work have aroused in me.

25

THE CAPITALIST STATE: REPLY TO NICOL POULANTZAS

RALPH MILIBAND

I very much welcome Nicos Poulantzas's critique of *The State in Capitalist Society* in the last issue of N.L.R.: this is exactly the kind of discussion which is most likely to contribute to the elucidation of concepts and issues that are generally agreed on the Left to be of crucial importance for the socialist project, yet which have for a very long time received altogether inadequate attention, or even no attention at all. While some of Poulantzas's criticisms are, as I shall try to show, unwarranted, my purpose in the following comments is only incidentally to 'defend' the book; my main purpose is rather to take up some general points which arise from his review and which seem to me of particular interest in the investigation of the nature and role of the state in capitalist society. I hope that others may be similarly provoked into entering the discussion.

1. The problem of method

The first such point concerns the question of method. Poulantzas suggests that, notwithstanding the book's merits (about which he is more than generous), the analysis which it attempts is vitiated by the absence of a 'problematic' which would adequately situate the concrete data it presents. In effect, Poulantzas taxes me with what C. Wright Mills called 'abstracted empiricism', and with which I myself, as it happens, tax pluralist writers.[1] Poulantzas quite rightly states that 'a precondition of any scientific approach to the "concrete" is to make explicit the epistemological principles of its own treatment of it'; and he then goes on to say that 'Miliband nowhere deals with the Marxist theory of the state as such, although it is constantly implicit in his work' [p. 293]. In fact, I do quite explicitly give an outline of the Marxist theory of the state[2] but

[1] *The State in Capitalist Society*, p. 172.

[2] Ibid., pp. 5, 93.

First published in New Left Review, *No. 59, 1970.*

undoubtedly do so very briefly. One reason for this, quite apart from the fact that I have discussed Marx's theory of the state elsewhere,[1] is that, having outlined the Marxist theory of the state, I was concerned to set it against the dominant, democratic-pluralist view and to show the latter's deficiencies in the only way in which this seems to me to be possible, namely in empirical terms. It is perfectly proper for Poulantzas to stress the importance of an appropriate 'problematic' in such an undertaking; and it is probably true that mine is insufficiently elucidated; but since he notes that such a 'problematic' is 'constantly implicit in my work', I doubt that my exposition is quite as vitiated by empiricist deformations as he suggests; i.e. that the required 'problematic' is not absent from the work, and that I am not therefore led 'to attack bourgeois ideologies of the State whilst placing [myself] on their own terrain' p. [293].

Poulantzas gives as an example of this alleged failing the fact that, while I maintain against pluralist writers the view that a plurality of élites does not exclude the existence of a ruling class (and I do in fact entitle one chapter 'Economic Élites and Dominant Class') I fail to provide a critique of the ideological notion of élite and do therefore place myself inside the 'problematic' which I seek to oppose. Here too, however, I doubt whether the comment is justified. I am aware of the degree to which the usage of certain words and concepts is ideologically and politically loaded, and indeed I provide a number of examples of their far from 'innocent' usage;[2] and I did in fact, for this very reason, hesitate to speak of 'élites'. But I finally decided to do so, firstly because I thought, perhaps mistakenly, that it has by now acquired a sufficiently neutral connotation (incidentally, it may still have a much more ideological ring in its French usage than in its English one); and secondly because it seemed, in its neutral sense, the most convenient word at hand to suggest the basic point that, while there do exist such separate 'élites' inside the dominant class, which Poulantzas describes by the admittedly more neutral but rather weak word 'fractions', they are perfectly compatible with the

[1] 'Marx and the State' in *The Socialist Register*, 1965.

[2] e.g. 'Governments may be solely concerned with the better running of "the economy". But the descriptions of systems as "the economy" is part of the idiom of ideology, and obscures the real process. For what is being improved is a *capitalist* economy; and this ensures that whoever may or may not gain, capitalist interests are least likely to lose' (op. cit. p. 79. Italics in original).

existence of a dominant class, and are in fact parts of that class. He suggests that the 'concrete reality' concealed by the notion of 'plural élites' can only be grasped 'if the very notion of élite is rejected' [p. 294]. I would say myself that the concrete reality can only be grasped if the concept of élite is turned against those who use it for apologetic purposes and shown to require integration into the concept of a dominant or ruling class: i.e. there *are* concepts of bourgeois social science which can be used for critical as well as for apologetic purposes. The enterprise may often be risky, but is sometimes legitimate and necessary.

However, the general point which Poulantzas raises goes far beyond the use of this or that concept. In fact, it concerns nothing less than the status of empirical enquiry and its relationship to theory. In this regard, I would readily grant that *The State in Capitalist Society* may be insufficiently 'theoretical' in the sense in which Poulantzas means it; but I also tend to think that his own approach, as suggested in his review and in his otherwise important book, *Pouvoir Politique et Classes Sociales*, a translation of which into English is urgently needed, errs in the opposite direction. To put the point plainly, I think it is possible in this field at least, to be so profoundly concerned with the elaboration of an appropriate 'problematic' and with the avoidance of any contamination with opposed 'problematics', as to lose sight of the absolute necessity of empirical enquiry, and of the empirical demonstration of the falsity of these opposed and apologetic 'problematics'. Poulantzas declares himself not to be against the study of the 'concrete': I would go much farther and suggest that, of course on the basis of an appropriate 'problematic', such a study of the concrete is a *sine qua non* of the kind of 'demystifying' enterprise which, he kindly suggests, my book accomplishes. After all, it was none other than Marx who stressed the importance of empirical validation (or invalidation) and who spent many years of his life in precisely such an undertaking; and while I do not suggest for a moment that Poulantzas is unaware of this fact, I do think that he, and the point also goes for Louis Althusser and his collaborators, may tend to give it rather less attention than it deserves. This, I must stress, is not a crude (and false) contraposition of empiricist versus non- or anti-empiricist approaches: it is a matter of emphasis—but the emphasis is important.

2. The objective nature of the state

Poulantzas's critique of my approach also underlies other points of difference between us. But before dealing with these, I should like to take up very briefly what he calls 'the false problem of managerialism'. Managerialism *is* a false problem in one sense, not in another. It is a false problem in the sense that the 'motivations' of managers (of which more in a moment) are not such as to distinguish the latter in any fundamental way from other members of the capitalist class: i.e. he and I are agreed that the thesis of the 'soulful corporation' is a mystification. But he also suggests that I attribute to the managers 'an importance they do not possess' [p. 297]. This seems to me to underestimate the significance of the 'managerial' phenomenon in the internal organization of capitalist production (which, incidentally, Marx, writing a hundred years ago, did not do).[1] Poulantzas for his own part chooses to stress 'the differences and relations between fractions of capital'. But while these *are* important and need to be comprehended in an economic and political analysis of contemporary capitalism I would argue myself that the emphasis which he gives to these differences and relations may well obscure the underlying cohesion of these various elements—and may well play into the hands of those who focus on these differences in order to deny the fundamental cohesion of the capitalist class in the conditions of advanced capitalism.

More important, however, Poulantzas also suggests that I attach undue importance, indeed that I am altogether mistaken in attaching *any* importance to the 'motivations' of the managers. Thus, 'the characterization of the existing social system as capitalist in no way depends on the motivations of the conduct of managers . . . to characterize the class position of managers, one need not refer to the motivations of their conduct, but only to their place in production and their relationship to the ownership of the means of production' [pp. 296–7]. I think myself that one must refer to both not because managerial 'motivations' are in themselves critical (and

[1] In fact, *his* formulations may go rather further than is warranted: 'A large part of the social capital is employed by people who do not own it and who consequently tackle things quite differently than the owner' (*Capital*, Moscow 1962, III, p. 431) 'This is the abolition of the capitalist mode of production within the capitalist mode of production itself, and hence a self-dissolving contradiction, which *prima facie* represents a mere phase of transition to a new form of production' (ibid., p. 429).

Poulantzas is mistaken in believing that I think they are)[1] but precisely in order to show why they are not. By ignoring them altogether, one leaves a dangerous gap in the argument which needs to be put forward against managerialist apologetics. This is why, I take it, Baran and Sweezy, for instance, devote a good deal of attention to 'business behaviour' in their *Monopoly Capital*.

This issue of 'motivations' also arises, in a much more significant and far-reaching way, in connection with what I have called the state élite and its relation to the ruling class. Poulantzas notes that, in order to rebut the ideologies which affirm the neutrality of the state, I bring forward evidence to show that members of that class are themselves involved in government, and also show the degree to which those who man the command posts of the various parts of the state system are, by social origin, status, milieu (and, he might have added, ideological dispositions) connected with the ruling class. But, he also adds, this procedure, while having a 'capital *demystifying* importance',[2] is not 'the most significant one' [p. 298]. His reason for saying this is so basic that I must here quote him at some length: 'The relation between the bourgeois class and the State is an *objective relation*. This means that if the *function* of the State in a determinate social formation and the *interests* of the dominant class in this formation *coincide*, it is by reason of the system itself' [p. 298].[2] Similarly, the members of the State apparatus 'function according to a specific internal unity. Their class origin—*class situation*—recedes into the background in relation to that which unifies them—their *class position:* that is to say, the fact that they belong precisely to the State apparatus and that they have as their *obtective function* the actualization of the role of the State. . . . The totality of this role itself coincides with the interests of the ruling class' [p. 299].[2]

I should like to make two comments about this. The first and less important is that Poulantzas greatly under-estimates the extent to which I myself do take account of the 'objective relations' which affect and shape the role of the State. In fact, I repeatedly note how

[1] e.g. 'Like the vulgar owner-entrepreneur of the bad old days, the modern manager, however bright and shiny, must also submit to the imperative demands inherent in the system of which he is both master and servant; and the most important such demand is that he should make the "highest possible" profits. Whatever his motives and aims may be, they can only be fulfilled on the basis of his success in this regard.' (*The State in Capitalist Society*, p. 34.)

[2] Italics in text.

government and bureaucracy, irrespective of social origin, class situation and even ideological dispositions, are subject to the structural constraints of the system. Even so, I should perhaps have stressed this aspect of the matter more.

But however that may be, I believe—and this is my second point—that Poulantzas himself is here rather one-sided and that he goes much too far in dismissing the nature of the state élite as of altogether no account. For what his *exclusive* stress on 'objective relations' suggests is that what the state does is in every particular and at all times *wholly* determined by these 'objective relations': in other words, that the structural constraints of the system are so absolutely compelling as to turn those who run the state into the merest functionaries and executants of policies imposed upon them by 'the system'. At the same time, however, he also rejects the 'long Marxist tradition [which] has considered that the State is only a simple tool or instrument manipulated at will by the ruling class' [p. 299]. Instead, he stresses the 'relative autonomy of the state'. But all that this seems to me to do is to substitute the notion of 'objective structures' and 'objective relations' for the notion of 'ruling' class. But since the ruling class is a dominant element of the system, we are in effect back at the point of total subordination of the state élite to that class; i.e. the state is not 'manipulated' by the ruling class into doing its bidding: it does so autonomously but totally because of the 'objective relations' imposed upon it by the system. Poulantzas condemns the 'economism' of the Second and Third Internationals and attributes to it their neglect of the State [pp. 292–3]. But his own analysis seems to me to lead straight towards a kind of structural determinism, or rather a structural super-determinism, which makes impossible a truly realistic consideration of the dialectical relationship between the State and 'the system'.

For my own part, I do believe that 'the state in these class societies is primarily and inevitably the guardian and protector of the economic interests which are dominant in them. Its "real" purpose and mission is to ensure their continued predominance, not to prevent it.'[1] But I also believe that within this 'problematic', the state élite is involved in a far more complex relationship with 'the system' and with society as a whole than Poulantzas's scheme allows; and that at least to a certain but definite and

[1] Op. cit., p. 265.

important extent that relationship is shaped by the kind of factors which I bring into the analysis and which Poulantzas dismisses as of no account.

The political danger of structural super-determinism would seem to me to be obvious. For if the state élite is as totally imprisoned in objective structures as is suggested, it follows that there is *really* no difference between a state ruled, say, by bourgeois constitutionalists, whether conservative or social-democrat, and one ruled by, say, Fascists. It was the same approach which led the Comintern in its 'class against class' period fatally to underestimate what the victory of the Nazis would mean for the German working-class movement. This is an ultra-left deviation which is also not uncommon today; and it is the obverse of a right deviation which assumes that changes in government, for instance the election of a social-democratic government, accompanied by some changes in the personnel of the state system, are sufficient to impart an entirely new character to the nature and role of the state. Both are deviations, and both are dangerous.

It is the same sort of obliteration of differences in the forms of government and state which appears in Poulantzas's references to the 'relative autonomy' of the state. He suggests that Marx designated Bonapartism as the 'religion of the bourgeoisie', and takes Marx to mean that Bonapartism was 'characteristic of *all* forms of the capitalist state' [p. 300].[1] I stand to be corrected but I know of no work of Marx which admits of such an interpretation; and if he had said anything which did admit of such an interpretation, he would have been utterly mistaken. For in any meaningful sense of the concept, Bonapartism has *not* been characteristic of all forms of the capitalist state—rather the reverse. What Marx did say was that Bonapartism in France 'was the only form of government possible at the time when the bourgeoisie had already lost, and the working class had not yet acquired, the faculty of ruling the nation'.[2] It is perfectly true that all states are in some degree 'autonomous', and Poulantzas misreads me when he suggests that I 'finally admit this autonomy only in the extreme case of Fascism' [p. 300].[3] What I do

[1] Italics in text.

[2] *The Civil War in France*, in *Selected Works* (Moscow 1950) I, p. 469.

[3] It is, incidentally, this recognition on my part of the 'relative autonomy' of the state which leads me, *inter alia*, to suggest that Poulantzas also misreads me when he states that my analysis 'converges with the orthodox communist thesis of *State monopoly capitalism*, according to which the present form of the State is

say is that Fascism is the extreme case of the state's autonomy in the context of capitalist society, which is not at all the same thing—and that between the kind of autonomy which is achieved by the state under Fascism, and that which is achieved by it under the conditions of bourgeois democracy, there is a large gulf, which it is dangerous to underestimate. This scarcely leads me to an apotheosis of bourgeois democracy. It leads me rather to say that 'the point of the socialist critique of "bourgeois freedoms" is not (or should not be) that they are of no consequence, but they are profoundly inadequate, and need to be extended by the radical transformation of the context, economic, social and political, which condemns them to inadequacy and erosion.'[1] Poulantzas's references to the sections of my book devoted to ideology also raise points of great substance. He suggests that both he and I 'have ended by considering that ideology only exists in ideas, customs and morals without seeing that ideology can be embodied, in the strong sense, in *institutions*'.[2] I myself must plead not guilty to the charge. What he, again most generously, calls, my 'long and excellent analyses' of the subject largely focus precisely on the institutions which are the purveyors of ideology, and on the degree to which they are part and parcel, as institutions, of the general system of domination—and I do this in relation to parties, churches, pressure groups, the mass media, education, and so on. What value my analyses may have lies, I think, in my attempted demonstration of the fact that 'political socialization' *is* a process performed by institutions, many of which never cease to insist on their 'un-ideological', 'un-political' and 'neutral' character.

The much more important point is that Poulantzas suggests that these institutions 'belong to the system of the State' and he proposes the thesis that this system of the State 'is composed of *several apparatuses or institutions* of which certain have a principally repressive role, and others a principally ideological role', and among these he lists the Church, political parties, unions, the schools, the mass media and, from a certain point of view, the family.[2]

I am extremely dubious about this. I suggest in *The State in*

---

specified by increasingly close inter-personal relations between the monopolies and the members of the State apparatus, by the "fusion of State and monopolies into a single mechanism"' (p. 71). In fact, I think this scheme to be *simpliste* and explicitly question its usefulness (*The State in Capitalist Society*, p. 11, ft. 2).

[1] Ibid., p. 267. [2] Italics in text.

Capitalist Society that the state is increasingly involved in the process of 'political socialization' and that it plays, in certain respects, an extremely important role in it.[1] But I also think that, just as it is necessary to show that the institutions mentioned earlier *are* part of a system of power, and that they are, as Poulantzas says, increasingly linked to and buttressed by the state, so is it important not to blur the fact that they are not, in bourgeois democracies, part of the state but of the political system. These institutions *are* increasingly subject to a process of 'statization'; and as I also note in the book, that process is likely to be enhanced by the fact that the state must, in the conditions of permanent crisis of advanced capitalism, assume ever greater responsibility for political indoctrination and mystification. But to suggest that the relevant institutions are actually part of the state system does not seem to me to accord with reality, and tends to obscure the difference in this respect between these political systems and systems where ideological institutions are indeed part of a state monopolistic system of power. In the former systems, ideological institutions do retain a very high degree of autonomy; and are therefore the better able to conceal the degree to which they do belong to the system of power of capitalist society. The way to show that they do, is not to claim that they are part of the state system, but to show how they do perform their ideological functions outside it; and this is what I have tried to do.

Finally, Poulantzas notes that my book says very little by way of 'political conclusions'. If by 'political conclusions' is meant 'where do we go from here?' and 'how?', the point is well taken. I have no difficulties in suggesting that the aim of socialists is to create an 'authentically democratic social order, a truly free society of self-governing men and women, in which, in Marx's phrase, the state will be converted "from an organ superimposed upon society into one completely subordinate to it" '.[2] But this obviously raises very large and complex questions which I did not believe it possible to tackle, let alone answer with any kind of rigour, at the tail-end of this particular book.

---

[1] Op. cit. pp. 183 ff.

[2] Op. cit., p. 277.

CONCLUSION

John Wakeford

There is much to indicate a substantial degree of clustering of power in modern Britain. When the new Director-General of the British Council was chosen in 1971, Lord Fulton explained to the House of Commons' Expenditure Committee why no public advertisement had been necessary:

> We consulted a wide range of people in important jobs in industry, trade unions, every university, the Royal Society, foundations, and all the bodies that would be likely to be able to turn up someone in a way that made you trust their judgement. . . . I think there is a lot of empirical evidence about this and I would be prepared to say that when filling this sort of post—it is like a vice-chancellor's post—if you do advertise you never appoint from the people who apply.[1]

For various reasons there are several strategies favoured in approaching the study of power and power relationships in Britain. There is however little systematic empirical evidence to substantiate the various interpretations of the situation to which such strategies give rise. For instance, in the context of a recent article Rex suggests as appropriate:

> 'A model of a ruling class effectively exercising economic and political power, while also organizing legitimation and consent to its rule.'[2]

Westergaard also favours a 'non-pluralist' perspective and delimits a dominant grouping thus:

> The dominant grouping is that of a small, homogeneous *élite* of wealth and private corporate property—politically entrenched in the leadership of the Conservative Party; strongly represented in, or linked with, a variety of public and private bodies; assured of the general support of the press, if not at the overt political level of the publicly-controlled mass media; its members sharing for a large part a common, exclusive educational background, and united by fairly close ties of kinship and everyday association. . . . It is an *élite* which, while its economic base is that of financial and industrial capital, yet has its own uniquely British features, in part inherited from the agrarian-mercantile nobility and gentry of the pre-industrial era. It is neither a tightly closed group—indeed much of its viability may derive from its absorbtive capacity—nor a monolithically united one. But internal divisions

[1] *The Guardian*, 12 April 1971.
[2] J. Rex, 'Power', *New Society*, 5 October 1972, Vol. 22, No. 522, p. 26.

remain generally confined to particular issues, and do not develop into major fissures of a durable kind.[3]

The basic notion of a 'power-elite' retains its appeal, though dilemmas stressed by 'pluralists', such as Dahl, are usually recognized and absorbed. Any approach based on a study of elite formation and on-going institutional connections remains a partial mode of documenting power relationships without the consideration of the processes by which decisions and policy alternatives are, or perhaps more significant are not, made, taken and implemented. Who influences such decisions? Who puts them forward, in terms of what options and priorities and on the basis of values and objectives of which individuals and groups involved? Most variants of the power elite thesis anyway are ripe with their own dilemmas in that they are not amenable to empirical confirmation or refutation; even when the criteria that are being employed are explicit, the data cited seldom unambiguously sustains and substantiates the particular interpretation propounded. Moreover, as was pointed out in the Introduction, whether such evidence as there is can be interpreted as substantiating the notion of a power elite is dependent not only on the initial conceptual and methodological assumptions that are made but also, in a wider sense, on the acceptance of a particular framework in which to ground the analysis. All sorts of other information could lead to different interpretations and possibly new insights going beyond a postulated intra-societal dominant grouping. The power-holders and the poor are both manifestations of inequality and we undoubtedly must, as Titmuss has advocated for poverty studies, 'take account of the changing agents and characteristics of inequality'.[4] Changes in the power structure must be examined more directly in the context of economic growth and political action.

Information, for instance, on the giant multinational companies and conglomerates must now have a place in any contemporary analysis of power, and we have included a discussion of some aspects of their growth in Britain.[5]

[3] J. H. Westergaard, 'Sociology: The Myth of Classlessness' in R. Blackburn (ed.), *Ideology in Social Science* (Fontana, London 1972), pp. 140–1.

[4] R. M. Titmuss, *Income Distribution and Social Change* (Allen and Unwin, London 1962), p. 87. See also S. M. Miller and P. Roby, *The Future of Inequality* (Basic Books, New York 1970); P. Chevigny, *Police Power* (Random House, New York 1969).

[5] 'American Investment in Britain' by Michael Hughes, pp. 157 ff. See also R. Jenkins, *Exploitation* (MacGibbon and Kee, London 1970).

Since 1967 there has been an unprecedented boom in merger and takeover activity in the City. Over the four years 1967–70 expenditure on acquisitions of subsidiaries by industrial and commercial companies totalled almost £5,000m. Between 1958 and 1970 one quarter of the net assets of quoted industrial and commercial companies were acquired by other companies.[6] Large firms now dominate the economy; the future of the British motor industry effectively rests in the hands of one company, as does the future of the British computer industry. Although large and international companies existed as far back as the seventeenth century it is only in recent years that takeovers of considerable size have become weekly occurrences: £50m paid by a hotel chain for a brewery chain, £67m by I.C.I. for an American chemical and pharmaceutical firm, a £300m bid for a firm producing baby foods and proprietary drugs from one of its competitors. In 1971 there were an average of four mergers a week in the City to a value in the year of over one and a quarter thousand million pounds. Companies based in one country buy into another. Companies with products in one field diversify into others, often by merger. Thus it has been estimated that by 1985 some 300 companies will control more than 75 per cent of the capital assets of the Western world.[7] Before then, in the non-communist world, it is forecast that key industries including car manufacture, computing and chemicals will each be effectively controlled by four or five multinational companies.[8]

Industrial wealth and power in the United Kingdom is increasingly concentrated in the hands of a small number of massive firms, and effectively concentrated in the hands of that minority within them who have a significant part in making major policy decisions. Whether or not such large organizations are as responsive to market forces as their smaller counterparts, they have the power to influence what the market will demand. The investment by I.C.I. or Courtaulds in a new industrial process is so great that an appropriate demand must be created and maintained to ensure

[6] A. Glyn and B. Sutcliffe, *British Capitalism, Workers and the Profits Squeeze* (Penguin Books, London 1972), p. 143.

[7] C. Levinson, 'Power of the Big League', *The Guardian*, 11 May 1971. See also *Fortune*, 15 May 1969, for a similar estimate. For an account of the mechanics of one massive merger see R. Jones and O. Marriott, *Anatomy of a Merger* (Cape, London 1970).

[8] See, for instance, *The Prospects for the UK Computer Industry for the 1970s*, House of Commons Paper 621–1, Stationery Office, London 1971.

that the market absorbs its product. The public is urged to purchase medicines of dubious value, dietary additives and substitutes, new aids to beauty, and amazingly fragile, rust-prone and potentially lethal motor vehicles. Joan Robinson points out, far from conforming to textbook economics, such firms in monopoly conditions tend to expand capacity, conquer new markets, produce new commodities and exploit new techniques! 'Modern industry is a system not so much of monopolistic competition as of competitive monopolies'.[9] Coupons, 'gifts' and trading stamps tend to replace genuine competition over price, quantity and quality. As Robinson points out, such firms manipulate not only the market economy but also national and international policy. Unfortunately for the sociologist they generally conduct their business with tact, discretion and in almost total secrecy. The recent investigation by the U.S. Senate into the International Telephone and Telegraph's involvement in American and Chilean politics may, however, provide some interesting material.[10]

I.T.T. could in itself be an important subject for the sociologist, the epitome of the multinational conglomerate—a single company operating hotels, hire cars, bakeries, insurance, house building, canteen food services, fire sprinklers, cellulose and publishing in more than seventy countries. It has over 400,000 employees and annual sales greater than the income of many of the countries, including Chile, where it does business. In Britain its subsidiaries manufacture KB Television sets, Rimmel cosmetics, Sherley dog food, Amplex and, under a contract with the Post Office, telephones. The influence of such firms, in particular the limitations they set on the effective powers of the British Government still awaits satisfactory study.[11]

Most Western capitalist countries are affected. But Japan too is now receiving the attention of the multinationals. During two months in 1970 the American car industry responded to the growing

[9] *Economic Heresies*, J. Robinson (Macmillan, London 1971), p. 103.

[10] There is a description of the same firm's attempts to persuade senior British civil servants and cabinet ministers to approve a new transatlantic communications cable in *American Inc.* by M. Mintz and J. Cohen (Dell, New York 1971).

[11] However some material has appeared on their influence in the United States and other countries. See for instance R. J. Barber, *The American Corporation* (MacGibbon and Kee, London 1970), Mintz and Cohen op. cit and 'Notes on the Theory of Imperialism' by P. Baran and P. Sweezy. *Monthly Review*, Vol. 17, No. 10 (March 1966).

share of their home market taken by Japanese firms by buying substantial stakes in two major companies—General Motors taking a 34 per cent interest in Isuzu Motors and Chrysler 35 per cent in Mitsubishi.

Some of these companies have already become in some ways so international that it is almost impossible to identify many of them with any single country. Nestlé, Shell and Unilever pursue their own corporate interest independent of their country of origin and the chairman of Ronson's British subsidiary has been quoted as advocating that an executive of a multinational company should

> set aside any nationalistic attitudes and appreciate that in the last resort his loyalty must be to the shareholders of the parent company, and he must protect their interests even if it might appear that it is not perhaps in the national interest of the country in which he is operating.[12]

In such companies while the management is often drawn from the native population, it is rare for this to be the case for more than a small minority of shareholders.

In the absence of concerted action by national governments to prevent companies exploiting their differences, the power of the multinational is considerable. Without such action it may allocate markets, switch production, move goods and transfer vast sums of money from one country to another, currency to currency, avoiding tax and exchange controls and having serious effects on the local pattern of employment. By 1966 a study by the Board of Trade showed that over one fifth of Britain's exports were accounted for by 'transactions between related concerns'. Integrated international companies such as IBM and to a lesser extent Ford, General Motors and Chrysler, may create serious problems for a host country by relatively minor alterations of their production schedules. Particularly since 1969 (when the production in several European subsidiaries of Ford was seriously affected by a strike at Dagenham) multinationals have been perfecting ways of ensuring that extended disputes in one country have little effect on the performance of the whole company.[13] Until a trade union can assemble considerable international support, its leaders are consigned in general to

[12] W. J. Kenyon Jones, quoted in C. Tugendhat, *The Multinationals* (Eyre and Spottiswoode, London 1971), p. 5.

[13] During the strike in March 1969 Henry Ford visited the British Prime Minister to discuss the situation in Ford Motors, now Britain's second largest single employer. By 1972 the new Ford models in Britain and Germany were almost identical.

negotiating with the management of the local subsidiary.[14] It is now considered by many economists that British subsidiaries of international companies were largely responsible for the build up of pressure against the pound before the 1967 devaluation. Their subsequent profits were then reinvested in many cases to extend their stake in the British economy.

The development is not limited to American firms, although, as Hughes points out, often their contribution is a major one. Some of the most sophisticated international firms such as Ciba and Alfa Laval originated in European countries and recent work has demonstrated that expansion across national frontiers is likely to become a general feature of large scale industry in capitalist societies—with several Western European and Japanese firms growing relatively faster than their American counterparts and joining them in the major international league.[15] In 1970 Hambros of London acquired control of one of the largest Italian private financial holding companies, La Centrale Finanziaria Generale, and Dunlop merged with Italian Pirelli.

Governments seem to have ambivalent feelings about such mergers. Despite its terms of reference the Monopolies Commission has been asked to examine few major mergers. Of the 430 mergers or proposed mergers that came within the provisions of the 1965 Act between 1965 and 1969, only 12 were referred for consideration and eight of these were not eventually judged by it to be against the public interest. One reason that companies initiate mergers is to achieve greater power and security for their management, for if any cost benefits are supposed to derive from the mergers of industrial giants, they are rarely able to make any quantitative estimates of them, and the prime motives actually cited by executives for takeovers are in terms either of selling or enlarging their market shares and lessening the problems of competitive trading by eliminating the competition. Throughout the

[14] The position of these companies has been compared to that of the Catholic Church. Tugendhat suggests that without a new industrial concordat between governments and companies, the former will be overshadowed as national rulers have been by the Church in the past. Tugendhat op. cit., p. 180 ff. Other relevant material can be found in C. Kindleberger (ed.), *The International Corporation: A Symposium* (M.I.T. Press 1970) and R. Vernon, *Sovereignty at Bay* (London 1972).

[15] See R. Rowthorn and S. Hymer, *International Big Business* 1957–1967 (University Press, Cambridge 1971). Many European firms are probably preparing mergers with British counterparts.

life of the last Labour administration 'industrial reorganization' was actively sponsored by the government largely to counteract international competition. The Industrial Reorganization Corporation, created by the Labour Government in 1966 with facilities to draw up to £150 million of government money, played an active part in the take over of AEI by General Electric, the merger of British Leyland with BMC and the creation of many other large companies by the merger of smaller ones. British firms so created were clearly identified with a 'national interest'.[16]

Governments, left-wing and right-wing, have to reckon with large foreign firms and international finance in addition to official international credit organizations such as the World Bank and the International Monetary Fund. The power and influence of such companies extend beyond that ordinarily considered in the legal concept of the firm. There is an Ombudsman to protect the citizen from the excesses of the state but no equivalent to protect him from the excesses of multinational and conglomerate companies.[17]

As was pointed out in the Introduction, questions relating to *cultural power* are fundamental to the study of power within Britain but this book cannot answer such questions. To what extent is there as Lockwood asks: 'manipulation of the lower classes, either by "tactical concessions" or through what the Webbs used to call "the capitalist domination of the mental environment" '.[18]

Beyond this, to what extent is there a prevailing climate of intellectual accommodation to disparities of power in this country?[19] It may be that such accommodation largely takes the form of benign neglect which permits the social scientist to concentrate his

[16] Turner gives a particularly illuminating account of the part played by senior members of the Labour Government in facilitating the B.M.C.–Leyland merger, including the dinner in October 1967 at Chequers to which the Chairmen of both companies were invited and assured that a successful merger would be good for the country. G. Turner, *The Leyland Papers* (Eyre and Spottiswoode, London 1971), pp. 120 ff.

[17] There is in any case an urgent need for a study of deviant behaviour in large companies along the lines of E. H. Sutherland's classic work on the criminal records of large American companies (*White Collar Crime*, Dryden, New York 1949). This could well cover offences against tax, safety and other legislation, but might also extend to 'grey areas' of security, pollution and redundancy practices and the misuse of confidential information such as in 'inside trading' (where individuals aware of imminent decisions use the knowledge to their own and their associates' benefit).

[18] See p. 269 above.

[19] Cf. A. W. Gouldner, *The Coming Crisis of Western Sociology* (Heinemann, London 1971), p. 299.

studies elsewhere, or it may be an abandonment, backed by a crude version of Dahrendorf's elegant but unoriginal thesis that there is 'impetus toward liberty' in social inequality generally, as such an inequality 'guarantees a society's ongoing dynamic historical quality'.[20] Westergaard isolates only some sections of centre and right-wing opinion who have been inclined to recognize the 'tenacious hold of inequalities as welcome evidence of their inevitability and moral necessity'.[21]

Perhaps we should not anticipate in Britain an equivalent 'assault on equality', a concerted rationalization of inequality, if not a new ideology of inequality, which has been documented in the United States.[22] But we need to inquire why, when incontrovertible evidence of persistent and substantial inequality has been with us for some considerable time, there is perhaps today a greater degree of reconciliation to prevailing conditions of social inequality than for many years. This should be a matter of concern to social scientists who explicitly and implicitly cooperate in refining the arguments and generally legitimating policy decisions by power holders which serve to reinforce the prevailing power distribution. Benign neglect should not prevail unchallenged.

[20] R. Dahrendorf, 'On the Origin of Inequality among Men' in A. Beteille, (ed.), *Social Inequality* (Penguin Books, London 1969), p. 42.

[21] J. H. Westergaard, op. cit., p. 152.

[22] See *Social Policy*, Vol. 3, No. 1, May/June 1972 which contains a critique directed at the work of Glazer, Banfield, Jensen, Herristein as providing an intellectual rationale for challenging the notion of equality in America, what S. M. Miller refers to as the 'Assault on Equality'. See also J. H. Westergaard, op. cit., 1972, pp. 156–8.

SELECTED FURTHER READING

This list is not intended to be exhaustive, but rather suggests some of the more important material on power published recently in the United Kingdom and other countries, particularly the U.S.A. We have not included reference to work from which extracts have been included in this book, or any of the vast literature concerned solely with the conceptual problems raised by the study of power. For this the reader is referred to R. Bell, D. V. Edwards and R. H. Wagner (eds.) *Political Power: A Reader in Theory and Research* (Free Press, New York 1969). Further references to material on power in advanced industrial societies may be seen in Ralph Miliband *The State in Capitalist Society*, from which we include an abstract.

ARCHER, MARGARET S. and GINER, S. (eds.) *Contemporary Europe, Class Status and Power* (Weidenfeld, London 1971).

ATKINSON, A. B. *Unequal Shares: Wealth in Britain* (Allen Lane, The Penguin Press, London 1972).

BALTZELL, E. D. *An American Business Aristocracy* (Free Press, Glencoe 1958).

BARBER, R. J. *The American Corporation: its power, its money, its politics* (MacGibbon and Kee, London 1970).

DOMHOFF, G. W. *The Higher Circles* (Random House, New York 1970).

DOMHOFF, G. W. and BALLARD B. B. (eds.) *C. Wright Mills and the Power Élite* (Beacon, Boston 1968).

FLORENCE, P. S. *The Logic of British and American Industry* (Routledge, London 1953, 2nd edition 1972).

FRANKEL, H. *Capitalist Society and Modern Sociology* (Lawrence and Wishart, London 1970).

GALBRAITH, J. K. *The New Industrial State* (New American Library, New York 1968).

GUTTSMAN, W. L. (ed.) *The English Ruling Class* (Weidenfeld, London 1969).

JONES, R. and MARRIOTT, O. *Anatomy of a Merger* (Cape, London 1970).

KELLER, S. *Beyond the Ruling Class* (Random House, New York 1963).

KOLKO, G. *Wealth and Power in America* (Praeger, New York 1962).

MILLS, C. W. *The Power Élite* (Oxford University Press, New York 1959).

OLSON, M. E. (ed.) *Power in Societies* (Macmillan, London 1970).

PERROTT, ROY. *The Aristocrats* (Weidenfeld, London 1968).

SAMPSON, A. *The New Anatomy of Britain* (Hodder and Stoughton, London 1971).

SCHONFIELD, A. *Modern Capitalism: the changing balance of public and private power* (Oxford University Press, London 1965).

THOMAS, H. (ed.) *The Establishment* (Anthony Blond, London 1959).

TUGENDHAT, C. *The Multinationals* (Eyre and Spottiswood, London 1971).

WILKINSON, R. *Governing Élites* (Oxford University Press, London 1969).

WITTFOGEL, K. A. *Oriental Despotism: a comparative study of total power* (Yale University Press 1957).

ZEITLIN, M. (ed.) *American Society Inc.* (Markham, Chicago 1970).

AUTHOR INDEX

SUBJECT INDEX